WOMAN'S BODY

Here are clear, unbiased answers to the questions that every woman, young or old, has about the way her body works. This book dispels the mysteries and taboos that have prevented women from fully knowing their own bodies. Now you can learn the real facts about fertility, pregnancy, birth control, sexual problems, body organs, diet, vitamins, weight, dependencies, drugs—and much more.

"A well-organized, diagrammatic (over 1,000 of them) book that provides answers to just about any question you might have about your personal physical being. . . . [*Woman's Body*] contains line drawings of things you've never seen, from angles you've never imagined, and it's an eye-opener."
—*The New York Times Book Review*

BANTAM BOOKS BY THE DIAGRAM GROUP

MAN'S BODY: An Owner's Manual
WOMAN'S BODY: An Owner's Manual

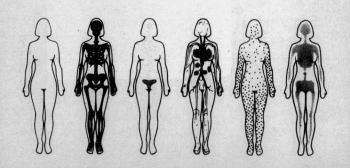

WOMAN'S BODY

An Owner's Manual
the Diagram Group

BANTAM BOOKS
TORONTO · NEW YORK · LONDON · SYDNEY · AUCKLAND

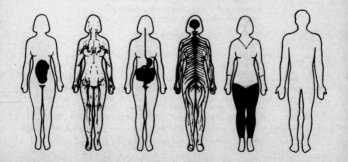

RL 10, IL age 13 and up

WOMAN'S BODY

*A Bantam Book / Published by arrangement with
Paddington Press Ltd.*

PRINTING HISTORY

Paddington Press edition/ May 1977
2nd printing . . . . June 1977

Psychology Today Book Club edition / June 1977
Playboy Book Club edition / July 1977
Macmillan Book Club edition / August 1977
The Woman Today Book Club edition / August 1977
Contemporary Book Club edition / November 1977
Literary Guild Book Club edition / January 1978

Bantam edition / April 1978

2nd printing . . . . . . October 1978	*5th printing . . . . October 1980*
3rd printing . . . . April 1979	*6th printing . . . . . September 1981*
4th printing . . . . . . February 1980	*7th printing . . . . . December 1983*

ISBN 0-553-24450-7

Published simultaneously in the United States and Canada

---

*Bantam Books are published by Bantam Books, Inc. Its trade-
mark, consisting of the words ''Bantam Books'' and the por-
trayal of a rooster, is Registered in U.S. Patent and Trademark
Office and in other countries. Marca Registrada. Bantam
Books, Inc., 666 Fifth Avenue, New York, New York 10103.*

PRINTED IN THE UNITED STATES OF AMERICA

O   16   15   14   13   12   11   10   9

CONTENTS

FOREWORD

For too long women have been the victims of the mysteries and taboos surrounding their own physical changes. Menstruation, sexuality, pregnancy, menopause, and aging are often experienced with fear, confusion, and sometimes even horror. The purpose of WOMAN'S BODY is to explain to every woman — in a straightforward and unbiased way — all of her body's functions and changes. WOMAN'S BODY makes even the most complicated body system comprehensible.

Because the language of medical experts is often complex and outside the experience of the average woman, the editors of WOMAN'S BODY have synthesized a vast amount of up-to-date medical research and statistical data and have translated it into clear and concise terms. To make this wide range of information even more easy to understand, the artists and designers have created hundreds of illustrations, charts, and diagrams. Individual panels, numbered for cross -reference, and a comprehensive index, enable the reader to find the answers to particular questions both quickly and easily.

All the material contained in WOMAN'S BODY has been presented to a team of practicing women physicians for their review and commentary. Because medical opinions and theories vary and often contradict each other, the editors have attempted to remain free of bias and to present as many points of view as possible. A selection of sources and a further reading list has also been included.

The words "average" and "typical" are often used in WOMAN'S BODY. They are reference points only, derived from statistical figures based on scientific surveys, and should not be made the basis of any judgment or personal assessment. The terms refer generally to what is or what happens in a large number of cases: not to what is necessarily best, or what should be.

WOMAN'S BODY has been created especially for the individual woman with the belief that a clearer understanding of the development and functioning of her body will increase her confidence and lead her to a fuller appreciation of herself.

A01-02

A01 The Moment of Fertilization

On the right below is shown the edge of a female ovum —
magnified about 25,000 times. The ovum is always by far the
largest cell that the body produces (despite its minuteness and
its great variations in actual size).

On the left are shown three spermatozoa, magnified in the same
way. The ovum has just been fertilized by the topmost sperm.
Immediately after fertilization the ovum's outer wall hardens to
prevent any more sperm from entering.

For a description of the process of
conception, see D03.

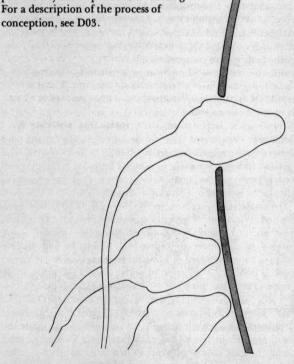

A02 Male or Female?

Female cell division (top section of diagram opposite) results in a
single ovum (a), containing an X chromosome. (The other cells
produced, shown by the white arrows, degenerate.)

Conception

Male cell division (lower section of diagram) results in four viable spermatozoa, two with a Y chromosome (**b**), and two with an X chromosome (**c**).

The ovum is fertilized (**d**) by one of the sperms with an X chromosome. So the resulting embryo (**e**) contains two X chromosomes, making it female.

Every body cell contains a "blueprint" of information, which decides how it functions. The information is carried on 23 pairs of chromosomes, which lie in the nucleus of the cell.

But because of special cell division, an ovum or a sperm only contains 23 single chromosomes. So when they unite, the new fertilized cell, from which the offspring grows, again contains 23 pairs of chromosomes — each parent having contributed half.

One pair of chromosomes decides the offspring's sex. In a woman, each of the pair is identical: they are both called X chromosomes. But a man has two chromosomes that do not match: one an X again, the other called a Y chromosome. Thus a sperm has either one X or one Y chromosome.

So if the ovum is fertilized by an X sperm, the resulting XX combination produces a girl.

If it is fertilized by a Y sperm, the XY combination produces a boy.

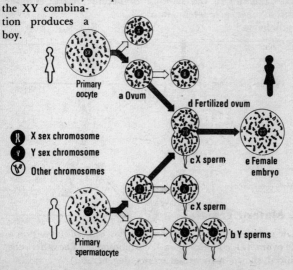

Primary oocyte

a Ovum

d Fertilized ovum

X sex chromosome

Y sex chromosome

Other chromosomes

c X sperm

e Female embryo

c X sperm

b Y sperms

Primary spermatocyte

A03-04

A03 Sex Differentiation

EXTERNAL

Until the 8th week after conception male and female fetuses still appear exactly the same. One week later — when the fetus is still only 1¼ in (3cm) long and weighs 2g — the external membrane has vanished from the genitals of the female fetus, giving entrance to a primitive vagina. Meanwhile, in the male, one end of the genital folds has begun to lengthen into a rudimentary penis. By the 11th week, the contrasting shapes of the external genitals are established.

INTERNAL

Inside the fetus the process is more complex and drawn out. In the undifferentiated fetus there are two tube systems: the Müllerian and the Wolffian ducts. But in the female, between the 7th and 9th weeks, the Wolffian tubes almost disappear, while the lower Müllerian tubes combine to form the vagina. Then, more slowly, through to the 34th week, the undifferentiated sex glands (gonads) turn into primitive ovaries, and the upper Müllerian tubes become the Fallopian tubes. In the male, in contrast, it is the Müllerian tubes that disappear. The gonads migrate to the scrotum to become testes, and the Wolffian tubes each develop into a vas deferens.

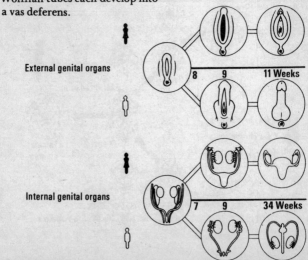

External genital organs

8   9   11 Weeks

Internal genital organs

7   9   34 Weeks

Fetal Growth

A04 The Growing Fetus

Human development in the nine months before birth is faster than at any time after. The drawings show the actual change in proportion of an average fetus in 4-week stages, beginning with the 8th week. As the fetus grows, it also shifts its position within the womb.

A05-06

A05 Birthweight

The 6-ft kangeroo gives birth to a less than 1-g baby; the blue whale a nearly 10-ton one. Human babies that have survived have ranged from under 2lb (0.9kg) to over 29lb (13.15kg) — but it is far healthier to be just an average 7lb 4oz (3.5kg).

In fact, the girls' average is slightly lower (just over 7lb-3.17kg) and the boys' correspondingly higher (7½lb-3.4kg). Girls' hearts and lungs are already marginally smaller at birth too (though their livers are heavier). All this is not because girls are born after shorter pregnancies than boys. In fact, there is a slight tendency for there to be more girls among the babies with unusually long pregnancies, and more boys among those with unusually short ones.

However, "premature babies" are quite often defined by

A06 Development

Crawling		
Sitting		
Walking		
Age in months		3

A newborn baby lies head down, hips high, knees tucked under abdomen. If she is held in a sitting position, her back is rounded and her head droops.

Between one and three months, she begins to lift her chin off the ground for a moment, and lift her head for a moment if held sitting. But if held standing, she sags at the knees and hips.

Babies

birthweight, rather than length of pregnancy. On this criterion, slightly more female babies are termed "premature," as slightly more are under 5½ lb (2.5kg) in weight. But really they are often "full-term low birthweight." Whether underweight or overweight, babies that are far from the average have less likelihood of survival. Average-weight babies have under a 2% death rate; 6- or 9-lb (2.72 or 4.08kg) babies a 3% one; 4½ or 10½ pounders (2.04 or 4.76kg) a 10% rate. Those that do survive are also more likely to be handicapped.

Perfectly normal babies vary greatly in their rate of development. Sitting up for a few moments without support can start anytime between 5 months and 1 year — walking without help anytime between 8 months and 4 years. Parents should not think that delay is always very serious, or that it is likely to have a lasting effect.

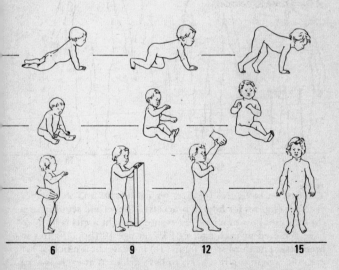

6 **9** **12** **15**

At about 6 months, she can support herself on her arms, lying or sitting, and can bear her own weight if held standing.

Between 8 and 10 months, she begins to be able to crawl on hands and knees, to sit and lean forward without support, and to hold herself upright.

At a year she can creep like a bear, on hands and feet, turn around as she sits, and walk with one hand held. At 13 months, she can walk alone.

A07 Growth, Height, and Weight

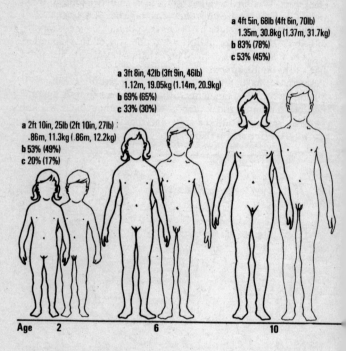

a 4ft 5in, 68lb (4ft 6in, 70lb)
1.35m, 30.8kg (1.37m, 31.7kg)
b 83% (78%)
c 53% (45%)

a 3ft 8in, 42lb (3ft 9in, 46lb)
1.12m, 19.05kg (1.14m, 20.9kg)
b 69% (65%)
c 33% (30%)

a 2ft 10in, 25lb (2ft 10in, 27lb)
.86m, 11.3kg (.86m, 12.2kg)
b 53% (49%)
c 20% (17%)

Age   2   6   10

The first set of figures (a) gives typical heights and weights for each age (figures for boys in brackets). The second set of figures (b) indicates how much of her eventual height a girl is likely to have achieved at each age, eg 83% at age 10 (boys' figures in brackets). The third set of figures (c) indicates how much of her eventual weight a girl is likely to have achieved at each age, eg 53% at age 10 (boys' figures in brackets).

Of course, such predictions are only averages. There are two reasons why a girl may be taller (shorter) than average for her age. She may be going to be a tall (short) adult. Or she may be advancing faster (slower) than usual to an eventual average

a 5ft 2in, 109lb (5ft 3in, 108lb)
   1.57m, 49.4kg (1.60m, 49kg)
b 97% (91%)
c 85% (70%)

a 5ft 4in, 125lb (5ft 8in, 143lb)
   1.63m, 56.7kg (1.75m,
   64.9kg)
b 100% (99%)
c 98% (92%)

a 5ft 4in, 128lb (5ft 9in,
   155lb) 1.63m, 58.1kg
   (1.75m, 70.3kg)
b 100% (100%)
c 100% (100%)

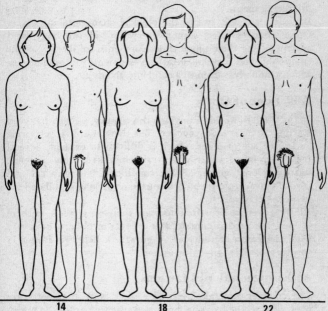

14   18   22

height: that is, she may be advanced (or behind) in her general development for her age.

The development of a child's permanent teeth gives a rough guide to this general rate of development. Compare the ages at which the teeth appear with the ages in G79. If they appear at the earlier age, the development is advanced; if at the later age, slow; if between, average.

It is interesting to note how much more slowly a child moves toward its eventual weight than its eventual height. At the age of 2, for instance, a child is already about one-half its adult height, but only about one-fifth its adult weight.

A08-10

A08 Puberty

Puberty is the time when a young person starts to be able to
have children. In a girl, eggs in the ovaries begin to mature,
and menstruation — probably the most important physical
development of puberty — begins. (In a boy, the testes start
producing sperm.)

But these are only two of the physical changes taking place.
Other changes affect almost every part of the body; and
accompanying these physical developments are the important
emotional and psychological developments of adolescence
which gradually transform a child into an adult.

A09 Time of Onset

In the Western world throughout this century, puberty has been
starting younger and younger. But there is still a very wide
variety of age of onset, which is difficult to explain. Several
factors seem to contribute: traits inherited from parents;
nutrition level; general living conditions; and physical and
psychological state (mental disturbance or long childhood illness can delay puberty).

All these seem to be more important than any effect — if there
is one — of race or climate. But the rate of puberty does vary
with the season of the year — growth in height is fastest in
spring, growth in weight in autumn.

A10 Hormonal Mechanisms

The changes that take place in a girl's body at puberty are
controlled by the hypothalamus — a specific part of the brain.
About 2 years before the onset of menstruation, the
hypothalamus starts to secrete substances known as "releasing
factors." These releasing factors travel to the pituitary gland at
the base of the brain, and cause chemical substances, or
"hormones," to be released. The first hormone produced is
called the follicle-stimulating hormone (FSH) because it
stimulates the growth of the follicles containing eggs in the
ovaries. Stimulated by FSH, the follicles produce estrogen,
which helps the growth of breasts and genitals.

The rising level of estrogen in the bloodstream has an effect on
the hypothalamus called "negative feedback." It causes a
reduction in FSH releasing factor, but also makes the

hypothalamus release a second substance — luteinizing hormone releasing factor. This in turn causes the pituitary to release luteinizing hormone (LH).

Luteinizing hormone causes one of the follicles to burst and release its egg for possible fertilization. The remaining collapsed follicle, known as the "corpus luteum," continues to secrete estrogen, and starts to secrete a new substance, progesterone, which prepares the lining of the uterus to receive and nourish a fertilized egg. If the egg is not fertilized, the levels of both estrogen and progesterone in the bloodstream fall, and cause the lining of the uterus to break down. The resulting bleeding constitutes the first menstrual period. This cycle repeats itself about once every 28 days, from puberty to menopause.

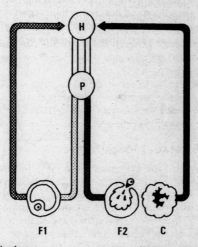

	F1		F2	C
☐ Releasing factors			H	Hypothalamus
▭ Follicle-stimulating hormone			P	Pituitary gland
▨ Estrogen			F	Follicle 1st stage
▧ Luteinizing hormone			F2	Follicle 2nd stage
■ Progesterone and Estrogen			C	Corpus luteum

A11-12

A11 Physical Developments

In girls, puberty begins at any time between the ages of 9 and 14, and ends between 14 and 18. (Boys generally mature later and more slowly than girls.) So some normal girls have completed puberty as others are just starting (especially as those who start early tend also to take less time over puberty). But on average, the changes start at about 11 and reach a peak at about 14. The order of events is also very variable, but changes in an average girl can be summarized.

PREPUBERTY
Breasts are undeveloped; there is no pubic or underarm hair; body shape is boyish.

EARLY PUBERTY (11-13)
Face becomes fuller; pelvis starts to grow to allow future childbearing; fat begins to be deposited on hips; breasts start to develop and nipples stand out; pubic hair begins to grow in the genital area; internal and external genitals begin to grow; vaginal walls thicken and menstruation may begin.

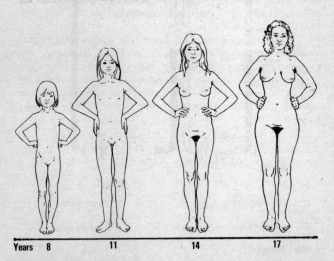

Years   8   11   14   17

LATE PUBERTY (14-16)
Breasts continue to grow; pubic hair thickens; underarm hair appears; menstruation occurs.

Puberty

MATURITY (17-18)

Body shape more full and rounded; growth of skeleton ceases; genitals mature; menstrual periods regular.

At the same time, more generally, many other tissues of the body increase in size. The voice deepens slightly (though not as much as in boys) due to the growth of the larynx. Blood pressure, blood volume, and the number of red corpuscles all rise. The heart slows down; body temperature falls; breathing slows down but the lungs' capabilities increase. Bones grow harder and change in proportion. By about 18, the bulk of growth is over — a typical girl has usually reached her full height and almost her full weight.

A12 Problems

In some rare cases, puberty can fail to occur at all, because of a hormone imbalance.

For most girls, however, the problems of puberty are usually psychological. Even such physical conditions as pimples and blackheads, excessive weight gain, and heavy perspiration are more embarrassments than anything else.

(See G14, K21, and G04.)

As a result of psychological changes, the adolescent girl may appear aggressive and rebellious, and may challenge the authority of parents and teachers (and perhaps even the police). A common but temporary problem is lethargy. Its causes may be psychological, but the physical effects of hormones, the "growth spurt," or just too many late nights, may be responsible.

A13-17

A13 Menstruation

Around every 28th day, from about the age of 12 to about the age of 47, a woman has a discharge of blood and mucus from the vagina. The discharge lasts from 2 to 8 days (4 to 6 is most usual) and may be preceded or accompanied by various unpleasant symptoms such as headaches and nausea (see A18). This, of course, is menstruation, or "the period" — the outward sign of the routine cycle of egg production and hormone change in a woman's body. It is a process that requires the wearing of pads or tampons (absorbent tubes placed in the vagina), if the menstruating woman is to avoid soiling her clothes.

A14 Egg Production

Each ovary contains groups of cells called follicles, which themselves contain immature eggs (ova). When the girl is about 12, these eggs begin to mature at the rate of one every 28 days or so — usually in alternate ovaries. (At birth, a female child's ovaries contain perhaps 350,000 immature eggs. Between puberty and menopause, only about 375 ever mature.)

As each egg matures, it bursts from the ovary — a process called ovulation — and passes into the Fallopian tube leading down from that ovary to the uterus.

A15 Process of Menstruation

If the egg is not fertilized by a sperm, it begins to degenerate 24 to 48 hours after leaving the ovary, and eventually passes unnoticed out of the body in the normal flow of fluid from the vagina. But meanwhile the uterus has been preparing to receive a fertilized egg. Hormones have caused the lining of the uterus to thicken, and to excrete a fluid so that the fertilized egg could be nourished while implanting itself. When no fertilization occurs, further hormone stimulation causes the thickened lining to crumble, and to be discharged along with a little blood through the vagina. This process is called menstruation.

Menstruation

A16 Journey of the Egg

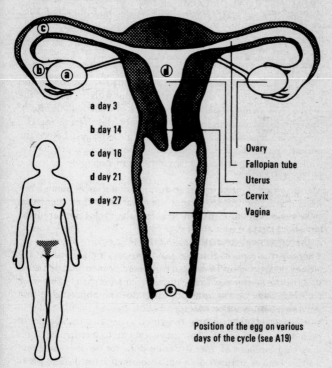

a day 3

b day 14

c day 16

d day 21

e day 27

Ovary
Fallopian tube
Uterus
Cervix
Vagina

Position of the egg on various
days of the cycle (see A19)

A17 Myths about Menstruation

Throughout history almost all societies have surrounded the menstrual process with myth and ritual. Even today, in some primitive cultures, the menstruating woman is thought to turn milk sour, turn food bad, damage crops, and even cause animals to abort! Elsewhere she may be completely isolated from the rest of the community in a special building. Modern Western society still preserves some old myths about menstruation — all of which can be ignored. It is perfectly safe for the menstruating woman to bathe, shower, swim, wash her hair, have intercourse, and take part in any other activity she wishes.

A18-19

A18 Problems of Menstruation

PREMENSTRUAL DISCOMFORT

Symptoms (most noticeable in the 7 days before the start of the period) can include headaches, backache, nausea, breast tenderness, psychological tension, and depression. Hormone treatment is used in some extreme cases.

PAINFUL PERIODS (DYSMENORRHEA)

Two types of dysmenorrhea are distinguished — spasmodic and congestive. Spasmodic dysmenorrhea begins with the onset of the period and involves pain in the lower abdomen ("cramps"), thought to be caused by contractions of the uterine muscle. Congestive dysmenorrhea is felt as a dull ache just before the period. Spasmodic period pains often disappear after pregnancy, while congestive pains can persist until the menopause.

IRREGULARITY

Menstruation is often irregular during adolescence. Some adult women also find, however, that the duration of their menstrual cycle varies from month to month. Regular cycles can vary from between 21 to 35 days.

ABSENCE OF PERIODS (AMENORRHEA)

There are two types of amenorrhea — primary and secondary. If a girl reaches the age of 18 without experiencing menstruation she is said to be suffering from primary amenorrhea. This rare condition may be the result of an endocrine abnormality and must be investigated by a doctor.

Secondary amenorrhea is the term used to describe the absence of periods in a woman who has already begun to menstruate. This may be quite normal: menstruation does not occur in pregnant women, and sometimes does not recommence until some weeks after the birth, especially if the mother is breastfeeding her child. Secondary amenorrhea, however, can also be caused by emotional stress such as shock, fear, tension, or depression, and also by endocrine disorders, illness, drug-taking, traveling, and poor general health.

HEAVY PERIODS

During a menstrual period, a woman usually sheds between 2 and 4 tablespoons of blood. Some women, however, discharge considerably more.

If menstrual bleeding is heavy or prolonged (and this often happens to women fitted with IUD's), iron-deficiency anemia can result (see H28). This can often be remedied by an iron-rich diet or a course of medicinal iron.

Heavy bleeding (and bleeding between periods) can sometimes be symptomatic of problems such as hormone disorders, fibroid tumors, or cancer of the uterus. Also, occasionally heavy periods can be caused by psychological factors. Metropathia hemorrhagica is one of the conditions caused by hormonal imbalance which can result in very heavy bleeding. If the condition does not respond to curettage (see L09) a hysterectomy may be needed.

In all cases of excessive bleeding a doctor should be consulted.

A19 Normal Menstrual Cycle

Day 1 onward: pituitary is already producing the follicle-stimulating hormone (FSH) — a new egg begins to mature in one of the follicles (a).

Day 4 onward: the follicle produces estrogen (E). As this builds up, it stimulates growth of uterine wall and breasts, halts FSH production, and stimulates the pituitary to release luteinizing hormone (LH).

Day 12 onward: LH causes the follicle to burst (b), releasing the egg, and makes the follicle develop into a "corpus luteum," producing progesterone (P) as well as estrogen.

Day 14 onward: P makes the uterine wall prepare for a fertilized egg and halts LH production. Without LH support, the corpus luteum degenerates (c), E and P levels fall, and eventually the uterine lining breaks up — menstruation (day 28). E no longer inhibits FSH, and the cycle begins again.

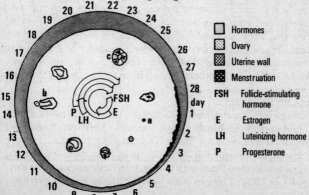

▨	Hormones
▨	Ovary
▨	Uterine wall
▨	Menstruation
FSH	Follicle-stimulating hormone
E	Estrogen
LH	Luteinizing hormone
P	Progesterone

A20-21

A20 The Average Human Being

The average woman is almost 5ft 3¾in (1.62m) tall. She weighs almost 135lb (61.2kg), her bust is 35½in (89cm), her waist 29¼in (74cm), her hips 38in (96cm). The maximum weight she reaches is about 152lb (69kg), and that is between the ages of 55 and 64.

The average man is just over 5ft 9in (1.75m) tall. He weighs almost 162lb (73.5kg), his chest is 38¾in (98cm) round, his waist 31¼in (81cm), his hips 37¾in (96cm). The maximum weight he reaches is about 172lb (78kg), and that is between the ages of 35 and 54. These figures are for people in the USA.

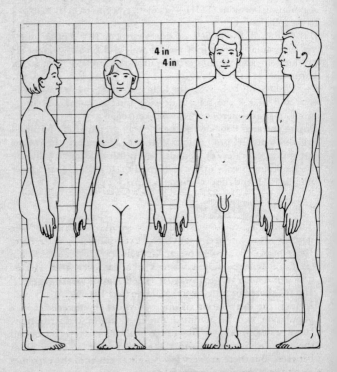

4 in
4 in

The End Product

A21 Normal and Abnormal

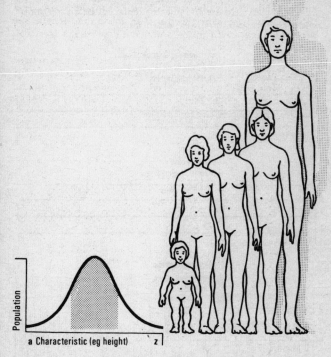

Population | a Characteristic (eg height) | z

The range of the normal is fairly small; the range of the
possible is fairly wide. A convenient example is height. In every
100 women, 95 are between 4ft 10in (1.47m) and 5ft 8in
(1.73m). But the tallest woman who has ever lived (whose
height has been verified) was 7ft 11in (2.4m) at death (age 27),
and the shortest $23\frac{1}{4}$in (59cm) at death (age 19).

In fact, the distribution of many physical characteristics in a
population can be summed up in a "normal distribution"
curve, as shown above. The range of the characteristic goes all
the way from a to z, and there are people at every point
between. But there are very few people at either of the extremes
— and very many in the central area.

A22-23

A22 Cell Life

The full-grown body is still changing constantly: each day, millions of body cells die and must be replaced. Below, we show some of their maximum life expectancies.

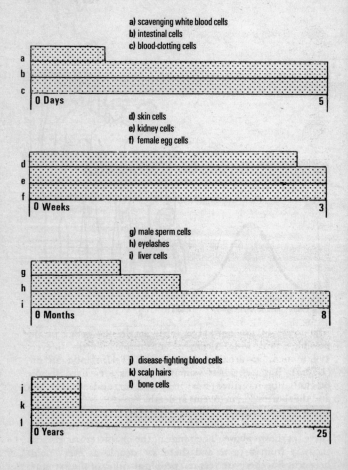

a) scavenging white blood cells
b) intestinal cells
c) blood-clotting cells

a
b
c
0 Days   5

d) skin cells
e) kidney cells
f) female egg cells

d
e
f
0 Weeks   3

g) male sperm cells
h) eyelashes
i) liver cells

g
h
i
0 Months   8

j) disease-fighting blood cells
k) scalp hairs
l) bone cells

j
k
l
0 Years   25

The End Product

A23 Woman and Man

This shows how some
characteristics of the typical
woman and man compare.

 Average brain weight

 Heart weight

 Quantity of blood

 Skin surface area

 Lung capacity (age 25)

A24 Ethnic Variations

No one now is very happy with the word "race": it has been too much a part of man's inhumanity to man. But patterns of ethnic variation — that is, fairly consistent differences in the physical characteristics of different peoples — do, of course, exist.

We are all aware of how people vary in stature, skin color, hair type, and facial features. But the ethnologist also notices such things as blood type, the ability to taste certain substances, and even the type of wax that forms in the ear. All these are part of the variety of human inheritance.

Three great ethnic groups — Caucasoid, Mongoloid, and Negroid — account between them for almost all of the world's population. We have tried to illustrate their typical characteristics. But sometimes the differences within each group are as large as those between them. Taking, for example, the old preoccupation, skin color, Negroids range from near black to sallow; Mongoloids from yellowish to flat white to deep bronze; and Caucasoids from fair pinkish in northern Europe to the dark brown people of southern India.

Another extreme variable is height. It is less totally inherited, and more immediately determined by environment, than other ethnic criteria. Not only does it range widely among individuals of a given people, but also betweeen different peoples of the same ethnic group.

A25 Ethnic Types

Basic facial characteristics

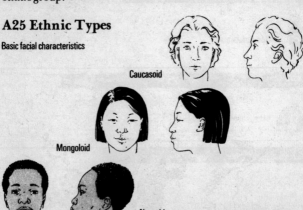

Caucasoid

Mongoloid

Negroid

Ethnic Variations

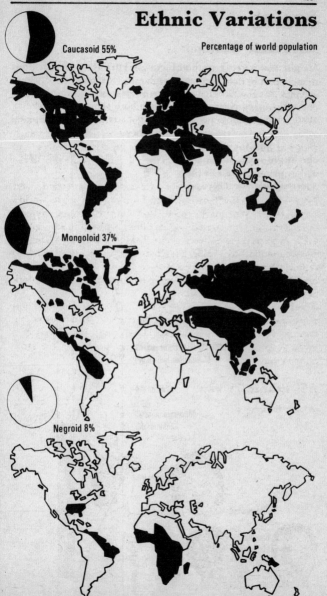

Caucasoid 55%

Percentage of world population

Mongoloid 37%

Negroid 8%

A26 Ethnic Variety

Height relates partly to ethnic factors — but little to overall ethnic group. Below, left, average heights for a sample selection of peoples reveal a jumbled sequence of Negroid, Caucasoids, and Mongoloids (eg Negroid peoples are both shortest and tallest). Also, even within a people, other genetic and environmental variations prevent too great a consistency.

Below, right, for example, the height range shows the tallest pygmy as tall as the shortest Sudanese Negro.

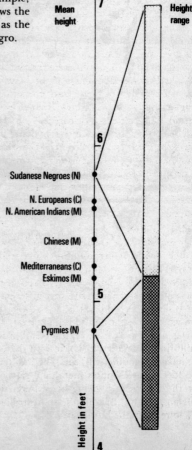

Mean height

Height range

7

6

Sudanese Negroes (N)

N. Europeans (C)
N. American Indians (M)

Chinese (M)

Mediterraneans (C)
Eskimos (M)

5

Pygmies (N)

Height in feet

4

(C) Caucasoid
(M) Mongoloid
(N) Negroid

Ethnic Variations

A27 Body and Climate

Animals of a species differ in coat color, size, limb length, and location of fat deposits, according to climatic conditions where they live. Some human variations are also related to climate.

ETHNIC FEATURES

The environment did not make people acquire inheritable characteristics — but it did decide which characteristics flourished. Those people who flourished bred among themselves, and passed on these features (which are not, of course, lost if the inheritor moves to a new environment).

Skin color is a well-known example. The extra melanin in dark skins gives added protection against the sun. Where the sun is no problem, pale skin allows better vitamin D formation (see H10). Yellow skin contains a dense keratin layer that reflects light well in deserts or snow. Dark eye color also protects against sunlight; and so do the thick, folded eyelids of Mongoloids. Negroid hair protects against heat on the scalp, but allows sweat loss from the neck. Straight hair, grown long, protects against the cold. Noses typically vary with air humidity. In dry conditions they are longer and narrower, so inhaled air is moistened. But the flat Mongoloid face developed as protection against the cold, and here the nose is not prominent and exposed. The Eskimos have taken this further, by developing facial fat.

OTHER VARIABLES

Other features, not entirely inherited, also vary with climate. Average weight is greater the colder it is. For instance, the average Eskimo woman is considerably heavier than the average Spanish woman. Body shape also varies: two bodies that weigh the same can have very different surface areas. Body area is larger the hotter it is, for a large area gives more skin from which to sweat and to radiate heat. Metabolic rate varies in the same way. A typical European has a "thermal equilibrium" of 77°F (25°C), ie with that temperature around her, naked, standing still, she shows no tendency to get hotter or colder. The Eskimo's metabolic rate is 15 to 30% higher than the European's, giving her a lower thermal equilibrium, while an Indian's, Brazilian's, or Australian's metabolic rate is 10% lower than the European's.

B01-02

B01 External Sex Organs

Most women are vague about the appearance and function of their sexual and reproductive organs. For unlike those of a man, those of a woman are almost entirely hidden, so that in a standing position the only obvious sign is the pubic hair. Collectively, the female external sex organs or genitals are known as the vulva. At the front, if one were looking between a woman's open legs, is:

a the mons veneris (mount of Venus) or mons pubis, a pad of fatty tissue over the pubic bone. From puberty (A11) this is covered with pubic hair. Extending downward and backward from the mons veneris are the

b labia majora (outer lips), two folds of fatty tissue which protect the reproductive and urinary openings lying between them. These outer lips change size during a woman's life and from puberty their outer surfaces are also covered with hair. Between them lie the

c labia minora (inner lips). These are delicate, hairless folds of 'skin quite sensitive to touch. During sexual arousal, they swell and darken in color (see B03). Below the mons area the labia minora splits into two folds to form

d a hood under which lies the

e clitoris. This is a small, bud-shaped organ and the most sensitive of the female genitals. The clitoris corresponds exactly to the male penis (see N02) and like it is made up of erectile tissue. During sexual excitement, the clitoris swells with blood and for most women is the center of orgasm. Just below the clitoris are the

f urethra — the external opening of the urinary passage which leads directly to the bladder — and the

g vaginal opening, the outside entrance to the vagina (see B02).

h The hymen, or maidenhead, is a thin membrane just inside the vaginal opening. It varies greatly in shape and size, and, in a virgin, it may be stretched or torn during the first experience of sexual intercourse, but quite often has already been stretched either by the use of tampons or during petting. If torn during intercourse there is usually some bleeding and possibly pain.

i The Bartholin's or vestibular glands lie either side of the vaginal opening. Contrary to previous belief, these glands play little part in vaginal lubrication. They may occasionally become infected (eg by gonorrhea: see L30).

Female Sex Organs

j The perineum is the triangular area of skin lying between the end of the labia minora and the anus. Below its surface are muscles and fibrous tissue that are stretched during childbirth.
k The anus lies below the perineum and is the external opening through which feces pass from the rectum.

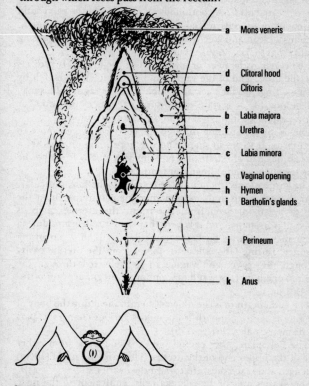

a	Mons veneris
d	Clitoral hood
e	Clitoris
b	Labia majora
f	Urethra
c	Labia minora
g	Vaginal opening
h	Hymen
i	Bartholin's glands
j	Perineum
k	Anus

B02 Internal Sex Organs

These are a woman's reproductive organs and consist of the vagina, uterus, Fallopian tubes, and ovaries.
a The vagina is a muscular passage, lying between **b**, the bladder and **c**, the rectum. It leads from the vulva upward, and at an angle, to the uterus. It is about 4-5in (10-12.5cm) long and capable of great distension. Normally the vaginal walls, which

B02-03

are lined with folds or ridges of skin, lie close together. During sexual intercourse, they stretch easily to take the male penis and extend even more considerably during labor to allow a child to be born. The vagina is usually moist, though moistness increases with sexual excitement and may also vary at different times of the menstrual cycle. A continuous secretion from the cervix and vagina of dead cells mixed with fluid lubricates the vagina, keeping it clean and free from infection. It is this self-cleansing quality that makes vaginal douching unnecessary.

d The cervix is the neck or lower part of the uterus. It projects into the upper end of the vagina and can quite often be felt by sliding a finger as far back as possible into the vagina. This may not be possible at certain times during the menstrual cycle or during sexual excitement if the uterus changes position.

e The os, a tiny opening through the cervix, is the entrance to the uterus. It varies in shape and size depending on whether a woman has had children, but remains very small. It cannot be penetrated by a penis, finger, or tampon.

f The entire uterus (including the cervix) is a hollow, muscular, pear-shaped organ and, in its nonpregnant state, is about the size of a lemon. Seen from the front, the uterine cavity is triangular in shape, and it is here that the fetus develops during pregnancy, pushing back the muscular walls in a surprising manner. During labor the fetus moves from the uterine cavity through the cervix and vagina to be delivered through the vaginal opening. (For a full description of pregnancy and birth, see D01 on.)

g The endometrium is the mucous membrane lining the body of the uterus. Once a month it undergoes various changes as part of the menstrual cycle (see A19).

h The Fallopian tubes extend outward and back from either side of the upper end of the uterus. They are about 4in (10cm) in length and reach outward toward the ovaries.

i The ovaries are the female egg cells, equivalent to the male testes (N05). They produce ova and also the female sex hormones, estrogen and progesterone. Once a month an ovum (egg) is released, which floats freely into the end of one of the Fallopian tubes. (For ovulation, see A14.)

Sexual Process

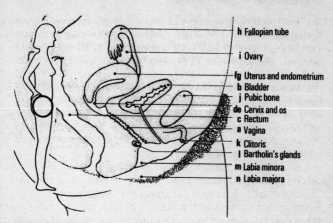

h Fallopian tube
i Ovary
fg Uterus and endometrium
b Bladder
j Pubic bone
de Cervix and os
c Rectum
a Vagina
k Clitoris
l Bartholin's glands
m Labia minora
n Labia majora

B03 The Sexual Process

Important changes take place in the body during lovemaking, as a result of muscular tension and the swelling of certain tissues with blood. These processes were first described in detail by William Masters and Virginia Johnson in their book, *Human Sexual Response* (1966).

The act of lovemaking can be divided into four stages: the excitement phase, the plateau phase, the orgasm, and the resolution phase.

EXCITEMENT PHASE

The duration of this phase varies according to the amount and effectiveness of the stimulation. General muscular tension begins, and heart rate and blood pressure start to increase.

PLATEAU PHASE

This is an extension of the excitement phase. If effective stimulation continues, sexual tensions increase and the desire for release of the tensions in orgasm is intensified.

ORGASM

The orgasmic phase usually lasts only a matter of seconds. Orgasms do, however, vary in intensity and duration from woman to woman and occasion to occasion.

RESOLUTION PHASE

When orgasm is over, the resolution phase begins. There is gradual muscular and physiological relaxation, and within 30 minutes the body returns to its unstimulated state.

B03-04

CHANGES IN THE BREAST

Early in the excitement phase the nipples become erect. Later, increased definition of the vein pattern in the breasts becomes obvious, and there may be an increase in the size of the breasts themselves.

In the plateau phase, the breasts continue to enlarge, and the areolae become prominent, so engulfing the nipples. Also, a pink mottling known as the sex flush may appear on the breasts. In the resolution phase, the areolae subside leaving the nipples prominent, and the breasts gradually resume their normal size.   **a** Areola **b** Nipple

EXTERNAL GENITAL CHANGES

In the excitement phase, the clitoris increases in length and diameter. The labia majora open and spread flat while the labia minora swell and extend outward. In the plateau phase, the clitoris shortens and may disappear under its hood. The labia majora swell further, and the labia minora change color from pink to red, or from red to deep red in a woman who has had children.

At orgasm, no particular changes are discernible, but during the resolution phase, the labia resume their usual color and size, and the clitoris returns to normal.

a Clitoris **d** Labia minora
b Urethra **e** Labia majora
c Vagina

INTERNAL GENITAL CHANGES

During the excitement phase, the vagina becomes moistened with a lubricant "sweated" through its walls. The uterus and cervix pull away from the vagina, and the inner $\frac{2}{3}$ of the vagina expands. During the plateau phase, the expansion of the inner vagina continues while the outer $\frac{1}{3}$ contracts, gripping the penis.

Sexual Arousal

The uterus continues to move away from the vagina.
At orgasm, the uterus and the lower $\frac{1}{3}$ of the vagina experience a wave of contractions.
During the resolution phase, the uterus, cervix, and vagina return to normal.

a Clitoris   **c** Cervix
b Uterus   **d** Vagina

B04 Erogenous Zones

These are the most erotically sensitive areas of the body, although, of course, they vary considerably from individual to individual. Stimulation by hand or mouth (or other light object) of any of these sensitive areas is not only an important part of intercourse, but can also be sexually satisfying in itself. It can lead to mutual masturbation or oral-genital sex, even though, traditionally, Western-style lovemaking follows a pattern of foreplay, intercourse, and orgasm. Many people — women and men alike — prefer sexual activity to end with the

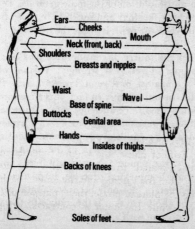

particular closeness of intercourse, and indeed many believe that lovemaking must always finish with vaginal intercourse; but to consider that stimulation of the erogenous zones of the body is only a prelude to, or substitute for, orgasm through vaginal intercourse, or even oral-genital sex play, is to limit the pleasures that it can bring.

B05 Oral Sex

The mouth and genitals are potentially the two most erotic areas of the body. This role of the mouth is clear from the practice of deep kissing. But though oral sex includes lip and deep kissing, and any oral contact with the body, it most often refers to oral-genital contact, ie cunnilingus and fellatio.

CUNNILINGUS

This is the stimulation by the mouth of a woman's genitals. The whole area from the tip and shaft of the clitoris to the anus, including the vaginal entrance, is highly sensitive and in most women responds even more intensely to oral contact than to stimulation by the fingers. The types of oral techniques used include kissing, licking, and sucking, and if these are used, most women attain orgasm very easily.

FELLATIO

This refers to oral stimulation of the male genitals. Techniques again include licking, kissing, and sucking, but also friction of the shaft and tip while the penis is inside the mouth.

ATTITUDES

Although oral sex is a source of considerable pleasure for both sexes, many people object to it strongly. Various objections have been raised against oral-genital sex, mainly that it is unnatural, sinful, or unhygienic. In fact, it is a common aspect of sexuality, widely used since ancient times. Its use today is as widespread, although often unadmitted. From a hygienic point of view, provided the genitals are kept clean, there are fewer and less harmful bacteria there than in the mouth. Likewise, both vaginal fluid and semen are just body fluids and usually tasteless. In female homosexual practice, in particular, use of oral sex is widespread — not only because vaginal penetration rarely occurs, but also because it is the most effective way for a woman to attain orgasm with a partner.

Sexual Arousal

B06 Orgasm

The female orgasm has possibly been the subject of more debate and literature than any other area of human sexuality. But, fortunately, since the work of Masters and Johnson in the 1960s, many of the myths and mysteries surrounding it have gone. It is now known that, although the experience and intensity of orgasm may vary considerably, the actual physical process of orgasm is always the same. The distinction between "vaginal" and "clitoral" orgasm is a myth.

REACHING ORGASM

Women vary greatly in what they respond to sexually, but the mons pubis, labia minora, clitoris, and vaginal entrance are almost always important. The clitoris is the most sexually responsive part of a woman's body, and in most cases fairly continuous clitoral stimulation is needed for orgasm. However, as the tip of the clitoris is extremely sensitive, constant direct touch can become painful. So for the majority of women, manipulation of the whole genital area of the mons pubis — by hand, tongue, or vibrator — is more pleasurable. During intercourse, movement of the penis in and out of the vagina provides continual clitoral stimulation by moving the labia minora backward and forward over the clitoral tip. The anus is another potentially erotic area, but it is not as easily penetrated as the vagina. For anal intercourse, lubrication — KY jelly, for example — is generally needed.

THE FEELING OF ORGASM

The time needed to reach orgasm varies from woman to woman and from occasion to occasion. Just before orgasm there is a feeling of tension lasting possibly 2-4 seconds when all the small muscles in the pelvis surrounding the vagina and uterus contract. This is followed by the orgasm itself, which may last 10-15 seconds. It is felt as a series of rhythmic muscular contractions, occurring every 0.8 seconds, first around the outer third of the vagina and spreading upward to the uterus. Both uterus and rectum also contract. In a mild orgasm there may be 3-5 contractions; in an intense one 8-12. Also during orgasm the muscles of the abdomen, buttocks, arms, face, legs, and neck may contract. Breathing is more rapid, and blood pressure climbs. All these return to normal and orgasm is usually followed by feelings of relaxation and peace.

MULTIPLE ORGASM

Women, unlike men, are capable of multiple orgasm. That is, immediately or shortly after a first orgasm, if a woman maintains her sexual excitement at the plateau level, she can move directly into a second orgasm. Some women can experience 3-5 orgasms within a few minutes, and up to 12 in one hour have been recorded.

EXPERIENCE OF ORGASM

Virtually all women are physically able to attain orgasm. But a recent US survey, *The Hite Report,* suggests that as few as 30% regularly achieve orgasm through intercourse. Kinsey's data, shown below, indicate that such orgasm does gradually become more frequent in long-term relationships — but that even after 20 years of a relationship, 11% of women never reach orgasm.

Nevertheless, it seems that the vast majority of women prefer intercourse to any other sexual activity, because of the closeness and affection associated with it.

Yet, despite the "sexual revolution" of the 1960s, women still seem to feel guilt about their own sexuality, and are reluctant either to initiate sexual activity or to communicate their sexual needs to their partners.

The diagram shows what % of women experience orgasm in marital intercourse, and how often they do so.

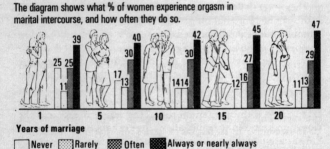

Years of marriage

☐ Never ▦ Rarely ▩ Often ■ Always or nearly always

B07 Entrance

The couple take up one of the positions that allow sexual intercourse to take place. The penis tip points at the entrance to the vagina.

Then the man may only need to push forward from his hips:

Sexual Intercourse

his penis slides immediately into the woman's vagina. Alternatively, in other positions, the woman lowers her vagina onto the man's penis.

But very often the following techniques are used:

a) either partner holds the penis, to help direct it into the vaginal entrance;

b) either partner holds the woman's labia apart to help the penis slide between them;

c) the penis is inserted only very gradually, beginning with the tip and progressing at first with several small forward movements and half retreats. This spreads the vaginal lubrication over the penis surface, and helps the vagina to accommodate itself gradually to the penis's size. (Also it is used as a tantalizing technique, to heighten the sensation of entrance.)

DELAYING ENTRANCE

Once physiological readiness has been reached, the penis can be inserted into the vagina. But a couple may choose to delay this for many minutes. During this time, they continue lovemaking without intercourse. In fact, during lovemaking, the highest levels of sexual excitement before intercourse are usually not reached until the body has been physiologically ready for some time. This is especially true of women, but also of men.

B08 Face-to-Face Positions

The number of positions for intercourse is almost endless. The choice of position depends on the mutual tastes and preferences of the couple. Among the most common, however, are front-entry positions with either the male or the female on top. Some typical examples are shown on the following page.

1 The so-called "missionary position" involves the couple lying face to face with the man on top. Penetration is easy and the close proximity of the bodies allows the exchange of caresses.

2 A variation of this position can be achieved when the woman's body is supported on a bed while the man kneels on the floor.

3 A further variation of the "missionary position" involves the man supporting the woman's body with his hands.

4 The female can take a more active part in lovemaking when she is above the man. This can be a satisfactory position for couples when the woman cannot bear the weight of her partner's body on top of her. The woman has considerable

B08-11

freedom of movement and her partner can caress her clitoris during intercourse.

5 The position in which the couple kneel facing each other with the woman on top again allows the woman to take an active part in lovemaking. It has the disadvantage that the man needs to support his weight on his hands so that he cannot easily caress his partner.

6 The partners face each other, both in a half-lying position with the weight supported on their hands. This has the disadvantage that neither partner can easily caress the other.

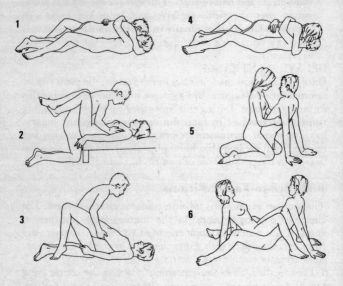

B09 Standing Positions

For successful intercourse in a standing position, both partners must be about the same height. If the woman is rather short, she can stand on a low stool, a pile of books, or even one step up some stairs, until she is at the correct height for easy penetration. Alternatively, her partner can pick her up and she

Sexual Intercourse

can clasp her hands around his neck, and her legs around his waist.

B10 Side Positions

If the couple lie side by side, they can caress freely as neither has to support the weight of the other.

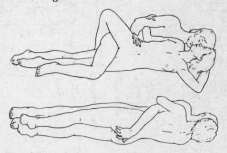

B11 Rear-Entry Positions

The advantage of all rear-entry positions is that they allow deep and satisfying vaginal penetration, and often increased pressure against the clitoris. Entry from the rear is the natural copulation position for most mammals, though many women have found the association offensive. But the extra stimulation

B11-14

of the woman that these positions allow makes them worthwhile and enjoyable for many couples.

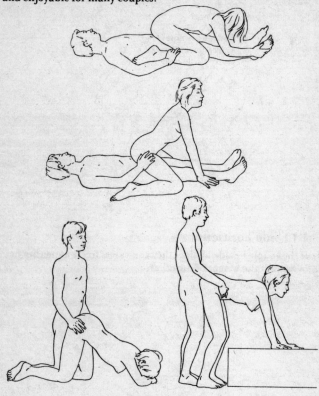

B12 Female Stimulation

Many intercourse positions rely on the movement of the man's penis and lower abdomen for the stimulation of the woman's clitoris. For many women, this kind of stimulation is insufficiently intense to produce orgasm.

Several positions can be adapted to allow for stimulation of the labia and clitoris by either partner's hand while intercourse is

Sexual Intercourse

taking place. Among the most useful are those involving rear entry, or those in which the woman is the active partner.

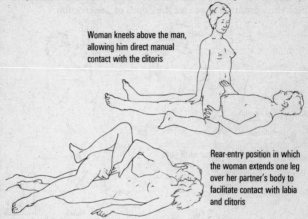

Woman kneels above the man, allowing him direct manual contact with the clitoris

Rear-entry position in which the woman extends one leg over her partner's body to facilitate contact with labia and clitoris

B13 Intercourse for Conception

To increase the chance of fertilizing an egg, the woman's body should be tilted so that the vagina is in a vertical position.

This position ensures that the ejaculated semen lies in a pool at the upper end of the vagina, near the cervix.

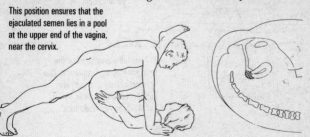

B14 Intercourse in Pregnancy

For women who have had a previous miscarriage, intercourse in the first 3 months of a pregnancy can sometimes be unwise. The doctor will advise on this when the pregnancy is first confirmed. Later in pregnancy, the woman's thickening waistline may make intercourse in more conventional positions uncomfortable if not impossible.

B14-15

A variety of positions can be adapted for use during pregnancy. Among the most suitable are rear-entry positions and those in which the woman can control the depth of penetration.

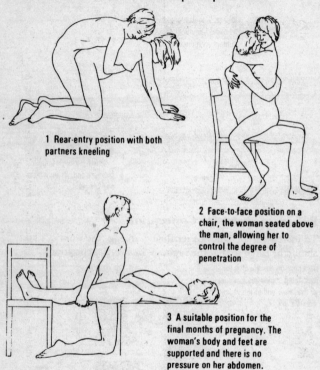

1 Rear-entry position with both partners kneeling

2 Face-to-face position on a chair, the woman seated above the man, allowing her to control the degree of penetration

3 A suitable position for the final months of pregnancy. The woman's body and feet are supported and there is no pressure on her abdomen.

B15 Growth of Sexual Experience

The information on the five subsequent pages is taken from the classic work by the American, Dr Alfred C Kinsey, and his associates (*Sexual Behavior in the Human Female*). Although their researches into the sexual behavior of American men and women are now some 30 years old, they are still the fullest and most reliable studies of their kind.

The first diagram shows what percentage of women have, by a

Average Female Experience

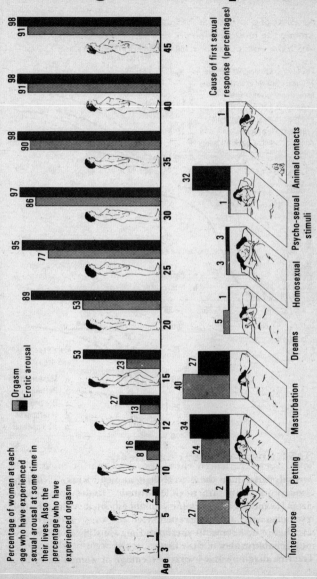

Percentage of women at each age who have experienced sexual arousal at some time in their lives. Also the percentage who have experienced orgasm

Orgasm
Erotic arousal

Age	3	5	10	12	15	20	25	30	35	40	45
Orgasm	1	4	16	27	53	89	95	97	98	98	98
Erotic arousal		2	8	13	23	53	77	86	90	91	91

Cause of first sexual response (percentages)

Intercourse	Petting	Masturbation	Dreams	Homosexual	Psycho-sexual stimuli	Animal contacts
27	34	27	5	3	32	1
2	24	40	1	3	1	

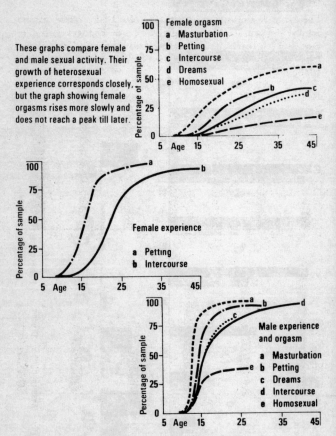

These graphs compare female and male sexual activity. Their growth of heterosexual experience corresponds closely, but the graph showing female orgasms rises more slowly and does not reach a peak till later.

Female orgasm
a Masturbation
b Petting
c Intercourse
d Dreams
e Homosexual

Female experience
a Petting
b Intercourse

Male experience and orgasm
a Masturbation
b Petting
c Dreams
d Intercourse
e Homosexual

given age, experienced either sexual arousal or orgasm; the second shows how these were first caused. Kinsey's findings showed just how rare so-called female "frigidity" is. Sexual arousal, and orgasm, begin in childhood. By the age of 35 only 2% of women have never experienced any sort of sexual arousal and only 9% have not experienced orgasm. For many women (40%), masturbation is the first source of orgasm, while petting is the main (34%) source of erotic arousal.

Average Female Experience

B16 Orgasm and Age

The diagram shows what percentage of sexually active women achieve orgasm at different ages. Response changes with age: most women reach their sexual peak during their late 20s and 30s. For many women there is then little change until the late 40s or early 50s.

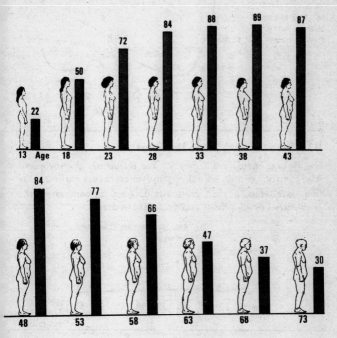

B16-18

Sexual outlets

Types of sexual outlet also vary with age. Taking five of the most likely activities, the graphs show what percentage they are of total sexual outlet. For example, between the ages of 13 and

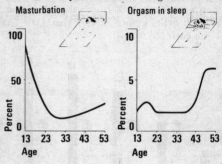

B17 Female and Male Patterns

On average men have orgasms more frequently than women. Also their maximum sexual responsiveness occurs earlier — by their late teens. It then gradually declines, in contrast to the later sexual development and decline in women.

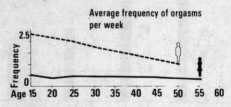

B18 Masturbation

Masturbation refers to stimulation of the genitals by hand or with some other object, usually to attain orgasm. It generally refers to self-stimulation, although mutual masturbation is common in both heterosexual and homosexual activity. At least 1 in 6 women masturbate at some time in their lives, and for many it is the most direct and successful means of achieving orgasm.

Masturbation

20 masturbation accounts for over 50% of a woman's sexual outlet; by her mid-30s this has declined to about 14%, and nearly 80% of her sexual activity is in heterosexual intercourse.

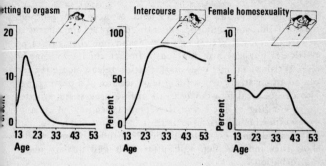

etting to orgasm   Intercourse   Female homosexuality

The graph compares the male and female experience of multiple orgasm. Kinsey found that 14% of the women with some sexual experience in his sample were capable of multiple orgasm.

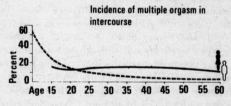

Incidence of multiple orgasm in intercourse

TRADITIONAL ATTITUDES

In our society, masturbation has been a subject more taboo than interpersonal sex. Traditionally the attitude was one of disapproval, reaching psychotic levels in the late 19th century. To some extent attitudes toward masturbation reflected those of society toward sexuality in general, but with an additional dimension caused by the fact that whereas interpersonal sex

B18-20

could be "justified" on grounds of love, marriage, etc, masturbation, by its very nature, was too blatantly an expression of an individual's inherent sexuality.

MODERN ATTITUDES

Since the researches of Kinsey and Masters and Johnson, masturbation is now more frequently recognized for what it is: a part of normal sexual experience and one that causes no particular physical or mental harm. In fact, the reverse may be seen as true. Not only does masturbation release acute tension due to an unsatisfactory sexual life or absence of a partner, but also can be used by women as a learning process for a better understanding of their sexual responses, leading in turn to greater fulfillment with a partner.

But despite more enlightened social attitudes, recent studies show that most women still suffer guilt and anxiety about masturbation.

B19 Cumulative Experience

The diagram opposite shows what percentage of women have experienced masturbation by a specific age. Some kind of sexual stimulation of the genitals often occurs in infants of only a few months, and Kinsey noted the case of a 4-month-old baby who experienced orgasm through self-stimulation. But generally, more conscious masturbation, resulting from natural curiosity about the sexual organs, begins between 2 and 5, and apparently begins somewhat earlier in girls than in boys. As the diagram shows, at least 60% of all women have masturbated at some stage by the age of 45. In general, masturbation is more common among older than younger women. Of women in their mid-40s, nearly 60% masturbate regularly as opposed to only 20% among adolescent women. Although this may be partly due to social factors, it does also reflect the general pattern of female sexual development.

Masturbation

Percentage of women at various ages who have
experienced masturbation at some time in their lives

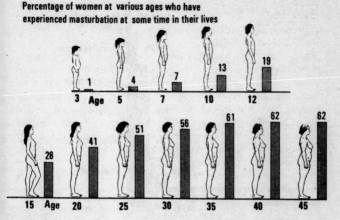

B20 Techniques

Women have various ways of masturbating, although the most
commonly used rely on stimulation of the clitoris. During her
life, a woman may use one or more of the methods described
below.

CLITORAL AND LABIAL

Well over 80% of women who masturbate regularly concentrate on direct stimulation of clitoris or labia. This is done in
various ways. One or more fingers can either be rubbed over or
around the clitoris, or the whole hand may be used to apply
steady and rhythmical pressure. (Few women masturbate by
actually rubbing the clitoral glans; more commonly they
massage the shaft or general clitoral area.) A pillow, vibrator,
or continuous stream of water from a faucet may be used
instead of the hands. Alternatively, some women masturbate by
crossing their legs, applying steady pressure from their thighs
onto the genital area. In addition, while using any of these
techniques, a finger or similar object may be inserted into the
vagina, although few women rely on vaginal insertion alone.
Slightly different from these methods is a technique used by
about 5% of women. In this a woman assumes a prone position
similar to that of a woman-on-top position in intercourse.
Although there may be some direct stimulation of the genitals,

B20-22

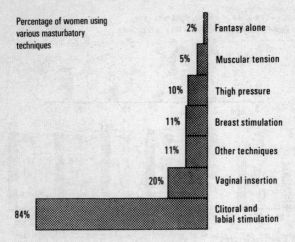

Percentage of women using various masturbatory techniques

2%	Fantasy alone
5%	Muscular tension
10%	Thigh pressure
11%	Breast stimulation
11%	Other techniques
20%	Vaginal insertion
84%	Clitoral and labial stimulation

possibly with a pillow, it is usually very slight, and a climax is achieved by rhythmical pelvic thrusting combined with a build-up of muscular tension similar to that during intercourse.

OTHER METHODS

In most women the breasts and nipples are highly sensitive and in a few cases their stimulation alone is sufficient for orgasm. Likewise, about 2% of women achieve orgasm through fantasy.

B21 Fantasies

Although it is usually assumed that sexual-erotic fantasies are a male prerogative, at least 50% of women always fantasize during masturbation and 70% sometimes do. To some extent the same applies during sexual intercourse. But only recently, in such publications as *My Secret Garden* by Nancy Friday, have women begun to admit to the variety and eroticism of their fantasies. Many women are still scared of such fantasies, fearing that they represent some sort of deviation or escape mechanism. While sexual fantasies do represent a degree of wish-fulfillment, they are also recognized as a natural and stimulating part of sexual activity.

Lesbianism

Percentage of women experiencing different types of fantasv
during masturbation

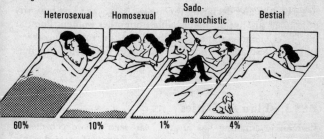

Heterosexual	Homosexual	Sado- masochistic	Bestial
60%	10%	1%	4%

B22 Homosexuality

The word "homosexual" is used, as with a man, to refer to
women who are attracted, emotionally and physically, to
members of their own sex. But, more frequently, female
homosexuals are known as lesbians, a name derived from the
Greek island of Lesbos, which, some 2600 years ago, was the
home of the poet Sappho. Many of her poems were beautifully
and movingly addressed to women, and from them comes the
term "Sapphic love" to describe love between women. It has
been suggested that the term "homoemotional" more accurately describes lesbianism, as such love between women is more
frequently characterized by its intense emotionalism than by its
sexual aspect. But, in our society, no matter which term is used,
the conventional interpretation of lesbianism has been
incorrectly one of perversion.

INCIDENCE

Statistics of actual numbers of lesbians in a population are
almost impossible to obtain. Because of secrecy, and even guilt,
surveys need not reveal the truth. Also, it is important to
distinguish between occasional incidents and a real preference.
Some degree of "homosexual" activity is common, either in pre-
adolescent sex play or in the schoolgirl crushes of adolescence.
It has long been thought that there are fewer lesbians than male
homosexuals in the population, although this is unlikely.
Perhaps 20% of women have at least one homosexual
experience to orgasm during their lives. But only perhaps 2-5%
of adult females in Western society are exclusively homosexual.
Although today more women are displaying their lesbianism

B22-24

more openly and declaring themselves "gay," the vast majority of lesbians are not distinguishable from other women. Popular images of the masculine-type "dyke" are, in reality, incorrect; and most lesbians are not identifiable by body type, mannerisms, dress, or occupation.

B23 Lesbian Activities

Lesbian lovemaking has always been seen in two completely different ways. On the one hand, there is considerable ignorance and fear among nonhomosexuals about lesbian procedure; while on the other hand, distorted presentations of lesbian activity have long been accepted as a source of erotic arousal in classical art, and today in hard-core pornography. Both views incorrectly assume that lovemaking between women is a preliminary to, or a substitute for, heterosexual intercourse. In fact, the reverse is true. What is notable is that lesbians can achieve a far greater sexual satisfaction with each other than many other women achieve in their heterosexual relations. Nearly all lesbian lovemaking results in orgasm for both women, a fact which may explain why men have tended to feel threatened by lesbianism. Many sexual activities are common to both lesbians and heterosexuals. In both there is mutual kissing and caressing, particularly of the breasts and genitals, and the general procedures of getting used to one another and of giving affection. By its very nature there is no pre-intercourse foreplay in lesbian lovemaking, and most activity centers around clitoral stimulation. The main techniques used are mutual masturbation and cunnilingus (kissing, sucking, and licking of the clitoris). Vibrators are commonly used for clitoral stimulation; the dildo, or artificial penis, is not used; in fact, its use has been a particularly pernicious and long-lasting myth. By definition, lesbians are attracted to other women and their lovemaking does not center on penis substitutes. One additional practice which is sometimes used is that of tribadism, where one woman lies on top of another and moves in such a way as to stimulate the clitoris of each.

A further myth is that each partner takes an exclusively "butch" (active male) or "femme" (active female) role. In sexual

Lesbianism

practice, if such roles are assumed, they usually alternate. This stereotyped view has confused nonhomosexuals and lesbians themselves, not only sexually but also in a social context. And this confusion has, to some degree, resulted in the ideological rejection of such roles as advocated by radical lesbians. A final and overriding myth is, perhaps, that all lesbians are first and foremost sexual beings, whereas they are no more sexually active or sexually obsessed than are most people. By comparison with male homosexuals, sexual promiscuity is rare among lesbians, as is prostitution. At the same time, particularly with the recent emergence of "gayness," and with the more open expression of female sexuality, promiscuity is neither more nor less frequent among lesbians than among heterosexual women.

B24 Theories

Until recently there have been few studies exclusively of lesbianism. Physical explanations such as hormone imbalance or congenital defects have been put forward, but findings are ambiguous and not generally accepted. In the past, lesbianism has also been defined in terms of neurosis or of immature development, but these are generalizations based on lesbians who have sought psychiatric help. One of the most sympathetic and recent theories is that of the psychiatrist Dr Charlotte Wolff. She emphasizes the bisexual nature of lesbianism, seeing an essentially bisexual element in the female anatomy (the clitoris). She explains lesbianism as a recognition, and rejection, from early childhood, of the "second sex" emotional attitudes and social position of women. Because of this she also says that lesbians are ideally suited to lead a move for the equality of women and the rejection of female/male stereotypes — which to some extent is the basis of Radical Lesbian ideology.

PROBLEMS

Society has so far tended to see lesbianism as abnormal. As a result, a woman who feels attracted to other women may fear the opinion of others, both within the family and society, and may even also have difficulty in admitting her sexual preference to herself. There has been some liberalizing of attitudes in society recently; also, with the development of the women's movement, some women have felt a commitment to lesbianism as part of a general rejection of any need for the male. However, other lesbians still feel the need to repress ordinary expression of their sexuality, and perhaps to play a token part in heterosexual relations. (In some cases such activity may be part of a genuine bisexuality.) Although lesbianism is now more organized, many lesbians remain isolated, unable to meet others.

B25 Bisexuality

Most of the confusion and disgust surrounding homosexuality exists because it is too frequently assumed that homosexuals deviate markedly from normality. There is very little evidence to support this. Instead it is believed by many, including Freud, Kinsey, and, more recently, psychiatrist Dr Charlotte Wolfe, that each person is inherently bisexual and, depending on conditioning, may choose a partner from the opposite sex (heterosexuality), the same sex (homosexuality), or both (bisexuality).

B26 Attitudes

Human societies have shown ambivalent and contradictory attitudes toward lesbians. On the one hand, female homosexuality has been regarded as a deviation, while on the other it has been ignored or ridiculed. These last attitudes, which reflect the approach of male-oriented societies toward women, have meant that female homosexuals have significantly escaped the same degree of legal persecution suffered by males. There are also far fewer historical references to lesbianism. It was accepted in ancient Greece and Rome. And it is also known

Sexual Problems

that the Mohave Indians of North America recognized and accepted a class of homosexual women.

But references to lesbians are scanty even during the Middle Ages when persecution of homosexuals reached fanatical proportions. In most European countries homosexuality was a capital offense. But significantly more sentences were carried out on males. Likewise, during the 1930s in New York, more than 700 males were convicted on homosexuality charges, but only one female.

MODERN ATTITUDES

During the 20th century lesbians have therefore had to fight two battles, one for basic recognition and one for acceptance. This began in the late 1920s with the publication in England of Radclyffe Hall's *The Well of Loneliness,* which aroused public disgust, and has continued more recently through the women's movement and the rise of Radical Lesbianism. Today lesbianism is out in the open for the first time. Despite its relative legal freedom (in Europe it is a crime only in Austria and Spain), lack of understanding about lesbians and discrimination against them — socially and economically — are still widespread.

B27 Sexual Problems

A wide range of problems can affect a woman's enjoyment of her sexuality. They may be physical or psychological in origin, but the result is the same — distress for both partners.

A very few women are truly frigid — that is, incapable of responding to any kind of sexual stimulation. But there are many who are temporarily unable to achieve orgasm. Some women find penile penetration or intercourse painful or even impossible; others have a partner with some kind of sexual difficulty. The purely physical problems are usually easy to identify; psychological problems can also be treated, but the origin of the problem must be traced first. Common underlying causes of psychological problems are feelings of fear, shame, or guilt about sexual response, or anxieties connected with pregnancy. Important in the treatment of such problems are the revolutionary sexual therapy techniques developed by Masters and Johnson.

B28-30

B28 Frigidity

Frigidity, or general sexual dysfunction, is a complex female complaint in which a woman derives little or no erotic pleasure from sexual stimulation. Treatment often takes the form of sensate focus therapy — a technique developed by Masters and Johnson. In sensate focus therapy the couple refrain from intercourse and orgasm for a period. During this time, they learn to caress each other's bodies until the woman is sufficiently aroused to initiate intercourse.

B29 Problems with Orgasm

For women, the most common sexual complaints are those to do with difficulty of reaching, or inability to achieve, orgasm.
REASONS
There are many complex reasons why women may experience difficulty in achieving orgasm, not only with a partner but also by themselves in masturbation. Shame about their sexuality, fear of actually examining their genitals, and therefore ignorance about their function, are among the main reasons for some women's avoidance of masturbation. Ignorance about the physiology of sex can equally prevent women from achieving orgasm with their partner. But in a female/male situation, other problems arise. Some of the most important are probably the refusal or inability of women to express clearly what they want from sex, and a deference to, or overprotectiveness toward, the male orgasm, at the loss of their own. This often leads to the practice by some women of faking orgasm within their relationship — a practice which ultimately can cause great strain on both people.
MASTERS-JOHNSON THERAPY
Masters-Johnson sex therapy divides the female problems with orgasm into two main categories:
a) primary orgasmic dysfunction — women who have never experienced orgasm; and
b) secondary orgasmic dysfunction — women who have previously experienced orgasm but whose ability to achieve it has since stopped.
Such women who have problems with orgasm are often very sexually responsive, enjoy intercourse, but are still unable to

Sexual Problems

continue their response beyond the plateau phase (B03).

Therapy consists essentially of encouraging an inorgasmic woman to bring herself to orgasm by masturbation (B18) either by hand or with an electric vibrator — a phallic-shaped sexual aid which, when held against the clitoral area, can bring a woman to orgasm. Once a woman can achieve orgasm easily by herself, her partner is brought into the therapy. Normal intercourse takes place during which the woman makes no attempt to achieve orgasm. Instead her partner brings her to climax either manually or with the vibrator. In general, after only a few sessions, the woman will be achieving orgasm during intercourse.

FEMINIST THERAPY

Feminists in the USA have started preorgasmic groups to tackle the same problem of female orgasmic dysfunction. They also concentrate on encouraging women to discover their own physical sexuality, but at the same time are examining some of the male-dependence roles mentioned above.

B30 Painful Intercourse

Discomfort during intercourse can make lovemaking an unpleasant experience for some women. There are several possible explanations for the discomfort.

VIRGINITY

In a woman who has not had intercourse, the hymen may be intact and unstretched (a). The first few times intercourse takes place there may be a little pain or even slight bleeding as the hymen is stretched or torn (b) to accommodate the penis. A very few women have tough hymens which need minor surgery.

VAGINISMUS

This is a comparatively rare disorder in which the muscles surrounding the vaginal entrance go into spasm when penetration is attempted. Treatment involves the woman learning, over a period of time, to insert first one, then two fingers into her vagina without experiencing muscular spasm. Her partner takes part in this and, when the woman's confidence is established, intercourse can take place.

B30-31

DISPAREUNIA

This is a general term for painful intercourse. The pain may be caused by several factors. Vaginal infections and irritations can be exacerbated by the friction of the penis moving in the vagina. Insufficient vaginal lubrication can cause pain. During normal stimulation, the vaginal walls secrete a lubricating fluid which facilitates entry by the penis. Pain results if the man attempts entry before the woman is sufficiently aroused or if he is wearing a condom. In the first case, entry must be delayed until the woman is fully aroused, and in the second, a lubricating jelly, or even saliva, will help solve the problem. A

 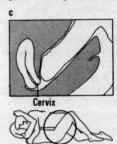

Cervix

common cause of pain in the pelvis is the penis hitting the cervix during particularly deep thrusts (c). Pelvic pain can also be caused by infections of the uterus, cervix, or Fallopian tubes, cysts or tumors on the ovaries, or tears in the ligaments supporting the uterus (following childbirth).

B31 Male Sexual Problems

IMPOTENCE

Many men experience a period of impotence at some stage in their lives. It can take two forms: inability to achieve erection, or inability to achieve orgasm despite erection. Most cases are caused by psychological factors such as fear of sexual failure, neurosis, or guilt. Treatment involves a series of Masters and Johnson sensate focus exercises similar to the therapy described in B28 for female frigidity.

PREMATURE EJACULATION

This is when the man reaches ejaculation too quickly for the woman to be sexually satisfied. Occasional occurrence is

Sexual Problems

normal, but consistent premature ejaculation can lead to self-consciousness, partner dissatisfaction, and impotence. The major cause of premature ejaculation is simply anxiety that premature ejaculation will occur. Unsatisfactory approaches to the problem include distracting the mind, use of anesthetic creams, drugs, and alcohol, and avoidance of touching the male genitals. Masters and Johnson evolved a successful therapy in which the woman manually controls and delays her partner's ejaculation.

EJACULATORY INCOMPETENCE

In this condition, which is less common than premature ejaculation, the man has no difficulty in achieving an erection, but cannot reach orgasm inside the vagina. The cause sometimes lies in traumatic incidents in the past, often in the context of a sexually restrictive upbringing.

The Masters and Johnson therapy begins with the masturbation of the man's penis to orgasm by the woman. Later the woman takes the penis into her vagina just before the male orgasm. When the man is confident about ejaculating into the vagina, he will then attempt penetration at a low level of sexual excitement.

C01

C01 Conception and Contraception

For pregnancy to occur, several conditions must be fulfilled: semen from the man must enter the woman's vagina;
the semen must contain healthy male sperm;
the sperm must find conditions in the vagina in which they can live;
the living sperm must make their way into the woman's uterus and (possibly) the Fallopian tubes;
they must find an egg there ready for fertilization;
and the egg, once fertilized, must be able to implant itself in the uterus.

By preventing any one of these, contraception is achieved. But it is important to note three things. First, that sperm may reach the vagina even if the penis does not enter it. Sperm ejaculated onto the vulva or surrounding skin can still swim into the vagina.

Second, that although conditions in the vagina are hostile to sperm, they can live there for 6 hours or more. So any barrier to prevent sperm moving up into the uterus must last at least this long after intercourse.

Third, that once sperm have reached the uterus they can live 4 to 5 days or more. So, to avoid conception, there must be at least this time gap between the arrival of sperm in the uterus and the arrival of the egg.

A normally fertile woman experiencing regular intercourse with a normally fertile man stands about a 60% chance of becoming pregnant in any one month. Therefore, for the woman who intends to have heterosexual intercourse, but not to have babies, some form of safe, effective contraception is essential.

The diagrams show the genital coupling and route of the semen. Ejaculation occurs in 2 stages. Rhythmic muscular contractions begin in testes and epididymides (a) and continue

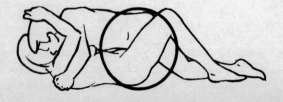

Conception and Contraception

along the vas deferns (**b**), also involving the seminal vesicles and prostate (**c**). Sperm and seminal fluid collect in the urethra inside the prostate. Then a sphincter relaxes, letting this semen pass down toward the penis. Contractions along the length of the urethra (**d**) cause ejaculation. Inside the woman's body, semen passes from the vagina into the uterus (**e**) and Fallopian tubes (**f**).

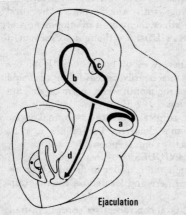

Ejaculation

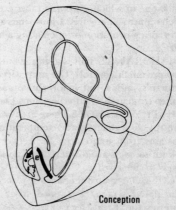

Conception

C02

C02 The Main Types of Contraceptive

There is a wide variety of contraceptive techniques in use today — none of which is ideal. Many concentrate on keeping sperm out of the uterus. Caps and condoms aim to provide a physical barrier; spermicides a chemical barrier. Withdrawal modifies the sex act, to try to keep sperm out of the female tract completely. Other techniques — generally more effective — concentrate on interfering with the ovum. The oral contraceptive pills usually affect the ovum's development and release. Intrauterine devices (IUDs) are thought to prevent it implanting in the uterus.

Finally, there are two other types of technique. "Rhythm" methods simply aim (not necessarily successfully) to avoid intercourse at those times of the month when sperm might find an ovum ready for fertilization.

Sterilization methods are surgical operations to make one partner incapable of having children. Techniques can be combined to give more effective contraception.

CONTRACEPTIVE TECHNIQUES
The remainder of this section will consider in detail the forms of contraception introduced here and located on the diagram opposite.

CONTRACEPTIVE PILL Oral contraceptives consist of small pills, one of which a woman takes every day for most or all of each month. There are various kinds and they have the effect of preventing ovulation or of creating a barrier to sperm (see C03-C07).

WITHDRAWAL This is a simple but not particularly effective form of birth control. The man withdraws his penis from the woman's vagina just before his orgasm, and so prevents the semen from getting into the vagina (see C15).

RHYTHM METHODS There are two rhythm methods of birth control — calendar and temperature. In both the woman abstains from intercourse for between 10 to 14 days of each month so as to avoid intercourse on the days when she is most likely to conceive (see C10-C12).

1 CONDOM is a rubber sheath placed on a man's erect penis. Ejaculated semen is trapped in it and so prevented from entering the vagina (see C09).

2 DIAPHRAGM is a rubber cap inserted by the woman into her vagina. It covers the entrance to the cervix, acting as a barrier to

Conception and Contraception

sperm (see C17).

3 SPERMICIDES are chemicals. Placed inside a woman's vagina, they both kill and act as a barrier to sperm (see C16).

4 INTRAUTERINE DEVICE (IUD) is a small device inserted into the woman's womb on a long-term basis. While in place, its effect on the uterus prevents implantation (see C08).

5a FEMALE STERILIZATION This consists of an operation on the Fallopian tubes, to prevent eggs passing from the ovaries to the womb (see C13).

5b MALE STERILIZATION (or "vasectomy") is a minor operation on the man's vas deferens which prevents sperm being ejaculated in the semen (see C14).

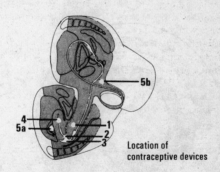

Location of
contraceptive devices

Most women change the type of contraceptive they use at least once or twice during their life.

BEFORE CHILDREN When a woman starts heterosexual activity, she will probably rely on the man to practice withdrawal, or to use a condom. Once regular relations are established, most young women prefer to use more effective and continuous methods like the Pill or one of the new IUDs.

FAMILY PLANNING Many women take the Pill between having children. Others use an IUD, or (less effectively) diaphragm, or condoms with spermicides. (An IUD can be removed by a doctor when conception is desired.) Some rely on the rhythm method, despite its failure rate.

AFTER HAVING CHILDREN Once a woman's family is complete, she may either return to a contraceptive that she has tried and liked, or she may at this point decide to be sterilized.

C03-04

C03 Contraceptive Pill

No other form of contraception has been as revolutionary as the "Pill." It is easy to use, reversible, and nearly 100% effective.

The Pill uses synthetic forms of the hormones estrogen and progesterone. These are produced naturally in the body for a few days in each menstrual cycle — and continuously during pregnancy. In each case, they have the effect of inhibiting output of FSH and LH hormones. FSH and LH are needed if follicles are to ripen for ovulation, and this is why no ovulation occurs during pregnancy. The contraceptive pill has a similar effect; and as no ovulation occurs, no ovum is available for fertilization by sperm.

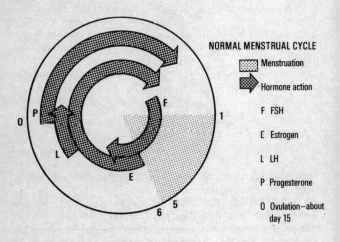

NORMAL MENSTRUAL CYCLE

Menstruation

Hormone action

F FSH

E Estrogen

L LH

P Progesterone

O Ovulation—about day 15

There are three main types of Pill:

a) the combination pill — so called because each active pill in the package contains both hormones;

b) the sequential pill, in which $\frac{3}{4}$ of the active pills contain just estrogen, and only the rest contain both hormones; and

c) the continuous pill, in which all pills contain progesterone alone, and which works rather differently.

The sequential pill has recently been withdrawn from use in some countries.

The Pill

C04 Taking the Pill

Taking the Pill is quite easy; the problem is to remember to do so. Most pills come in packages of 21 which are designed to aid memory. To start oral contraception, the first day of a period counts as day 1. Pill-taking begins on day 5, whether bleeding has stopped or not. It continues until day 25 when the last pill is taken. A gap of 7 pill-free days follows before the next course, during which menstruation occurs. For women who have difficulty in remembering this sequence, combined and sequential pills are available in packs of 28. But the extra pills are dummies.

The first package of pills may not give complete protection, and for the first 2 weeks a second contraceptive should be used.

If a combined pill is forgotten, it should be taken within 12 hours of the usual time even if it means taking 2 in 1 day. If more than 2 are missed and the gap between pills is more than 36 hours, then the pack should be finished but a second contraceptive also used.

It is important not to forget to take the continuous pill, and it must be taken at the same time every day.

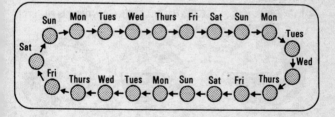

C05-07

C05 Types of Pill

COMBINATION PILL This is the most widely used and effective type. The woman takes one standard pill each day for 21 days, starting on the 5th day after menstruation begins, and ending on the 25th day. There is a gap of 7 days during which no hormone is taken, and menstruation occurs; then a new package is started.

As well as preventing ovulation, the combination pill:

a) affects the uterus lining, so implantation could not occur;

b) causes the cervical mucus to thicken, forming a chemical barrier to sperm.

SEQUENTIAL PILL This is closer to a woman's natural cycle, but less effective. Again, 21 pills are taken, starting on the 5th day after menstruation. But the first 14 pills contain estrogen alone; only the remainder contain both hormones. Ovulation is prevented, but the uterus lining and cervical mucus are unaffected.

CONTINUOUS PILL There are 28 pills in each pack, all active and all containing synthetic progesterone only. One is taken every day, even during menstruation. They work mainly by their effect on the uterus lining and cervical mucus, rather than on ovulation.

COMBINED PILL CYCLE   SEQUENTIAL PILL CYCLE   CONTINUOUS PILL CYCLE

▭	Menstruation	
➡	Hormone action	

5	First pill	5	First estrogen-only pill
25	Last pill	19	First estrogen/
e	Estrogen		progesterone pill
p	Progesterone	25	Last pill

p Progesterone only

C06 Side Effects

Most women experience some side effects on the Pill. There

The Pill

may be headaches, nausea, swollen or tender breasts, heavier periods, and vaginal discharge. But not all women experience these, and most symptoms disappear within the first few months. If they do not, a change of brand may remove any unpleasant side effects.

No woman should take the Pill without consulting a doctor. All pills, and especially high-estrogen ones, carry a risk of blood clotting. The resulting thrombosis may be fatal. This is more likely in women over 35, and pregnancy itself carries higher risks. Other disorders a doctor must consider before prescribing the Pill include hepatitis, diabetes, migraine, and epilepsy. There is still no proof that the Pill causes cancer. But estrogen can aggravate some types of existing cancer. Cervical smears are an important part of the medical examination that accompany the Pill, and a cancerous condition would be found in good time. Doctors still disagree on how long a woman should stay on the Pill. On average, women tend to use it for 3 to 4 years. To regain fertility, a woman only needs to stop taking the Pill. But it may be some months before her ovaries are functioning normally and conception can occur.

C07 Depo-Provera

This is based on similar hormonal principles to the oral pill, but is given by injection: 150mg is injected every 3 months, or larger doses every 6 months. It is given to an estimated 1 million women in about 70 countries — mostly developing ones. But in the USA and UK, use of the drug is only very rarely allowed. In its favor is its effectiveness, when other methods fail through lack of motivation or care. Against it are its possible side effects and links with disease. Symptoms in some women may include:

a) disruption of menstrual bleeding, which may be prolonged, heavy, unpredictable, or absent altogether;

b) vomiting, dizziness, moodiness, headaches, and weight gain; and

c) rectal bleeding.

Links with disease include:

a) an established link with subsequent infertility in some women;

b) established links with blood-clotting disorders; and

c) possible links with breast and cervical cancer.

Co8

C08 Intrauterine Device (IUD)

The IUD, also known as the "coil" or "loop," is a small plastic device for insertion into the uterus. It may be left there for several years, and while in place works as a contraceptive almost as effective as the Pill without requiring much attention. Intercourse can occur without restriction. Once the IUD is removed, fertility returns in 1 to 12 months.

Comparable practices date back to biblical times, when camel drivers inserted pebbles into the uteri of female camels, to keep them from becoming pregnant.

Yet how an IUD works is uncertain.

Theories include:

a) that an IUD makes the ovum pass down the Fallopian tube too rapidly for fertilization or implantation;

b) that it interferes with the lining of the uterus, so that implantation cannot take place; and

c) that it interferes directly with the implantation process.

The IUD is very effective while in place — though some doctors advise use of a spermicide as well around ovulation. But it may fall out, especially during the first few months or at menstruation. Early IUDs were too large for women who had not had children. Recently smaller designs, usable by all women, have appeared. However, the failure rate may be a little higher.

Many women experience side effects with IUDs — usually heavy periods and/or pain. For this reason, about 25% of women fitted have their IUD removed.

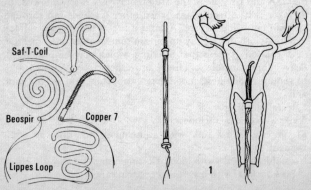

Saf-T-Coil

Beospir   Copper 7

Lippes Loop

1

IUDs and Condoms

IUDs may also aggravate infection, or (rarely) cause it. There is also a slight risk of perforation of the uterine wall, but significant damage is rare.

If pregnancy does occur, the IUD can be removed, as it increases the risk of miscarriage. Otherwise though, most types have no effect on a fetus.

Many doctors advise renewal of the IUD every 2-3 years.

Lippes Loop and Saf-T-Coil are the most commonly used IUDs for women who have had children.

For those who have not, the Copper 7 (and the similar Copper T) are the most common. These both have copper wound around the stem, and this aids their contraceptive effect.

INSERTION

1 An IUD must only be fitted by a trained person. Some require an anesthetic, but most are packed in a thin plastic inserter, which may be passed without difficulty through the cervical canal into the uterus. This is easiest during or just after menstruation.

2 The IUD is then pushed through the inserter and takes up its normal shape inside the uterus. The insertion takes only a few minutes. Some women experience discomfort similar to a heavy period pain. This can last for 24 hours with some slight bleeding.

3 The IUD has nylon threads (or a stem projection) left hanging through the cervix into the vagina. As a result, a woman can — and should — make regular checks to ensure her IUD is still in place.

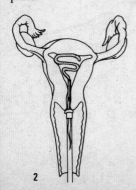

2

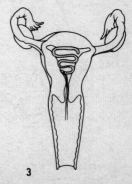

3

Co9

C09 Condom

The condom ("sheath," "rubber," "French letter") is still probably the most widely used contraceptive. It has a long history, dating back some hundreds of years, and was popularized as a protection against venereal disease. When used carefully, preferably with a spermicide, it is an effective means of birth control.

The condom consists of a thin rubber sheath, about 7in (18cm) long, open at one end and closed at the other. It fits tightly over the man's erect penis. When he ejaculates, his semen is trapped in the sealed end. This prevents sperm from entering the vagina.

USING A CONDOM

The condom is taken out of the package rolled up, and is unrolled onto the erect penis just before intercourse. (The actions of this can be incorporated into lovemaking.)

At least 1in (2.5cm) at the tip should be left empty of air to help prevent bursting or leakage. After ejaculation, the man withdraws his penis before his erection subsides. While withdrawing, he should hold the condom so that it does not come off.

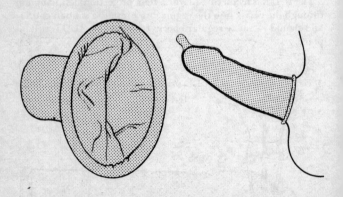

IUDs and Condoms

TYPES

There are various types of condoms — plain ended or teat ended — and they can be of different colors. Some people complain that condoms reduce sensitivity: lubricated brands claim to be an improvement.

For easier insertion, it is better for a woman to use spermicidal cream or jelly, which gives the advantage of extra contraceptive effectiveness. Condoms have kept their popularity largely because they do not need medical supervision and can be obtained and carried around easily. They are sold in sealed packages and have a maximum shelf life of 2 years, away from heat. Their chief disadvantage is that, due to the annoyance of interrupting lovemaking, some couples may decide to "take the risk" of intercourse without contraception.

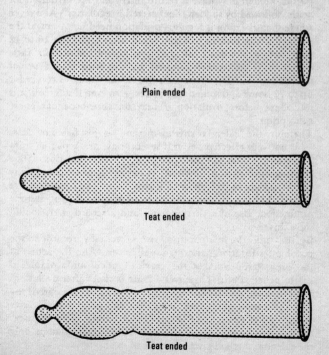

Plain ended

Teat ended

Teat ended

C10-11

C10 Rhythm Method

With this method, a couple do not have intercourse during the part of the woman's menstrual cycle during which she can conceive, ie when a fertilizable egg is available.

The menstrual cycle lasts (in principle) 28 days. During this, the egg is available for fertilization for only about 1 day — the 24 hours that follow ovulation. However, there is no direct sign of ovulation, only of menstruation. Ovulation typically occurs halfway between the menstruations — on about the 15th day. So a woman can count forward 14 days from the start of her last menstruation to guess when ovulation will occur. But the menstrual cycle is seldom perfectly regular. In most women, menstruation is erratic when periods return after the birth of a baby, and in a quarter of women it is always fairly erratic. (Other women may have a record of regular menstruation for years, followed by sudden, unexpected irregularity.) Also, even where menstruation is regular, ovulation need not occur at the midpoint, the 15th day. It can occur anywhere from 16 to 12 days before the start of the next menstruation. In fact, ovulation is sometimes induced by the stimulus of sexual intercourse. Finally, sperm can live in the woman's cervix for up to 72 hours and sometimes longer — so even if intercourse is four days before ovulation it may on rare occasions cause conception.

Therefore the "calendar rhythm method" — just based on dates — is not very effective, even if several days are kept free from intercourse around the likely date of ovulation. The "temperature rhythm method" is better. A woman normally has a sudden rise of about 1°F (0.6°C) in body temperature during the day of ovulation, due to increased progesterone production. Use of a thermometer and a record chart should show this rise.

By the time the temperature rise is actually recorded, the possible fertilization period is usually over. (Also the action of the progesterone makes the cervical mucus unfavorable to sperm penetration.) This gives a "safe period" after ovulation, from the temperature rise up to (and including, if desired) the next menstruation. But it gives no safe period after menstruation since there is no way of telling when the next ovulation will occur. Between menstruation and ovulation, only the calendar method gives any indication of safety.

The Rhythm Method

C11 Temperature Rhythm Method

The temperature should be taken first thing on waking, before any activity (even getting out of bed). A rectal thermometer is preferable to an oral one.

The circle shows the pattern of temperature during the menstrual cycle. Low temperatures are at the outside, high at the center. There is an abrupt rise at ovulation (about day 14).

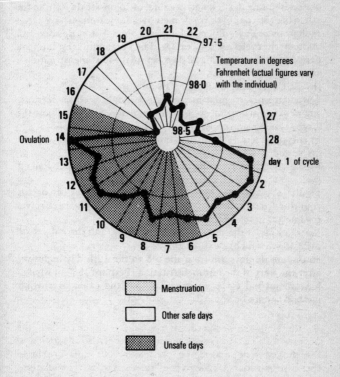

Temperature in degrees Fahrenheit (actual figures vary with the individual)

Ovulation

day 1 of cycle

Menstruation

Other safe days

Unsafe days

C12

C12 Calendar Rhythm Method

REGULAR MENSTRUATION

Suppose a woman had menstruation regularly every 28 days. Ovulation would be most likely on the 15th day of the cycle, but could happen anytime from the 13th to the 17th — a period of 5 days. Since sperm can live 72 hours and even longer, 4 days before this are also unsafe. And since the egg may still be fertilizable 24 hours after ovulation, the day after the 5-day period is unsafe too. This gives a total of 10 unsafe days, from the 9th to the 18th day of the cycle inclusive. Some women have cycles as short as 21 days, others as long as 38 days — but this does not matter if the cycles are still regular. The woman still abstains for a period of 10 days, starting 20 days before the next menstruation is expected.

IRREGULAR MENSTRUATION

A woman with irregular menstruation should keep an accurate record of her menstrual cycle for a year beforehand, and note the shortest and longest cycles. She must then calculate as follows:

a) she subtracts 19 from the number of days in her shortest cycle; and

b) she subtracts 10 from the number of days in her longest cycle.

Figure (a) gives the earliest day on which pregnancy can occur, counting from the start of the last menstruation; figure (b) gives the latest.

For example, if the shortest cycle is 25 days, and the longest 29:

a) 25-19 = 6; and b) 29-10 = 19.

So the unsafe days are from the 6th to the 19th day inclusive, after the start of the last menstruation. Perhaps 15% of women have menstrual cycles so irregular that the calendar rhythm method cannot be applied.

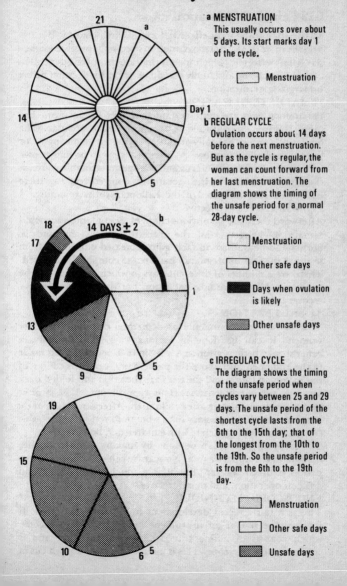

The Rhythm Method

a MENSTRUATION
This usually occurs over about 5 days. Its start marks day 1 of the cycle.

☐ Menstruation

b REGULAR CYCLE
Ovulation occurs about 14 days before the next menstruation. But as the cycle is regular, the woman can count forward from her last menstruation. The diagram shows the timing of the unsafe period for a normal 28-day cycle.

☐ Menstruation

☐ Other safe days

■ Days when ovulation is likely

▨ Other unsafe days

c IRREGULAR CYCLE
The diagram shows the timing of the unsafe period when cycles vary between 25 and 29 days. The unsafe period of the shortest cycle lasts from the 6th to the 15th day; that of the longest from the 10th to the 19th. So the unsafe period is from the 6th to the 19th day.

☐ Menstruation

☐ Other safe days

▨ Unsafe days

C13-14

C13 Female Sterilization

Sterilization is the most effective form of birth control. But it is also the most final — a last solution. As yet, no reversible method has been perfected, which means that a person considering the operation must be absolutely certain of her or his decision before undergoing sterilization.

FEMALE STERILIZATION

For women who are quite certain that they do not want any more children, sterilization is becoming more popular. The operation consists basically of cutting, tying, or removing all or part of the Fallopian tubes. As a result, eggs can no longer pass from the ovaries to the uterus and the sperm is unable to reach the eggs. Provided that the operation is done correctly — there have been rare instances of the Fallopian tubes rejoining — sterilization is 100% effective.

Afterward there are no obvious changes. Sexual interest should remain unchanged, and the menstrual cycle continues as normal. Some women, in fact, gain increased enjoyment from sex once the fear of pregnancy has been so completely removed. There are a number of different ways in which a woman can be sterilized. All require hospitalization but the time needed for recovery varies.

TUBAL LIGATION

This is the most commonly used method of sterilization for women. It can be done in various ways. Traditionally, a general anesthetic is given and a 2-3in (5-7.5cm) incision made in the abdomen, just above the pubic hair. A piece is cut out of the Fallopian tubes, and the ends are then tied and folded back into the surrounding tissue. This type of operation is often performed immediately after childbirth. After some days in the hospital, it is then necessary for a woman to rest for some weeks (which for a working woman with children may be difficult).

The same operation can be done by making a much smaller incision in the upper vagina. No scar is visible and the recovery period is much shorter. But it is a much more skilled and difficult operation, and therefore rare.

ENDOSCOPIC TECHNIQUE

This is a fairly recent development in female sterilization. It involves the use of an instrument known as a laparoscope, which consists of a fine tube which conducts light and is connected to a telescope. This is inserted through a small cut in

Sterilization and Spermicides

the abdomen — it can also be inserted through the vagina — and is used to light up and inspect the Fallopian tubes. Very fine forceps are inserted, either through the same cut or through a second smaller one, and an electrocurrent which cauterizes the Fallopian tubes is passed along them. Afterward, there are only 2 tiny scars and the recovery time is very short.

HYSTERECTOMY
Until quite recently, hysterectomy, which involves the complete removal of the uterus (see L10), was a fairly widespread means of sterilization. However, it is not now generally recommended for birth control purposes, though it is an operation that many women unfortunately have to undergo for other reasons (see L11).

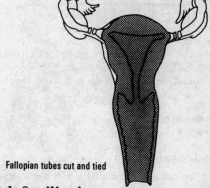

Fallopian tubes cut and tied

C14 Male Sterilization

VASECTOMY
A vesectomy is a safe, simple, surgical operation in which each vas deferens — the duct leading from each testis to the penis — is cut and tied off. As a result, the semen a man ejects no longer contains sperm.

Apart from instances where the cut tubes have rejoined, the operation is always completely effective. It does not alter a man's ability to have an orgasm or to ejaculate. But the operation is rarely reversible, which again means that a man must be absolutely sure before undergoing a vasectomy. The operation is quite short and generally lasts under half an hour.

C14-16

For the majority of vasectomy operations, a local anesthetic only is needed. Either 1 or 2 very small cuts are made on or near the scrotum. A piece about 1cm long is removed from each duct, the cut ends then being folded back and tied. Once the operation is over, the man can generally return straight home and can be back at work within 2 or 3 days. The most common aftereffects are likely to be some soreness and bruising. A vasectomy is not immediately effective as there are usually some sperm stored in the seminal vesicles, above the cut. For this reason, a second method of contraception must be used, until two successive follow-up tests of the semen show negative sperm counts (perhaps 2 or 3 months after the operation).

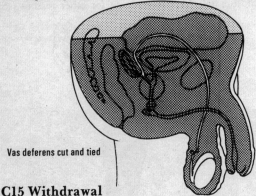

Vas deferens cut and tied

C15 Withdrawal

Withdrawal (or coitus interruptus) is the oldest and simplest method of birth control. The man takes his penis out of the woman's vagina just before his orgasm. His semen is ejaculated outside her body. Used with great care, withdrawal may be effective, but only if every drop of semen is not only kept out of the vagina but also right away from the vaginal lips. It is impossible to be sure of this because:

a) some fluid containing live sperm may "weep" from the penis before orgasm; and

b) in the pleasure of orgasm, the man may not withdraw properly.

Continued use of withdrawal can also be frustrating. The woman in particular may not be able to relax through fear that the man may not withdraw.

Sterilization and Spermicides

C16 Spermicides

These are chemical products which are inserted into the woman's vagina before sexual intercourse. They act in 2 ways: by killing the sperm, and by creating a barrier of foam or fluid through which sperm cannot pass into the uterus.

Spermicides come in various forms: creams, jellies, aerosol foams, foaming tablets, suppositories, and C-film, a fairly recent spermicide-impregnated plastic. But used by themselves, none of these is at all reliable as a contraceptive. If used, they should be combined with another method, such as cap or condom.

Creams, jellies, and aerosols are sold with a special applicator. Using this, the woman squirts the chemical high up into her vagina.

This should be done as near to intercourse as possible, and certainly no more than one hour before, as effectiveness is only temporary.

Using an applicator

Suppositories and tablets come in solid form and must be inserted by hand deep into the vagina.

Suppositories are cone-shaped and melt at body temperature; tablets dissolve and foam in the vagina's moisture. Both should be inserted 15 minutes before intercourse.

The new C-film consists of a small square of soluble plastic which can either be inserted into the vagina or placed on the tip of the man's penis before it enters the vagina. It dissolves, releasing spermicide, but is no more reliable than other spermicides (and less so than some).

Some women find that spermicides irritate their genitals.

C17

C17 Contraceptive Caps

DIAPHRAGM (DUTCH CAP)

The diaphragm is the best-known example of caps that fit across a woman's cervix to act as a barrier to sperm. The diaphragm is a domelike rubber device. Its rim contains a coiled spring. By itself the cap is not particularly safe, but used carefully in conjunction with spermicides it is quite effective. For most women before the Pill was introduced, the diaphragm was the safest method of contraception available to them.

Putting a diaphragm in place is not very difficult, though at first it needs practice. The woman holds its edges together and pushes it by hand into the vagina so that the bottom edge rests against the rear of the vagina and the top edge rests against the vaginal wall behind the bladder. The spring causes the diaphragm to regain its circular shape so that it is held in place. Before insertion, 2-4in (5-10cm) of spermicidal cream or jelly should be squeezed onto the inside (closest to the cervix) or both sides of the cap. The cap

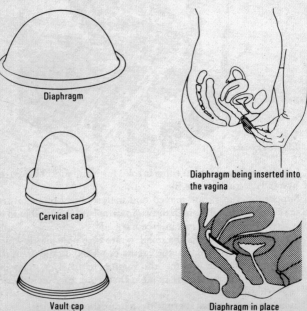

Diaphragm

Cervical cap

Vault cap

Diaphragm being inserted into the vagina

Diaphragm in place

The Cap

should be put into the vagina not more than 2-3 hours before intercourse. After intercourse it should be left in place for at least 6-8 hours while the sperm die. If intercourse occurs again in that time, more spermicide should first be introduced into the vagina without disturbing the cap.

Diaphragms vary in size. An initial fitting by a doctor or nurse is essential, and the cap should be checked for fit every 6 months, after a pregnancy, or if more than 10lb (4.5kg) is gained or lost in weight. At home, the cap must be washed after use, according to instructions, and checked carefully for holes.

CERVICAL CAP

This is much smaller, and fits onto the cervix. It is no longer used except in special cases.

VAULT CAP

A vault cap is much more rigid than other caps. It fits across the top end of the vagina and is held in place by suction.

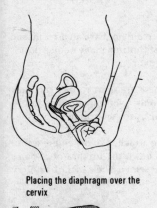

Placing the diaphragm over the cervix

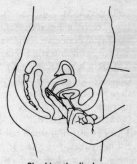

Checking the diaphragm

Cervical cap in place

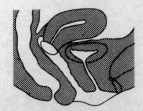

Vault cap in place

C18-19

C18 Unsatisfactory Methods

MORNING-AFTER PILL

This should only be seen as an emergency measure. It consists of giving a woman large doses of estrogen about 3 days after unprotected intercourse. The estrogen affects the uterus lining and implantation is prevented. The side effects are undesirable and may be harmful.

LACTATION

Breastfeeding mothers were once thought to be unable to conceive in the first 6 weeks after childbirth, if their periods had not returned. But in fact, though the likelihood of conception is reduced, contraception is still necessary.

DOUCHE

Douching — washing out the vagina after intercourse — is a completely ineffective method of birth control. Not only can sperm reach the cervix within 90 seconds, but the effect of squirting liquid into the vagina could be to help the sperm on their way.

NO ORGASM

It was once believed that if a woman did not have an orgasm, she would not conceive. This is obviously untrue; many women do not have orgasms but still become pregnant.

AMERICAN (GRECIAN) TIPS

Claimed to increase sensitivity, these are short rubber condoms that fit over the tip of the penis only. Not only do they fail to increase sensitivity, they are also likely to come off in the vagina.

GAMIC APPLIANCE

This consists of a small rubber bag attached to the end of a thin rubber tube. The tube is pushed down the urethra of a man's penis, so that when he ejaculates the semen is held in the bag. Very rarely used, this method is likely to cause damage to the urethra or infection.

C19 Effectiveness of Techniques

THE ODDS OF BECOMING PREGNANT

It is misleading to make a hard and fast statement about the effectiveness of contraception. As the table shows, there is a difference between effectiveness in theory and success in practice. For example, the combined pill has a theoretical effectiveness of 99.9%. In practice, this drops to between 95% and 98%, as out of 100 women using it for a year, between 2 and 5 become pregnant. Failures happen for various reasons. The method itself can fail, or a couple can fail either to use it correctly or even to use it at all.

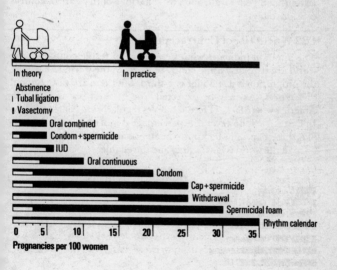

In theory   In practice

Abstinence
Tubal ligation
Vasectomy
Oral combined
Condom + spermicide
IUD
Oral continuous
Condom
Cap + spermicide
Withdrawal
Spermicidal foam
Rhythm calendar

0   5   10   15   20   25   30   35

Pregnancies per 100 women

C20 Contraception Today

Contraception today, even with its faults, has reached a fairly high level of sophistication. Yet of the world's fertile women, probably less than a third actually use contraception regularly. There are various reasons for this discrepancy. Outside Europe and North America, women in most parts of the world know little about modern contraception. Anticontraceptive laws still exist in some countries, while in others social or religious attitudes create further barriers. Despite the enormous increase in family planning programs, facilities are often inadequate. Statistics on this page are based on surveys done by the International Planned Parenthood Federation and give some idea of the state of contraception today.

C22 World Use of Contraceptives

The diagram indicates what percentage of fertile couples in the world are regularly using contraception. In the world as a whole, the proportion is just under one-third, but there are vast regional differences. As may be expected, the greatest use is in North America where 80% of fertile couples regularly use contraception. In East Africa, however, the percentage is well under 2%. Figures like these can only be approximate, as information from some parts of the world is both scanty and unreliable.

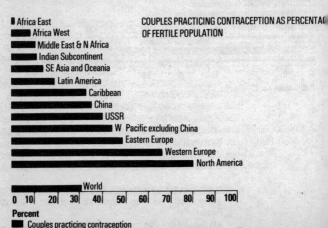

■ Africa East
■ Africa West
■ Middle East & N Africa
■ Indian Subcontinent
■ SE Asia and Oceania
■ Latin America
■ Caribbean
■ China
■ USSR
■ W Pacific excluding China
■ Eastern Europe
■ Western Europe
■ North America

COUPLES PRACTICING CONTRACEPTION AS PERCENTAG OF FERTILE POPULATION

World

| 0 | 10 | 20 | 30 | 40 | 50 | 60 | 70 | 80 | 90 | 100 |

Percent
■ Couples practicing contraception

World View

C21 Contraceptive Education

Unwanted pregnancies are common among teen-age girls, yet most are reluctant to use birth control. To encourage them, UK family planning workers produced a conventional comic strip — part of which is shown here — giving accurate information about contraception.

Taking the world as a whole, traditional methods of contraception — cap, condom, rhythm, withdrawal — are used by just over half the couples who regularly use contraception. But this varies from region to region. Sterilization is used by 61% of those using contraceptives in India; but in other parts of the world it is fairly uncommon. In Latin America, West and North Africa, and the Middle East, if contraception is used at all, it is mainly the Pill or IUD. Perhaps surprisingly, the traditional methods are still the most widely used in Europe.

DISTRIBUTION OF METHODS USED BY PRACTICING COUPLES

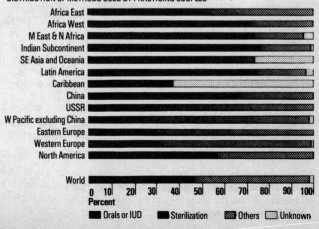

Do1

D01 Events in Pregnancy

At some stage in their lives most women experience the desire to have children. But it need no longer be the unplanned, haphazard process that it once was. Today a woman can decide first whether to have children, and if so, when.

But for women embarking on their first pregnancy, fear of the unknown is still a common emotion. Probably no other event causes as much apprehension and anxiety. For a woman to avoid this it is important for her to understand what is happening to her body and to her unborn child during the 9 months of pregnancy and the birth that follows. This chapter describes the various stages from fertilization to labor, including some of the potential problems.

FERTILIZATION AND IMPLANTATION

After sexual intercourse one male sperm fertilizes a female egg. A week later this attaches itself to the lining of the uterus and the embryo starts shaping into a miniscule human being.

EMBRYO TO FETUS

By the 8th week the embryo is recognizably human. Now termed a fetus, during the next 7 months its organs will increase 120 times in weight.

PREGNANCY

The absence of menstruation is the first sign for most women. Other changes follow such as morning sickness, breast enlargement, and swelling of the abdomen. Good antenatal care aims to prevent any complications and to ensure the good health of mother and child.

BIRTH

For many women this is the most alarming aspect of pregnancy. Relaxation and an understanding of the stages of labor and delivery help to make childbirth easier and allow a woman greater participation.

COMPLICATIONS AND RISKS

Complications may be unavoidable, eg miscarriage. But some risk factors that may affect the unborn child, such as smoking, can be controlled by the mother.

The timetable on the following pages gives a rough guide to certain milestones and occasional problems in pregnancy. Some events relate to the mother-to-be, while others involve the development of the fetu'

Events in Pregnancy

Detailed developmental changes in mother and child appear in sections D11 and D13.

Most people think of pregnancy lasting 9 months. But calendar months vary in length. Our chart irons out these variations by showing a time span of 40 weeks. These can be divided into nine 31-day months (279 days) or ten 28-day (lunar) months.

Traditionally, most doctors use lunar months for pregnancy calculations, dating the onset of pregnancy from the first day of the last menstrual period, despite the fact that conception occurs about 14 days later.

Some dates shown are only approximate. There are large variations in the timing and even appearance or non-appearance of certain signs or symptoms. One factor that especially affects some variations is whether the mother-to-be is expecting her first baby or a second or subsequent child.

Do1

D01 EVENTS IN PREGNANCY

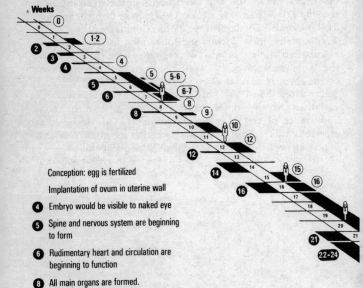

Weeks

Conception: egg is fertilized

Implantation of ovum in uterine wall

4 Embryo would be visible to naked eye

5 Spine and nervous system are beginning to form

6 Rudimentary heart and circulation are beginning to function

8 All main organs are formed. Embryo is recognizably human, and is termed a fetus. Length approx 1in (2.5cm)

12 End of period of greatest susceptibility to drugs taken by mother

14 Fetus can now swallow and urinate. Thumbsucking occurs. Placenta has formed.

16 X-ray (undesirable at this stage) would show fetal skeleton. Fetal heart may be heard. Sex may be distinguishable. Growth of fine body hair (lanugo) starts.

21 Position of fetus in womb changes until 28th week

22-24 Fetal eyelids open and hands grip

25 Fetal length approx 13in (32cm)

28 Fetus is legally viable. If born at this stage it has a 5% chance of survival

34 In certain cases position in womb may be corrected by manipulation

36 Head drops into mother's pelvic cavity (except in first pregnancy, when it drops at start of labor)

38 Babies born before this date and weighing less than 5lb 8oz (2.5kg) are termed premature

40 Baby is born. Approx length 20in (50cm). Weight 7½lb (3.4kg)

Events in Pregnancy

0 Start of last menstruation

1-2 Intercourse

4 1st missed period

5 Urine test can reveal pregnancy (12 days after 1st missed period)

5-6 Veins may be prominent. Breasts may be soft and enlarged. Areolae (areas around nipples) may be darker and show milk ducts.

6-7 Morning sickness may begin. Gums may soften. Stretch marks may appear on breasts.

8 Physical diagnosis of pregnancy possible (enlarged womb, soft cervix)

9 Fluid (colostrum) may be squeezed from breasts

10 Doctor can feel contractions of the womb

12 Morning sickness usually stops now

15 Pigmentation of breasts may occur. In dark women, a line may be seen from navel to pubic bone

16 Abdominal protrusion of womb visible

Craving for unusual foods sometimes occurs in later pregnancy

17-20 Mother may feel fetus moving (sometimes called "quickening")

24 Womb may now be felt at navel level

29 Average increases:
weight 19lb
breasts 14oz
heartbeat 14,000 per day

30 Navel begins to flatten

35 Ribs spread out to accommodate lungs displaced by uterus.
Possible pains from trapped nerves.
Traveling should be curtailed

36 Womb moves up to the ribs. The mother has to lean back to keep balance; but the level of the womb may drop ("lightening"); bladder irritability can recur. Uterine contractions increase in frequency. Gynecologist may have mother X-rayed if he suspects a contracted pelvis likely to cause problems at birth

40 Uterus contracts rhythmically to produce labor pains; membranes in womb rupture and discharge

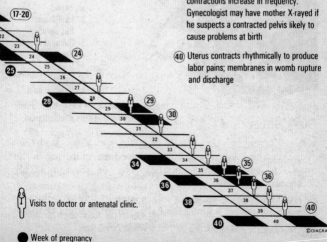

Visits to doctor or antenatal clinic.

Week of pregnancy

©DIAGRAM

Do2-03

D02 Ejaculation

EJACULATION

Sperm have more than 1ft (0.3m) to travel before reaching the female vagina. At ejaculation muscular contractions in the testes (a), epididymides (b), and along the vas deferens (c) propel the sperm toward the penis. On their way they mix with the seminal fluid secreted from the seminal vesicles (d), and prostate (e). The resulting semen is then propelled through the urethra (f) into the woman's vagina (g, h).

SPERM PRODUCTION

Sperm cells are formed inside the testes at a rate of about 200 million a day. While developing, they are stored in the epididymides. Each sperm is about 1/500th of an inch long, and takes 60 to 72 days to mature. By contrast, in a woman just one mature egg is produced a month.

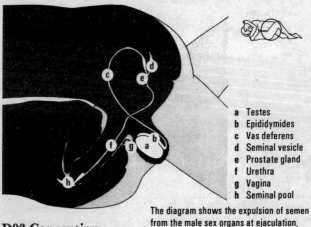

a Testes
b Epididymides
c Vas deferens
d Seminal vesicle
e Prostate gland
f Urethra
g Vagina
h Seminal pool

The diagram shows the expulsion of semen from the male sex organs at ejaculation.

D03 Conception

1 Development of the female egg. In the 2 weeks before ovulation a number of egg follicles have been maturing in the ovary. A week before ovulation one of these suddenly accelerates its growth.

2 Ovulation. The mature egg bursts from its follicle. Muscular contractions propel it along the Fallopian tube. If not fertilized within 24-48 hours, the egg will degenerate.

Ejaculation and Conception

3 Intercourse takes place. About 400 million sperm are ejaculated by the man into the female vagina. Of these, only one sperm will fertilize the ovum. The sperm travel fast, possibly covering 1in (2.5cm) in 8 minutes; also muscular spasms may aid them.

4 The sperm arrive at the cervix. The seminal fluid has liquified, and about half the original sperm have died in the acidic conditions of the vagina. The remainder pass through the cervical mucus. Normally a barrier to sperm, at ovulation the mucus can be easily penetrated.

5 Sperm reach the top of the uterus. There are possibly only 6,000 of the original number left, but it has taken them well under an hour to arrive. About half the sperm now turn into the wrong Fallopian tube.

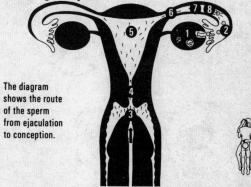

The diagram shows the route of the sperm from ejaculation to conception.

6 Remaining sperm swim into the top of the Fallopian tube that contains the matured female ovum. Conditions are favorable and sperm may survive here for up to 72 hours. Should ovulation not have taken place, sperm can therefore wait for a newly developed ovum to arrive.

7 A few hundred sperm complete their journey along the Fallopian tube to the female ovum. Enzymes released by the sperm heads now break down the ovum's outer wall.

8 Fertilization. One male sperm penetrates the ovum. The cell wall immediately hardens, preventing other sperm from entering, and the nuclei of the two cells fuse together: a new human life is conceived.

Do4

D04 The First Four Weeks

The diagrams represent the process of fertilization and development during the first four weeks of life. The path of the ovum, from fertilization to implantation in the uterus, is traced with an enlarged cross section of the various stages of development.

1 Fertilization **2** First cell division, 1 day
3 Morula stage, 4 days **4** Blastocyst stage, 7 days
Implantation occurs at this stage
5 Internal cells differentiate, 10 days
At this stage
nourishment is drawn
by diffusion from the
uterus by the
chorionic villi (a)
6 Embryo (b) and yolk
sac (c), 15 days
7 Umbilical cord (d)
develops, 20 days
8 25 days

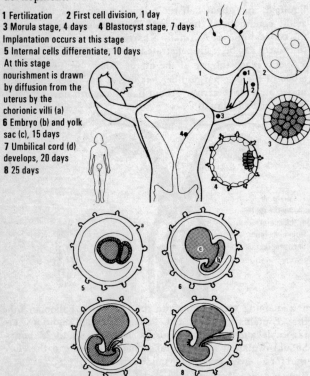

Fertilization occurs in the Fallopian tube within a day of ovulation (see A16 and D03). There may be as many as 100,000 sperm in the Fallopian tube, or as few as 100.
But more than one sperm is needed to produce enzymes to break down the ovum's wall. The nuclei fuse (**1**) and the ovum wall hardens, preventing the entry of other sperm.

Fertilization and Implantation

Soon after fertilization the ovum begins to divide, first into two (2), then into four, and so on. The first division takes about 24 hours. Subsequent divisions take less time. The small bundle of cells, now called a morula, looks like a mulberry (3). The ovum at this point will normally be about to enter the uterine cavity.

Helped by a little uterine fluid, the cells of the morula are separated by a small space. The outer cells flatten into a cellular wall, the trophoblast, and the remaining cluster of cells, the blastocyst, moves to one side (4). The amniotic sac, placenta, and fetus develop from these cells.

By about the 7th day, small projections, the chorionic villi, will have formed on the trophoblast. These burrow into the uterus wall. The embryo undergoes continual cell differentiation (5-8).

Cell differentiation takes place with each cell division. Thus this is a vital stage of development. Seemingly disproportionate repercussions, ie the stunted growth of an organ of the body, can occur from the damage or loss of one cell alone.

Implantation in the uterus establishes a basis of embryonic nutrition. After about 18 days, the nervous system begins to form and it continues to develop until a few weeks after birth.

By the end of the first month, the embryo is about 4mm long, about the size of a tapioca grain, with millions of cells intricately organized to carry out specific functions. A primitive heart is now formed. The embryo is already 10,000 times bigger than the original ovum.

Implantation

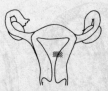

The enlarged sections of the blastocyst (below) show how it burrows into the uterus wall (endometrium).

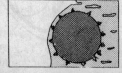

D05-06

D05 Multiple Fertilization

Since the advent of fertility drugs, multiple births have become increasingly common. The drug, which stimulates the growth of follicles, may cause the release of more than one ovum from the ovary.

A single ovum may also split 3, 4, or 5 times — still utilizing a single placenta, as in the case of identical twins.

Triplets, quads, and quins may develop from 3, 4, and 5 ova, with 3, 4, and 5 placentae, and 3, 4, and 5 amniotic sacs respectively. But other combinations can, and do, occur: eg triplets may be the product of one ovum plus one that has split, as in identical twins.

Quads may be the result of two split ova, or of two single ova plus one split one. The sharing of the placenta is dependent upon whether or not the ovum has split. On rare occasions when the uterus is stretched to its ultimate capacity, the same amniotic sac may be shared.

IDENTICAL TWINS are the result of one ovum splitting soon after fertilization. (Siamese twins are the product of a splitting which for some reason has been arrested before completion.) The fetuses lie within separate sacs of amniotic fluid, though they share the same placenta. The latter means that they will be of the same blood group. The splitting of the ovum means that they will share the same genetic structure, ie be of the same sex with very similar features, hair, etc.

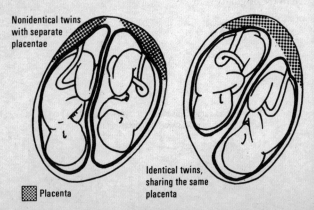

Nonidentical twins
with separate
placentae

Identical twins,
sharing the same
placenta

▨ Placenta

Fertilization and Implantation

NONIDENTICAL TWINS are the result of two ova being fertilized by two sperm. Thus they may or may not be of the same sex, blood group, etc. They will only share the general resemblances of any two children born of the same parents. Multiple births tend to be a trait inherited and carried by women rather than men, ie the tendency to release more than one ovum from the ovary is an exclusively female distinction.

D06 Ectopic Pregnancy

If the fertilized egg does not reach the uterus within seven days, the tiny armlike protrusions (chorionic villi) which will have formed by then will burrow into the wall of the Fallopian tube. The latter will become sorely distended as it can only stretch to a limited extent. The chorionic villi will continue to burrow into the wall in search of nourishment — which is obviously restricted. Eventually they will break through the muscular wall or into an artery causing bleeding, pain, and the loss of the embryo. (Surgery is always necessary.)

Occasionally, however, the embryo will escape into the cavity of the abdomen, and the chorionic villi will burrow into the wall where eventually a placenta will develop. Healthy babies which have developed within the abdomen have occasionally been delivered (by Cesarian section).

Ectopic pregnancies are not uncommon, and since the same hormones are secreted as in a normal pregnancy, causing the naturally anticipated reactions, they are not always detected until discomfort is felt. One in every ten women who have had an ectopic pregnancy is liable to have another. They are often due to prior inflammation of the Fallopian tube.

D07-08

D07 The Uterus

The tiny embryo has embedded itself in the wall of the uterus.
Up to the 8th week, the uterus contains the growth without
enlarging.

Between the 4th and 8th weeks of life, the embryo develops from
a small limbless object resembling a white kidney bean 4mm
long into a miniscule but complete human being all of 40mm
from head to toe.

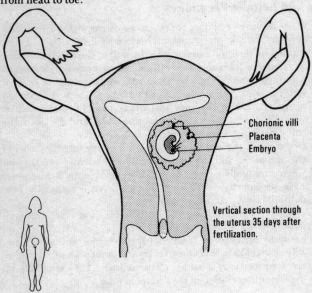

Chorionic villi
Placenta
Embryo

Vertical section through
the uterus 35 days after
fertilization.

D08 Development of the Embryo

By the end of the first 2 months, the initial formation of the
organs is complete. The sex of the embryo is apparent by the
50th day.

The embryo starts off as soft tissue. But by the 40th day, the
skeleton of cartilage is growing and, by the 45th day, the first
bone cells appear.

We can follow the development, for example, of the arms, as
an external feature, and the heart, as an internal organ.

The Embryo

The arms appear as buds at 30 days. By the 40th day, they differentiate into hands, and lower and upper arms. The fingers are in outline only. By the 50th day, the arms are growing and the fingers have separated. (The legs and feet develop in the same way as the arms but correspondingly later.) The heart continues to form for about 2 months, but at 30-35 days it takes over circulation of the blood, which had hitherto been circulated via the umbilical cord and the placenta.

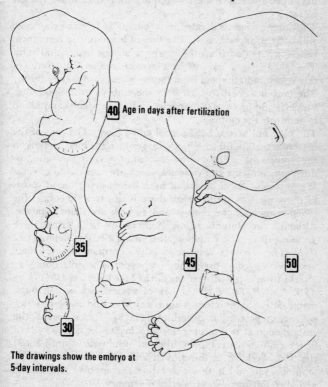

Age in days after fertilization

The drawings show the embryo at 5-day intervals.

Do9

D09 The Support System

THE PLACENTA develops during the first 10 weeks of life from the spot where chorionic villi first burrowed into the uterine wall. The remaining chorionic villi surrounding the embryo die.

The placenta, which looks like a bath cap roughly 8in (20cm) in diameter, and about 1lb (0.45kg) in weight when fully developed, has a maternal (outer) and embryonic (inner) surface.

The outer surface is divided into roughly 20 lobes of chorionic villi and tiny blood vessels. The flow of blood to and from these vessels is supplied from the mother's uterine artery and vein. The inner surface, covered by a layer of amnion, has a series of tiny vessels radiating out from the umbilical cord at the center.

The umbilical cord, which links the embryo to the placenta, supports and protects two arteries and a vein which carry blood to and from the embryo.

The placenta acts as both a pool and a filter. The cells of the maternal surface fill with blood from which the blood vessels on the embryonic surface draw not only oxygen but also, by diffusion, proteins and vitamins which are essential to growth. Waste products will be drawn from the embryo's blood vessels in the same way. But though there is this free exchange, the blood systems of the mother and embryo are quite separate. Although the placenta is largely protective in function, there are some drugs and viruses against which it has no defense (see D64). The placenta also produces the hormone progesterone, upon which the pregnancy depends. The placenta, or afterbirth, is expelled after the birth of the baby (see D34).

THE AMNIOTIC SAC (or bag of waters) is a sac of tough membrane, the amnion, within which a fluid (largely water with some protein) is contained. The sac forms around the embryo soon after it has become attached to the uterus wall. In it, the embryo has complete freedom of movement until about the 30th week. It is the growth and gentle pressure of the amniotic sac which slowly enlarges the uterus, and so the abdomen, giving the overt sign of pregnancy.

The fluid cushions the embryo from knocks, etc. It maintains a constant temperature and thus insulates the embryo, providing a level of water-conditioned central heating. It absorbs the

The Embryo

waste excreted by the embryo, and is also the medium with which the fetus first learns to swallow.

In cases of multiple birth, each fetus normally develops in its own sac. On average, at the 36th week of pregnancy, the sac contains about 2.4pt (1.1 liters). By the 40th week, however, roughly $\frac{1}{3}$ of this will have been lost.

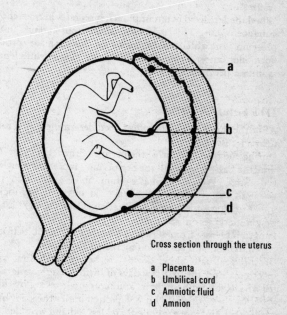

Cross section through the uterus

a Placenta
b Umbilical cord
c Amniotic fluid
d Amnion

D10-11

D10 Hormones

At ovulation, the follicle which releases the ovum changes its function to become the corpus luteum, which produces estrogen and progesterone.

Estrogen prevents more ova developing, while progesterone prepares the lining of the uterus for a possible implantation (see A19).

When the fertilized ovum implants, it secretes human chorionic gonadotrophin. This maintains the corpus luteum until the placenta — which takes over the function of producing hormones after 3 months — has developed sufficiently to maintain pregnancy.

D11 Fetal Growth

After the sex of the embryo has been determined, it is referred to as a fetus.

During the next 7 months, the organs of the fetus grow. By the time the baby is born, all the organs have increased their weight 120 times. Weight increases from about 1oz (28.3g) at 8 weeks to $7\frac{1}{2}$lb (3.4kg), on average, at birth. It has increased 5,000 million times since fertilization. Over the next 20 years, weight increases only 20 times.

Length increases from 40mm at 8 weeks to 20in (50.8cm), from crown to heel, at birth. It has increased $12\frac{1}{2}$ times.

Growth gradually slows down just before birth, but rapidly speeds up after the first few days of birth. Besides general fetal growth, head and body hair, and nails are growing by the 18th week. By the 30th week, fat is deposited under the skin, making it smoother and more rounded, and less red and wrinkled.

Eyelids, which have been growing, close over the eyes in the 9th week, to open again in the 22nd.

8   12

The Fetus

On the internal front, at 14 weeks the heart pumps 6pt (2.83 liters) a day. By the 18th week, it can be heard externally by placing an ear on the mother's abdomen. At around 38 weeks, the heart pumps 720pt (340 liters) per day. The total blood content is 0.6pt (0.28 liters).

Muscular reflexes develop on eyelids, palms, and feet, and the swallowing reflex starts at the 14th week. Thumbsucking also takes place around this time.

Fetal movements, or "quickening," can be felt at the 18th week. Urination into the amniotic fluid begins around the 14th week. Premature live birth is possible at 22 weeks, but survival prospects are poor. Births at 24 weeks, though, can often be kept alive in intensive care units, by open-heart surgery and use of special respirators.

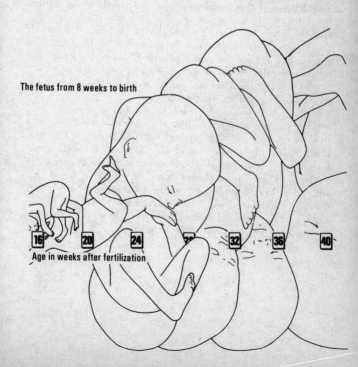

The fetus from 8 weeks to birth

Age in weeks after fertilization

D12

D12 Rhesus Incompatibility

There are various systems of grouping blood types. Within a system the groups are usually incompatible. If an incompatible group is introduced into the body (ie in blood transfusion), antibodies will be produced to inactivate the influence of the "foreign" blood type. In the case of blood incompatibility, the consequences can be far-reaching. One system of grouping is called the rhesus system, discovered in experiments on rhesus monkeys in 1940.

Blood is denoted rhesus positive if it contains the rhesus factor. If it does not contain the factor, it is rhesus negative. Most people (85%) are rhesus positive. Normally this is of no consequence; however, problems can arise in pregnancy when a rhesus negative woman is carrying a rhesus positive child. (If the father is rhesus positive, this is likely in three out of four pregnancies.) In the course of labor or birth, it is quite likely that the child's blood will get into the mother's blood system. If this happens, antibodies will be produced in the mother to protect her against the rhesus positive blood of the baby. But these antibodies are small enough, in a subsequent pregnancy, to pass through the placenta, and so inactivate the blood of the fetus, if it is again rhesus positive.

The dangers increase with each subsequent pregnancy. In a severe case, the fetus may suffer from anemia, jaundice, or a weak heart. One in 200 pregnancies is complicated in this way. If the child is likely to be moderately affected, it is usually given a complete transfusion of rhesus negative blood shortly after birth. As there is no rhesus factor in negative blood, no antibodies are formed, and within 40 days the baby's own rhesus positive blood will have replaced the transfused blood, which is broken down as normal in the liver. In serious cases, the fetus can be transfused while still in the uterus.

The Fetus

How rhesus incompatibility works:
a) a small amount of fetal rhesus positive blood enters the blood system of the mother, whose own blood is rhesus negative.
b) This causes the mother to produce antibodies to inactivate the rhesus positive blood.
c) During a subsequent pregnancy, the mother's antibodies pass through the placenta and inactivate the fetal rhesus positive blood.

+ Rhesus positive blood of fetus

○ Antibodies

D13

D13 Pregnancy

SIGNS AND SYMPTOMS

Usually the first sign of pregnancy is amenorrhea (absence of menstruation—see A18). But if periods are normally irregular, the time of ovulation is uncertain and so amenorrhea is not a definite diagnosis of pregnancy.

The most noticeable physical manifestation of pregnancy after the 3rd month is the swelling of the abdomen as the uterus expands beyond the pelvis. (The swelling causes stretchmarks which often remain after birth.)

Between the 4th and 5th months, the mother feels the fetal movements ("quickening") for the first time. The sensations are faint at first but get stronger. From the 5th month, the fetal heart can be heard with a stethoscope and fetal movements seen from the outside.

The mother's weight gradually increases (on average by between 25 and 30lb—about $11\frac{1}{2}$ to $13\frac{1}{2}$ kg). She will begin to feel tired because of her shape and size, and so become lethargic, increasingly so toward the end of pregnancy.

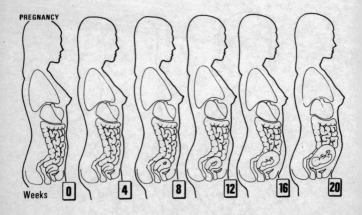

PREGNANCY

Weeks **0** **4** **8** **12** **16** **20**

Pregnancy

Her posture changes, as she has to lean back to balance the baby's weight. Because of this, backache is often experienced. Eventually she may have to walk with a waddling movement, with her legs slightly apart.

Most symptoms of pregnancy, some of which cause discomfort (in turn causing insomnia), result from the changed hormone levels and the increased pressure of the growing fetus.

HORMONAL EFFECTS

a) Emotional changes. The altered hormone levels of pregnancy cause changes in emotional states. There seems to be a general pattern common to most women (though not all). In the first 3 months, there are often extreme changes in mood, with an ambivalent response to pregnancy. During the 2nd trimester, the woman has accepted the fetus and prepared for it: she has adjusted to the hormonal changes.

b) Morning sickness (see D01). About $\frac{2}{3}$ of women experience this, usually from the date of the first missed period until the 2nd or 3rd month, when it often ceases abruptly. It varies in severity, from nausea in the morning only, to vomiting during

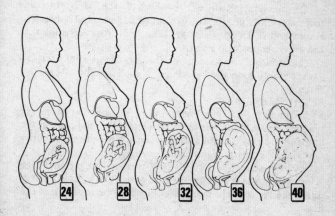

24   28   32   36   40

D13-14

the day. The exact cause of morning sickness is not known, though it is thought that the increase in estrogen is responsible. The body eventually adjusts but, while nausea continues, it is a good idea to eat small frequent meals rather than large ones. Dry toast in the morning may help, and greasy spiced foods should be avoided. For a minimum diet, see D55.

c) The breasts start to enlarge in preparation for lactation. They may itch, tingle, or feel heavy, and are sometimes painful. Their veins become prominent. By the 16th week, they start to secrete a thin fluid from the nipples (colostrum). The areolae become mottled due to increased pigmentation. (Increased pigmentation may also appear on the face and external genitals, and a dark line may run from the navel to the genitals.)

d) Appetite. As the fetus grows, so does the mother's appetite (see D55). But pressure and reduced motility of the stomach induced by hormones reduce the capacity for large meals. There may be cravings for certain foods. With some women, this craving extends to the truly unusual — coal for example — and is then known as pica. By contrast, certain foods and substances may become repulsive for some women. Coffee, meat, alcohol, wine, and greasy foods are examples.

e) Constipation. Reduced motility of the large intestine increases the possibility of constipation, and therefore hemorrhoids. Dried fruit or bran will ease constipation. Laxatives should be avoided.

f) "Heartburn." Relaxation of the esophagus sphincter can cause regurgitation and heartburn. A good diet should ease this situation.

FETAL PRESSURE

a) Frequent urination. The pressure of the uterus on the bladder makes urination more frequent. This happens in the 2nd and 3rd months and also near term, when the fetus settles down into the pelvis ("lightening," or engagement: see D01).

b) Varicose veins (see G100). Fetal pressure on the main leg veins in the groin may cause varicose veins. The veins in the legs dilate as a result of the pressure of blood trying to return to the heart.

Pregnancy

D14 Pregnancy Testing

HCG TEST

The test for pregnancy is made on the woman's urine. It takes about 2 minutes to carry out and is 95% accurate after the 40th day of pregnancy. The test is based on the fact that the placenta secretes large quantities of human chorionic gonadotrophin (HCG) within 40 days of the last menstruation.

For the test, a drop of a substance which neutralizes HCG (anti-HCG) is combined on a glass slide with a drop of the woman's urine. A minute later, another substance is added (latex rubber particles with HCG). If there is no HCG in the urine, the anti-HCG will fix onto the HCG in the latex rubber particles, forming milky lumps or "curds." This is a negative result. But if the woman is pregnant, the HCG in her urine will be fixed by the anti-HCG in the first mixture and, when the rubber and HCG is added, there will be no anti-HCG left to combine with the added HCG. The particles will not form lumps but remain smooth.

The test should not replace clinical diagnosis, as mistakes can and do occur.

CLINICAL DIAGNOSIS (6-10th week)

The two stages of the examination are quite painless; they cause mild discomfort only if the woman is not relaxed. A speculum is inserted into the vagina in order to look at the cervix, which is a bluish color in pregnancy. Then, after removal of the speculum, the doctor gently inserts two fingers into the vagina, while pressing on the abdomen with the other hand, in order to feel whether the uterus has enlarged.

The test will also show up any abnormal swellings in the uterus, while a "Pap" smear (see L43) is often taken at the same time to check for cancer of the cervix.

D15

D15 Antenatal Care

Antenatal care is to ensure that every pregnant woman maintains good health, learns about child care, has a normal delivery, and bears healthy children. She (and hopefully her partner) will learn what is happening to her and what to expect.

Antenatal care has reduced maternal and infant mortality.

CLINICAL VISITS

The woman goes to her doctor or antenatal clinic to have her pregnancy confirmed.

The approximate date of the birth will be determined and the doctor will carry out:

a) a full consultation entailing discussion of past illnesses and operations, of present health, of any complaints now that she is pregnant, and consideration of her anxieties and questions; and

b) a general and then obstetrical examination, which will reveal any conditions which may affect the pregnancy, for which treatment will be given, and which enables the doctor to anticipate possible complications. Any previous pregnancies, miscarriages, or abortions will be considered.

The physical examination entails a general medical checkup, a urine test, blood test, and blood pressure test, and obstetrical abdominal and pelvic examinations.

URINE TEST is taken to see if albumin, signifying a kidney disorder, or sugar, which may suggest diabetes, are present.

BLOOD TEST determines blood type, rhesus factor (see D12), and iron content, and any presence of syphilis (see D56).

BLOOD PRESSURE TEST (which is taken at every antenatal visit) will show whether toxemia of pregnancy may occur. Its cause is unknown, but its effects can be severe. The arteries supplying the uterus go into spasm, reducing the blood supply to the placenta, with possible fatal results to the fetus.

ABDOMINAL EXAM checks muscle tone and possible enlargement of liver and spleen. (Also, after the 12th and 28th week, checks that growth and position of the fetus in the uterus is correct.)

PELVIC EXAM identifies pelvic structure and dimensions, and an internal test is made as part of pregnancy confirmation (see D14). Breasts and nipples will also be examined, and legs for signs of varicose veins.

Antenatal Care

The mother-to-be continues her antenatal visits every month until she is 7 months pregnant, then every 2 weeks until she is 9 months, with a weekly checkup till the birth. Visits will be more frequent if any previous illnesses (eg diabetes, heart disease, hypertension) are likely to cause complications. At each visit, the baby's position in the uterus will be checked (see D30).

When the fetal head settles down into the pelvic cavity ("lightening"), this suggests that the mother's pelvic shape and size are normal. An examination will be made to ascertain the position of the fetal head, and a cervical check made at the same time.

ILLNESS

Any fever, chill, heavy cold, or other illness during pregnancy should be reported immediately to the doctor.

German measles contracted up to the 12th week of pregnancy may interrupt the development of the fetus and lead to deafness and heart defect in the child (see D56).

WEIGHT GAIN

A gain of 25 to 30lb (11.3 to 13.6kg) from conception to birth is normal. Any more than this is unnecessary and even undesirable.

At term the fetus weighs 7 to 8lb (3.2 to 3.6kg), and the amniotic sac and placenta $2\frac{1}{2}$ lb (1.1kg).

The mother carries the balance as fats and fluids in her tissues.

DIET

Eating for two is definitely out!

A woman's average Calorie requirement is about 2,300; the fetus requires only an extra 300. So intake should only increase slightly. It is important that extra emphasis is put on proteins, vitamins, and minerals (see D55). Whole foods are preferable to refined. But vitamin and mineral supplements should only be taken on the doctor's advice.

GENERAL CARE

Bathing is safe and relaxing. Water in the vagina is best avoided, but is only dangerous if forced in under pressure. The genitals and breasts should be kept clean, as secretions become heavier during pregnancy. Dental care is also important, as the gums become softer and so more easily injured by food and toothbrushes. Injured gums are susceptible to infection which can cause loss of teeth (see G80).

D15-16

Drinking and smoking should be kept to a minimum, and it is best not to smoke at all. Some women who normally smoke find that they do not want to during pregnancy. Douching is unnecessary, as the vagina is self-cleansing, and in pregnancy it can be dangerous.

Unless there is a history of miscarriage, or possibility of complications, intercourse during pregnancy will not harm the fetus. Near term, intercourse in some positions may be uncomfortable for the woman, disturbing for the fetus, and difficult to achieve; but see Intercourse in Pregnancy, B14.

D16 Antenatal Exercises

RELAXATION helps to relieve tension during pregnancy and labor. A comfortable position is important for practicing it. The floor, a bed, or chair are all suitable. In the later stages of pregnancy, lying on your side may be more comfortable than on the back. Concentration on each part of the body is necessary to learn relaxation. After practice a sensation of "floating" can be felt.

BREATHING exercises should be practiced during pregnancy to gain control over the different muscles involved in breathing, which will be used in various ways in labor.

In early labor, slow, deep breathing is used, relaxing during contractions. Later on, rapid, shallow panting is used, speeding up as each contraction intensifies.

THE POSTURE of a pregnant woman is altered as the abdomen enlarges. Strain on the back and abdomen can be avoided by learning a good posture, which can be obtained by pressing the whole spine length against a wall, tucking the buttocks and abdomen in, keeping the head up and shoulders back, and maintaining this posture. Humping and hollowing the back mobilizes it and prevents it aching.

LABOR POSITIONS can be practiced to strengthen the inner thigh muscles and control of breathing.

Antenatal Care

1 Relaxation practice
2 Breathing exercises
3 Posture exercises
4 Labor exercises

1a

1b

2a

2b

3a

3b

3c

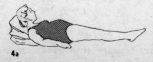

4a

4b

D17-18

D17 Complications in Pregnancy

The majority of pregnancies are completely normal, but there are some (about 30%) in which complications may develop. If left unattended, these conditions can become serious, but the main purpose of antenatal care is to detect potential dangers and, where possible, to prevent them from happening.

The chart shows which unusual symptoms should be reported immediately to a doctor and what the possible causes of such symptoms may be.

DANGER SIGNS	POSSIBLE CAUSES
Severe abdominal pain, possibly with slight bleeding, in first few weeks of pregnancy.	Ectopic pregnancy
Vaginal bleeding with or without abdominal pain in the first 28 weeks of pregnancy.	Threatened miscarriage
Vaginal bleeding with or without abdominal pain after the 28th week of pregnancy.	Premature separation of placenta (abruptio placenta, if pain; placenta praevia, if painless)
Severe swelling of fingers and face, with blurred vision and headaches, after the 20th week of pregnancy.	Toxemia of pregnancy
Gush of water from the vagina at 28-36th week.	Rupture of membranes (bursting of amniotic sac)

D18 Miscarriage

About 1 in 6 women miscarry, and a threatened miscarriage is the usual cause of bleeding in the first half of pregnancy. Known more correctly as a spontaneous abortion, it occurs most often at the 6th or 10th week. The fetus detaches itself from the uterus and is expelled. Most common reasons are:
a) major abnormality in the fetus (about 50% of aborted fetuses are found to be abnormal);
b) death of fetus;
c) faulty hormone production;
d) anatomical defect or functional abnormality;
e) illness or infection;
f) defective sperm or ovum;
g) psychological conditions.
There are different kinds of miscarriage at different stages of

Complications in Pregnancy

pregnancy: threatened, inevitable, complete, incomplete, and missed are the most usual. The symptoms of a threatened miscarriage will generally appear during the first few weeks. Bleeding, red or brown, without pain, occurs (**a**). At this stage, it is uncertain whether the miscarriage will occur, and in 80% of cases the threat passes and pregnancy continues. But if the cervix opens, then the miscarriage is considered inevitable (**b**). A complete abortion means the uterus empties itself of the entire pregnancy. Incomplete abortion (**c**) leaves varying amounts of tissue in the uterus and a D & C is required (see L09). In a missed pregnancy, the fetus has died but remains in the uterus. It is eventually aborted and a D & C is usually given. A miscarriage can be a tense and despairing time, and many women still feel expectant of the birth even though they are no longer pregnant. But miscarriage is often a sign that the fetus was defective, and so rejected; and, after a first miscarriage, the chance that the next pregnancy will be successful is high.

The diagram shows three main
types of miscarriage:
a Threatened
b Inevitable
c Incomplete

D19-22

D19 Ectopic Pregnancy

The diagram shows an ectopic pregnancy and possible areas where one might develop. Bleeding and pain in early pregnancy (6th-12th week) may be caused by an ectopic pregnancy. In this condition the fertilized egg has failed to reach the uterus and has implanted within a Fallopian tube. For a full description, see D06.

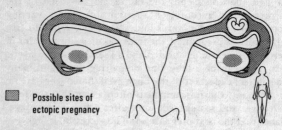

Possible sites of
ectopic pregnancy

D20 Displaced Placenta

Hemorrhage after the 28th week may be caused by 2 fairly rare conditions:
a placenta praevia, in which the placenta lies in the lower part of the uterùs; and
b abruptio placenta, in which the placenta separates prematurely from the uterus.
A woman with placenta praevia will be hospitalized after the 28th week. A Cesarian may be necessary, but in 20% of cases delivery is normal. Most cases of abruptio placenta continue normally, and in only 25% is separation too great for the infant to survive.

a

b

Complications in Pregnancy

D21 Rupture of Amniotic Sac

A sudden gush of water from the vagina after the 28th week generally means that the amniotic sac in which the baby grows has burst and amniotic fluid is escaping. If this occurs before the 28th-36th week, it may often precede premature labor.

The woman is hospitalized and drugs or sedatives may be given to discourage labor. After the 36th week, labor will be allowed to continue or will be induced as the baby is sufficiently mature to survive.

D22 Toxemia of Pregnancy

Toxemia of pregnancy is a serious condition that can occur in late pregnancy. It affects 7-12% of women having their first baby and 3-6% of those having subsequent children.

SYMPTOMS AND SIGNS

There are 3 main warnings:

a) edema (swelling due to water retention) of fingers, face, or legs;

b) raised blood pressure; and

c) protein in the urine.

Excessive weight gain is also associated with toxemia.

PROGRESS

Toxemia goes through 2 stages.

a) Preeclampsia. This rarely occurs before the 20th week and the conditions are those mentioned above. (Some degree of edema, particularly of the legs, is, however, common in pregnancy. It becomes dangerous when associated with other symptoms.) As preeclampsia progresses, vision becomes blurred and the woman will suffer severe headaches.

b) Eclampsia is the final and most severe stage, and may be fatal. Fits, followed by unconsciousness or coma, are characteristic. It is particularly dangerous for the fetus (see D66).

TREATMENT

Today toxemia rarely develops to a final stage. This is almost entirely due to antenatal care, where the symptoms can be detected early on. For this reason alone, regular attendance at the antenatal clinic is vitally important.

Bed rest and a restricted diet are generally sufficient to prevent toxemia from developing. Diuretic pills may be given to get rid of excess water and salt. For more severe cases, hospitalization is necessary so that the condition can be checked.

D23-25

D23 Preparing for Childbirth

Labor and delivery are, for many women, the most alarming aspects of pregnancy. As with the physical changes of pregnancy itself, an understanding of the processes involved helps to relieve anxiety. A woman has 9 months to prepare for birth, and in order to participate fully in the experience she should become acquainted with all the available possibilities. Each woman's experience is personal and individual: whether she delivers at home or in a hospital, with or without drugs, should in the final analysis be for her to decide.

D24 Natural Childbirth

Natural childbirth is the process of giving birth without the automatic use of drugs or obstetrical techniques. The idea was popularized in the 1930s by the English doctor, Grantly Dick-Read. It is based on the assumption that much of the pain of childbirth is caused by tension, itself due to the woman's anxieties and fears about labor. If these are eliminated, tension is relieved and pain will be lessened. The keynote to relaxation in labor is an understanding by the woman of all aspects of pregnancy and birth. Armed with this knowledge, Dick-Read maintained, the woman can approach labor with confidence.

PSYCHOPROPHYLAXIS

The psychoprophylactic method of childbirth was introduced by a French doctor, Fernand Lamaze. He felt that relaxation was not enough, and introduced prelearned muscular and breathing exercises to be used by the woman during labor. With these a woman is no longer helplessly passive, but can actively participate in the process of birth.

Although the theory and exercises are the basis of childbirth preparation today, few women actually give birth without drugs — nor should a woman feel she has failed if she is not one of those few.

Preparing for Childbirth

D25 Home or Hospital

Forty years ago it was normal for a woman to have her child at home. In Holland, over half of all deliveries are still carried out in the home, with absolute safety. In the US and Britain, however, home births are now extremely rare. The dying practice of midwifery and the increasing accent on the safety and well-being of both mother and child have meant that most doctors prefer to deliver in a hospital where the facilities for any possible complications are immediately available. However, given an absence of complications, there is no reason why a woman who wishes to do so should not deliver her child at home. The advantages are obvious — your own room, a familiar atmosphere, and possibly the presence of friends can greatly ease the doubts and tensions of labor.

Most women feel safer delivering in a hospital, though. It is always recommended that a woman have her first child there. After the first birth, it is often possible to predict whether the next will be normal. The risks of pregnancy and labor rise for the third and subsequent births, and for mothers under 17 and over 35 — so these are usually delivered in a hospital. A pregnant woman will also be admitted for a hospital birth if there is any evidence or suspicion of possible difficulty or danger — toxemia, diabetes, rhesus incompatibility, prematurity, multiple birth, difficult fetal position, small pelvis. Unfortunately, the choice of a home or a hospital delivery today largely depends on the facilities available. The main aim of doctors has been to lower the risks, and even though hospital birth is not essential for many women, it has become part of a routine for greater safety.

D26-27

D26 Breathing Exercises

The diagram shows four types of breathing used during labor:
a   deep chest breathing for early first stage;
b   shallow chest breathing used in the middle stage;
c   shallow rapid breathing (panting) for transition; and
d   expulsion, in which the breath is held while the woman bears down to push against the baby.

At the beginning of labor, deep abdominal breathing helps to relieve pressure. Once contractions increase so that they harden the abdominal wall, the woman switches to deep chest breathing. She continues to change as labor progresses, each time alternating her normal breathing (between contractions) with the learned form used during the contractions. Once delivery begins, expulsion breathing is used.

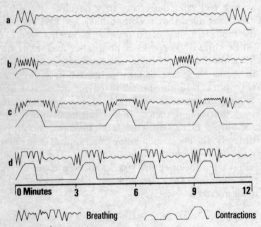

D27 Drugs in Labor

A woman who delivers in a hospital can use a variety of pain-relieving or pain-killing drugs. There are 2 kinds: analgesics and anesthetics.

ANALGESICS These relieve pain and may be taken orally, inhaled, or injected. During early labor, painkillers are rarely necessary, but narcotics such as Demeral (Pethidine) may be given. Barbiturates, also used in the past, are now not generally given, as they can cause breathing to stop in some cases.

Preparing for Childbirth

INHALANT ANALGESICS can be self-administered and the intake controlled as needed. There are 2 types: trilene and nitrous oxide ("laughing gas"), and they are used for dilation and delivery (see D31 and D34).

REGIONAL ANESTHETICS are widely used. Injected into the woman's body at a specific point, the anesthetic completely blocks off pain. The epidural block is probably the most efficient and is becoming more available. Anesthetic is injected into the epidural cavity, which lies between the spinal cord and its covering, the dura. It numbs the entire region from the lower abdomen to the feet, and can be readministered during labor. Although an effective pain reliever, it can lessen the mother's ability to push and may result in a forceps delivery (see D41). Other regional anesthetics include the pudendal nerve block, given immediately before a forceps delivery, and the caudal block. Both anesthetize the pelvis. A paracervical block is injected into the plexus, making the cervix and upper vagina completely insensitive. A regional anesthetic is also given before an episiotomy (see D34). Drugs used in labor are carefully supervised, but most do cross the placenta and can make the newborn infant drowsy and slow to suck. These effects, although undesirable, are temporary and should be weighed against the possible long-term effects on a woman of a painful and distressing labor.

The diagram shows the nerve supply for the uterus, cervix, and vagina. Most of the nerves for this area collect together at the paracervical ganglion or plexus (a). When local anesthetic is injected here, the cervix and upper vagina are desensitized, without impairing the ability of the uterus to proceed with labor.

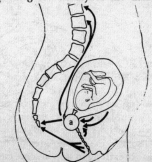

D28

D28 Labor

Women often find that their experiences during labor differ. However, most labors follow a similar general pattern.

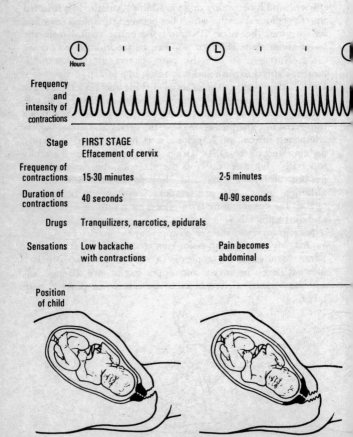

	Hours	
Frequency and intensity of contractions		
Stage	FIRST STAGE Effacement of cervix	
Frequency of contractions	15-30 minutes	2-5 minutes
Duration of contractions	40 seconds	40-90 seconds
Drugs	Tranquilizers, narcotics, epidurals	
Sensations	Low backache with contractions	Pain becomes abdominal
Position of child		

Experience of Childbirth

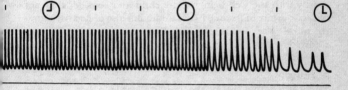

	SECOND STAGE	THIRD STAGE
Dilation of cervix	Delivery	Afterbirth
2-3 minutes	2-5 minutes	5-10 minutes
40-90 seconds	60-90 seconds	
Epidural	Trilene, nitrous oxide, paracervical block	Ergometrine
The "show" Amniotic sac ruptures (if not earlier)	Possible nausea "Bearing down"	

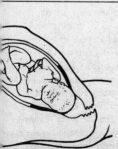
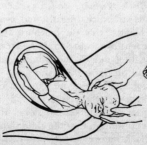

D29

D29 Alternative Birth Styles

The possibly damaging effects on a woman of a prolonged, painful, and distressing childbirth are now well recognized. But recently the accent has moved from the effects of birth on the mother to the effects of birth on the child. It is argued that the methods of delivery commonly used can have a lasting and detrimental effect on a child. There are 3 main advocates of a new approach to birth: R. D. Laing, the Scottish psychologist; Frederick Leboyer, the French obstetrician; and the American psychoanalyst, Elizabeth Fehr. All concern themselves primarily with the well-being of the child and consider that not only is it aware of its time in the womb but also of its arrival into the world. They feel that its initial impressions are critical to its future development, and that being dangled upside down and slapped on the bottom are both unnecessary and damaging.

R. D. LAING

Laing argues that cutting the umbilical cord too soon is a major cause of birth traumas. The cord linking mother and newborn child still carries on its functions of providing blood, oxygen, and nutrients, even after the actual birth. Immediate severance causes unnecessary shock to the baby, which can be avoided by leaving the cord uncut until it has naturally ceased to function. It used to be common practice not to cut the cord until it stopped pulsating. Doctors today tend to cut it while it is still performing transitional duties. Laing believes that if the cord is left for 4 or 5 minutes, until the baby's own circulation has taken over, the process is more natural and nontraumatic.

FREDERICK LEBOYER

In his book *Birth Without Violence*, Leboyer also advocates not cutting the umbilicus until it has ceased to function. In addition, he believes that the newborn child's eyes, ears, and skin are hypersensitive, and should be treated gently and with respect. Struggling out of the womb into bright lights and noise, being put on hard scales and hung upside down (which immediately forces the spine into an unaccustomed angle) are all alien to a being who has been 9 months in the womb. Leboyer suggests that lights and noise in the delivery room should be at a minimum, that the child should be placed on the mother's stomach before cutting the cord, and that after the

Experience of Childbirth

cord is cut, the child should be placed in a bath of water at body temperature and allowed to move and "open up" in a calm, unhurried way. Certainly Leboyer has noted that a baby born in this way opens its eyes and begins smiling immediately — one cry, as opposed to a torrent of tears and red-faced rage, having satisfied everyone of its ability to breathe.

ELIZABETH FEHR

The late Elizabeth Fehr believed that a traumatic birth left a permanent impression. She introduced into psychoanalysis the process of "rebirthing," by which a person retraces his life backward toward birth. As a result of her investigations, she concluded that auditory hallucinations suffered by schizophrenics might well be related to sounds heard by the child as it struggled from the womb. Her work has given added impetus to the movement for gentler birth styles.

D30-31

D30 Fetal Positions

These are the positions in which the baby can lie in the mother's pelvis just before labor begins. The face-down position may cause remolding of the skull. A transverse lie can usually be manipulated into another position; uncorrected, it requires a Cesarian section (see D40).

Frequency of birth positions

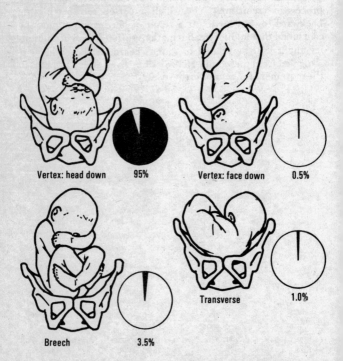

Vertex: head down   95%

Vertex: face down   0.5%

Breech   3.5%

Transverse   1.0%

Labor

D31 Duration of Pregnancy

Pregnancy normally lasts between 36 and 42 weeks from fertilization.

LABOR

Throughout pregnancy the uterus undergoes slight contractions known as Braxton Hicks contractions. As the pregnancy nears term, these contractions become more frequent and intense.

Labor itself has three distinct stages. In the first stage, the cervix is "effaced" and "dilated," to allow the fetus to pass without damaging it. The second stage is the actual delivery of the baby; the third, delivery of the placenta.

FIRST STAGE

Before delivery can begin, the uterus must undergo a change in shape to permit the fetus to pass through the cervix. The upper uterus pulls the lower uterus and cervix up around the head of the fetus.

This process takes about 8 hours for women having their first child (primigravidae), and may take 4-5 hours for those having their subsequent children (multigravidae). By the time effacement is completed, contractions are occurring about every 3 to 5 minutes, and lasting 40-90 seconds. The mucous plug lodged in the cervix throughout pregnancy is displaced as the cervix begins to dilate to allow the baby a free passage through. The process, a continuation of effacement, reveals the amnion surrounding the baby's head. If the amnion has not been ruptured already, it is usually ruptured during dilation, either by the baby's head or by the doctor delivering. This releases a quantity of amniotic fluid (see D09). To allow the baby to pass, the cervix must dilate to accommodate its head, which is about 4in (10cm) in diameter.

As dilation proceeds, contractions become more frequent and intense; by full dilation they will be occurring every 2-3 minutes and lasting 60-90 seconds.

Dilation takes from 3-5 hours for a woman having her first child, and less for subsequent children.

D32-33

D32 Induced Labor

Labor may be induced artificially if the health of the mother or fetus is in danger. There has also been a tendency for births to be induced for the convenience of hospitals. Labor will normally begin within 24 hours of induction, and tends to be shorter than a spontaneous labor. But the contractions follow the same pattern as spontaneous labor, even though each stage takes much less time.

The frequency of induction varies greatly from place to place. The following are the main conditions in which induction is justified.

PREECLAMPSIA is the major medical cause of induction, accounting for 50% of such cases. It is characterized by high blood pressure, edema, and proteinuria in the woman (see D22). Although the danger to her is slight, danger to the fetus increases with severity. Should eclampsia (a type of epilepsy) develop, the mortality rate is very high for mother and fetus.

POSTMATURITY accounts for 35% of inductions. If the fetus remains in the uterus after term, it will continue to grow, making for a difficult birth. Placental function begins to fall off after the 40th week, and there is a tendency toward mental damage in postmature babies.

HEMORRHAGE (10% of inductions) is caused by the placenta separating from the uterus before birth. In difficult cases

D33 First Stage of Labor

The cervix and uterus as labor begins

Contractions every 15-30 minutes

Partial effacement
Contraction and retraction of the uterus shorten the neck of the cervix.

Contractions every 10 minutes

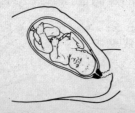

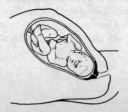

Labor

Cesarian section is required.

RHESUS INCOMPATIBILITY (see D12) necessitates induction in severe cases.

DIABETES in the mother, if untreated, results in a high mortality rate for both mother and fetus. But antenatal checks will reveal diabetes (D15) if it has not been detected previously, so mortality is not a problem. Treatment must be carefully controlled. Even so, fetuses tend to be puffy and fat, and thus difficult to deliver. They will usually require induction by the 38th week.

METHODS OF INDUCTION

There are two methods: surgical and medical.

SURGICAL INDUCTION involves the artificial rupture of the amniotic sac, below the fetus. About a pint of fluid is drained off, and labor usually begins within 24 hours. The rupturing of the sac does not in itself make for any difficulty in delivery.

MEDICAL INDUCTION involves intravenous infusion of oxytocin, to stimulate uterine contractions. The oxytocin is given throughout labor — though not for more than 10 hours.

Many procedures in obstetrics, including induced birth, have become controversial issues in some countries: their justification has been in question. Lack of information as to the reasons for their use exacerbates the situation, causing resentment between women and hospital staff.

Full effacement

Contractions every
5 minutes

Partial dilation
Continued contraction and
retraction dilate the cervix.

Contractions every
2-5 minutes

Full dilation
The fetus is able to pass
through the cervix
without damaging it.

Contractions every 2-3
minutes

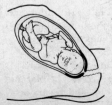

D34-35

D34 Delivery

TRANSITION TO SECOND STAGE

The transition to the 2nd stage is characterized by feelings of pressure in the low pelvis, backache, and often nausea and leg cramps. At this point, when tension rises, it is helpful and comforting for the woman's partner or friend to prompt her to do her antenatal breathing exercises.

Contractions continue, once every few minutes, and there is an increasingly uncontrollable desire to push or bear down — like trying to relieve severe constipation. However, it is not safe to bear down until full dilation has been achieved, as the cervix may tear.

SECOND STAGE

When the cervix is fully dilated, bearing down can begin. The baby is now being pushed out of the uterus and down the vagina, and will be delivered in anything from 5 to 40 minutes.

If there is danger of the perineum (B01) being torn by the baby's head, an episiotomy may be performed: the doctor makes an incision from the vagina obliquely down toward the anus. This cut is sewn up after the delivery is completed.

The fetus begins its journey on its side, head first (but see D30). Contractions of the uterus force the fetus down into the pelvis. The head is rotated downward beneath the pubic arch and, as the head is born, it rotates back to its original position. The shoulders and then the breech follow the same pattern of rotation as they are delivered, and the baby is born.

The 2nd stage is now completed — in primigravidae it takes up to one hour, in multigravidae less.

Mucus is extracted from the mouth and nose of the baby, who may be suspended upside down to drain mucus from its lungs. The umbilical cord is clamped and cut, sometimes immediately and sometimes after several minutes; in a week the stump of the cord will dry out and fall off.

The baby on delivery is wet and covered in a fatty substance, vernix. As oxygen begins to circulate in the lungs, the baby's color will change gradually from bluish to pink.

THIRD STAGE

The placenta is delivered within 30 minutes of the baby. As birth occurs, the uterus retracts quite markedly. The placenta is not capable of contraction or retraction, and shears away

Birth

from the uterus. Light traction on the cord aids its delivery.
Once delivered, the placenta is checked to ensure none is left inside the uterus, since this could lead to infection and hemorrhage.

CHECKS

The baby is checked just after birth for congenital malformations (see D65). It will be given a vitamin K injection to help blood clotting in case of hemorrhage, and silver nitrate eye drops to help protect the eyes. Heart and lung functions are checked. A handprint or footprint is taken to check for mongolism, and a mouth smear to check for PKU (see D54).

D35 Positions For Delivery

The diagrams show the positions currently used for delivery. The dorsal, in which the woman lies flat on her back with her knees up and separated, and the left lateral, in which she lies on her left side, knees toward her chest, are the most typical in many countries. But the lithotomy position is the one usually used in the USA.

FIRST STAGE

During the early stages, there is little active work a woman can do, and generally she remains up and about, waiting for the contractions to increase in frequency. Once labor is fully established and she is in bed, she should choose the most comfortable position.

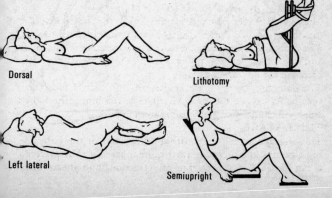

Dorsal

Lithotomy

Left lateral

Semiupright

D35-36

During the first stage, it is not advisable for her to lie flat on her back. Sitting propped up on pillows or lying on one side improves the flow of blood through the uterus, providing more oxygen for the baby. During transition itself, a woman can squat, sit upright, use any position which helps her the most.

SECOND STAGE

This is the time when the mother can most actively participate in labor, and she should choose the position in which she can work the best — changing at any time if she wishes. Many women find they can push best by clasping their legs, drawing them up to the abdomen.

THIRD STAGE

Once the baby is born, the dorsal position is generally used for the delivery of the placenta.

D36 Second Stage of Labor

SECOND STAGE OF LABOR

Full dilation signifies the beginning of delivery. The woman "bears down" to help expel the baby.

The baby's head passes through the cervix and rotates to squeeze beneath the pubic arch.

Contractions every 2-5 minutes

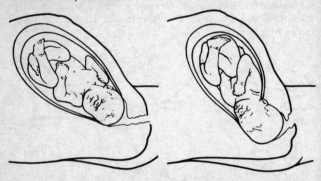

Birth

The head is born, and rotates back to its previous position. The baby's shoulders rotate to pass through the pelvis.

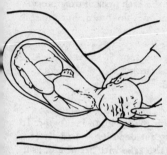

The right shoulder, then the left, is born.

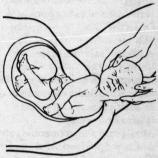

The baby breathes spontaneously. Mucus is cleaned from its face and air passages. The umbilical cord is clamped.

THIRD STAGE
The placenta is delivered within 30 minutes of the baby.

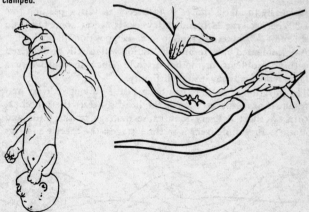

D37-40

D37 Premature Birth

A premature baby can be defined by weight: under 5lb 8oz (2.5kg). But low birthweight full-term babies have totally different problems from the true premature baby — who is better defined as one born before the 36th week of pregnancy.

Often the cause of premature labor is unknown, but possibilities are:

a) lack of antenatal care;
b) poor health;
c) some maternal diseases (eg diabetes);
d) fetal congenital abnormalities;
e) multiple pregnancy; and
f) small placenta.

After birth, the premature baby is placed in an incubator. Its skin is red and wrinkled, lacking fat deposits — body heat is hard to maintain. Problems can also arise with breathing, as its respiratory system is underdeveloped. It cannot suck well, and has a feeble cry. But if adequately cared for, it will become as healthy as a full-term baby.

D38 Breech Birth

Normally the fetus moves from breech to vertex position (see D30) between the 24th and 28th week. However, some fail to do so, and 3.5% of fetuses remain in breech position till birth.

A normal-sized baby in breech position will usually be delivered with no problems for mother or child. But a small pelvis or a large fetal head may lead to difficulty.

The duration of delivery can be critical — a long delivery may result in oxygen starvation if the head squeezes the umbilical cord. A short delivery may cause damage to the fetus and mother. Breech delivery is in three stages: the breech and legs

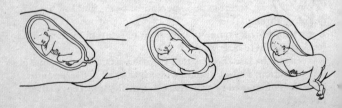

Problem Births

are born first, then the shoulders, and finally the head. Forceps are usually used to help ease the head out gently and avoid injury (see D41).

D39 Multiple Births

Twins are born on average once every 85 births, triplets once every 7,500 births, quadruplets once every 650,000, and quintuplets once every 57,000,000 births (see D05).

Difficulties may arise in multiple births. They tend to be premature, and so must be delivered in a hospital. Labor is usually straightforward as each baby is small. The birth canal is dilated after the birth of the first baby so that subsequent ones are born easily.

Toxemia of pregnancy and anemia occur more frequently in a multiple pregnancy.

The maternal death rate in twin pregnancies is 2-3 times greater than in a single pregnancy. In 1 in 14 twin births, one twin dies, and with larger multiple births the likelihood of fetal death rises steeply.

D40 Cesarian Birth

Cesarian section is an operation carried out on a pregnant woman to deliver her baby, if this is not possible through the vagina.

Reasons for it include:
a) fetal distress;
b) low-lying placenta (see D20);
c) very small pelvis;
d) obstructive fibroids;
e) transverse fetal position; and
f) previous uterine injury.

General anesthetic is given before the operation. A cut is made below the navel into the abdomen and uterus, and the baby is delivered through this.

It is possible for a woman to have several Cesarian sections, but four is thought to be enough.

It is only in the last 25 years that Cesarian section has become a safe operation. Now it accounts for 10% of all deliveries in the USA. It is often used in preference to a difficult forceps delivery (see D41).

D41-43

D41 Forceps Delivery

Frequency of forceps delivery varies greatly from country to country. In the USA, an average of 50% of births involve forceps. About 6% of births in the UK are forceps deliveries.

Forceps are used in the 2nd stage of labor to aid the progress of the fetus, and are used in the following circumstances:

a) slow or no fetal progress;

b) maternal distress, eg preeclampsia (see D22), exacerbated by the effort required during labor;

c) fetal distress.

APPLICATION

Forceps consist of two curved blades that interlock and fit closely around the fetal head. One blade is inserted into the uterus and located in position around the head. The other blade is then inserted and, when positioned, locked into the first blade. Gentle traction draws the fetus down through the vagina. Local anesthetic and episiotomy may be needed in

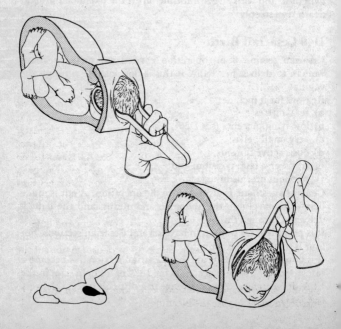

Problem Births

forceps delivery.
CONDITIONS
a) The cervix must be fully dilated to allow insertion of the forceps blades. Damage will be caused to the cervix and vagina if the fetus is pulled through before dilation.
b) The amniotic membranes must be ruptured, if they are not already, and bladder and rectum empty.
c) The forceps can only be applied to the fetal head.

D42 Vacuum Extraction

Vacuum extraction is used as an alternative to simple forceps delivery, and is very popular in Scandinavia and the UK.
Vacuum extraction can be started before the cervix is fully dilated. A metal cup is inserted into the vagina and placed against the fetal head. It is connected to suction equipment, the vacuum formed being strong enough to allow the fetus to be gently pulled out of the uterus.
Scalp tissues are sucked into the cup, but within a few hours of delivery any swelling subsides.

D43 Emergency Birth

In 80% of cases, a woman can deliver without any problems; but if a birth begins unexpectedly, the help of a doctor or hospital should always be sought. If no help is available, then it is best simply to give encouragement to the mother, and let nature take its course without interference. Let the mother "bear down" (push against the baby) as soon as she wants to; do not worry whether full dilation has occurred, for any damage to the cervix can be repaired later by minor surgery. Show her how to push during contractions, by holding her breath, raising head and shoulders, and pulling the knees up. Pain is not normally a problem, if the atmosphere is kept calm and quiet.
After the birth, clean the mucus from the baby's mouth and nose. Breathing should begin within 30 seconds. Do not cut the cord. Keep mother and baby warm.
More than $\frac{1}{2}$pt of blood from the uterus (not the placenta) signifies hemorrhage. In this case only, the abdomen should be massaged to try to ease the bleeding.

D44-45

D44 After the Birth

For about 10 days after birth, there is a steady loss of a bloody substance, called lochia, from the vagina, as the placental site and uterine lining break down.

The breasts produce colostrum for the first few days. This is then replaced by milk. Sometimes the breasts are overfull and painful. For a day or two after the birth, the mother may experience some constipation and difficulty in urinating; or she may urinate involuntarily, especially when coughing or laughing. This is caused by muscle slackness in the pelvic area and is best treated by early mobilization and reassurance. Changes in hormone balance often cause the mother to be depressed and weepy for a short while after giving birth. This is called the "3rd or 4th day blues," named after the time it usually occurs.

Menstruation normally returns after about 24 weeks if the mother is breastfeeding, or 6-10 weeks if not. Ovulation starts in the first case after about the 20th week. Women who do not breastfeed can therefore become pregnant much sooner; while of those who do, the longer they breastfeed, usually the lower the likelihood of pregnancy, although this is not always the case.

POSTNATAL EXAMINATION

This takes place after 6 weeks. The position of the uterus is checked, and the mother is asked if she has any pain or discomfort in the abdominal area, or any vaginal discharge. Often a blood test is made to check for anemia. Blood pressure is always measured.

A vaginal inspection is made to see that any stitches from an episiotomy have healed, and if there is any inflammation, or erosion, of the cervix (25% of mothers have it to some degree after giving birth). Mostly it is self-healing, but treatment is required if it persists (see L07).

Postnatal Care

D45 Changes in the Uterus

The puerperium is the time when the uterus and other genital organs gradually return to their normal size.

The uterus, cervix, and vagina undergo immense stretching during pregnancy and labor; but within 6 weeks of the birth evidence of the pregnancy is difficult to find. The uterus weighs, after birth, about 2½ lb (1kg) and, after 2 weeks, about 11oz (350g). In rare cases the uterus retroverts following pregnancy (see L05).

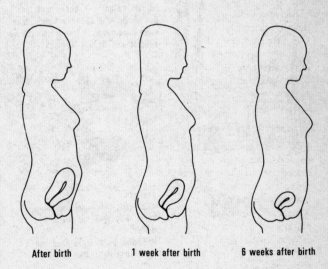

After birth   1 week after birth   6 weeks after birth

D46

D46 Postnatal Exercises

These are important for most women, as they retone muscles (especially those of the pelvic floor), stimulate blood circulation, and promote good posture.

They should be done as many times as possible a day as soon as the mother is up and about. Some abdominal exercises can be performed while feeding the baby (see Exercise 1) or around the home (see Exercise 2).

Exercise 1
Tighten abdominal muscles while sitting in correct posture position.

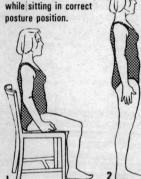

Exercise 2
Stand straight, pull in abdomen and buttocks. Tighten up inside.

Exercise 3
Lie relaxed on floor, knees bent, feet flat (a). Draw in abdomen tightly, then raise head (b). Hold few seconds, lower head slowly. Repeat 10 times.

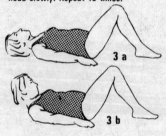

3 a

3 b

4 a

Exercise 4
Alternately hollow (a) and hump (b) back, abdominal muscles held tightly.
Hollowing back, move head and hip first to right, then to left (c).

4 b

4 c

Postnatal Care

Exercise 5
Lie flat on floor, back straight (a). Feet must be held by another person or a heavy item of furniture. Cross arms on chest, raise body to forward position (b), then lie back (c). Arms can be stretched forward above head before lying back.

5 a

5 b

5 c

Exercise 6
Lie on back, legs straight. Move feet up and down, and round in circles (a). Tighten kneecaps, tense leg muscles (b). Ankles crossed, press thighs together, tighten up inside (c).

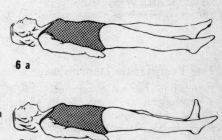

6 a

6 b

6 c

D47-49

D47 After the Birth

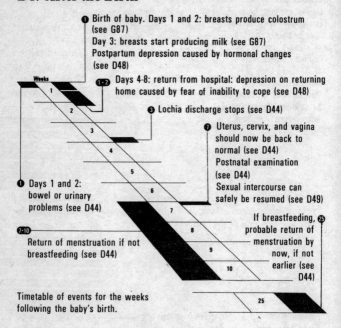

❶ Birth of baby. Days 1 and 2: breasts produce colostrum (see G87)
Day 3: breasts start producing milk (see G87)
Postpartum depression caused by hormonal changes (see D48)

Weeks

1-2 Days 4-8: return from hospital: depression on returning home caused by fear of inability to cope (see D48)

❸ Lochia discharge stops (see D44)

❼ Uterus, cervix, and vagina should now be back to normal (see D44)
Postnatal examination (see D44)
Sexual intercourse can safely be resumed (see D49)

❶ Days 1 and 2: bowel or urinary problems (see D44)

7-10
Return of menstruation if not breastfeeding (see D44)

If breastfeeding, **25** probable return of menstruation by now, if not earlier (see D44)

Timetable of events for the weeks following the baby's birth.

D48 Postpartum Depression

Postpartum depression, or "baby blues," is rapidly being acknowledged as a significant aftereffect of childbirth. Though its intensity ranges from mere anxiety to severe psychosis, most women experience depression of some kind during the postnatal period.

It is not confined to first-time mothers: some women experience depression after the birth of each of their children.

Almost every mother goes through a "low" period about 3 days after the birth, roughly coinciding with the time the breasts begin to produce milk rather than colostrum. Many more women, however, experience severe depression on return from hospital. These feelings may last only a matter of days, but,

After the Birth

particularly in a woman who is physically run down, may persist for a few months.

Among the feelings most commonly experienced during depression are confusion, shock, insecurity, inadequacy, fear of inability to cope with the baby, and even disappointment about its sex or appearance. Many women are frightened because they cannot rationalize their anxieties, and many fear a deterioration of their relationship with their partner. Postpartum depression is often attributed to hormonal imbalance following childbirth, but evidence is as yet inconclusive since depression has been noted in adoptive as well as natural mothers. Probably the single most important cause of postpartum depression is society's glorification of motherhood, which sets up uncertainty and guilt in women who doubt their ability to be loving, caring mothers.

Treatment for the depression can involve drugs, but it is usually preferable to treat the cause rather than the symptoms. If the mother receives help, support, and constant reassurances from her family, friends, and other mothers, the chances of a quick recovery are high.

D49 Intercourse

Medical opinion generally favors delaying the resumption of intercourse until after the postnatal examination. Some people, however, argue that problems are unlikely, provided that there is no vaginal discomfort and the discharge of lochia has ceased. In any case, it is wise to wait until you feel ready. Reduced sexual interest after childbirth may be due to emotional upheaval or a lowered estrogen level. Other problems include muscular cramps during intercourse or pain from stitches after an episiotomy. Pregnancy is possible before menstruation resumes or during lactation. A diaphragm used before the birth will no longer fit and the Pill should not be used if breastfeeding. Condoms with spermicides are recommended.

D50

D50 Breastfeeding

More and more women in Western countries are choosing to breastfeed their babies. Most doctors welcome this, for they regard breastfeeding as the safest and most natural method of infant feeding, and many mothers agree that it is an enjoyable and rewarding experience (see G87 for details of milk production in the breast).

Some women, however, are uncertain about breastfeeding. Perhaps they have commitments that would make it impossible; or they may find the whole idea distasteful. And for some women who had planned to breastfeed, problems arising after the birth force them to turn to bottlefeeding. Current breastfeeding propaganda may make mothers who are bottlefeeding their babies feel inadequate and uncaring. This should be ignored; although breastfeeding is preferable for most babies, the vital physical contact between mother and child can be as intimate, warm, and loving whether the baby is fed by breast or bottle.

Mothers who do decide to breastfeed should ensure that they take sufficient rest — tension and the inability to relax can reduce the milk supply.

Diet is another important factor. The lactating mother should ensure that she eats a high-Calorie diet with particular emphasis on foods rich in protein, vitamins, and calcium (see D55).

After the Birth

BREAST OR BOTTLE?

BREASTFEEDING	BOTTLEFEEDING
Milk instantly available, at correct temperature, and sterile	Milk needs mixing and (usually) heating. Equipment must be sterilized
Antibodies protect the baby against some infections for first 6 months	No equivalent
Breast milk is cheaper than formula milk	Some expense — bottles, milk, teats must be purchased
Mother cannot tell how much milk the baby has taken without test weighings	Mother can see at a glance how much milk the baby has taken
Mother's health and well-being affect the milk supply	Milk supply independent of the mother
Milk supply usually adjusts itself to the baby's needs but cannot always meet the occasional need for extra milk	Extra feeds present no problem but can overfeed
Some drugs can be passed to the baby via the milk	Mother's medications do not affect the baby

D51-53

D51 Risks in Pregnancy

Abnormalities at birth can be caused by various factors — some hereditary, some environmental — and every expectant mother worries about them. On this page we list some of the chief dangers in pregnancy. Although the fetus is well protected, its development can be seriously affected by many of the risks mentioned.

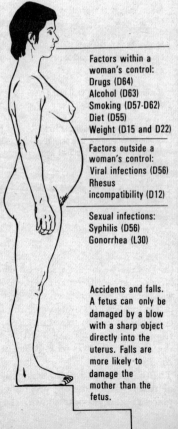

Factors within a woman's control:
Drugs (D64)
Alcohol (D63)
Smoking (D57-D62)
Diet (D55)
Weight (D15 and D22)

Factors outside a woman's control:
Viral infections (D56)
Rhesus incompatibility (D12)

Sexual infections:
Syphilis (D56)
Gonorrhea (L30)

HEREDITARY FACTORS. Some genetic disorders can be inherited by an infant. Examples are hemophilia, sickle cell anemia (see D54).

AGE. Congenital abnormalities are more likely to occur in babies born to women under 16 and over 40.

VACCINATION. Smallpox and German measles vaccinations should not be given during pregnancy. Others should be avoided, but some can be given after the first 14 weeks.

ENVIRONMENT. There are many factors in the environment that can put an unborn infant at risk. Air pollution, water pollution, and a degree of radiation are unavoidable today. A woman can lessen this risk by avoiding X rays, although today these are generally only given in order to detect and prevent a greater risk.

Accidents and falls. A fetus can only be damaged by a blow with a sharp object directly into the uterus. Falls are more likely to damage the mother than the fetus.

Risks in Pregnancy

D52 Amniocentesis

This is the method by which amniotic fluid is extracted from the uterus, and analyzed for possible fetal abnormalities. Such abnormalities can now be detected early in pregnancy.

Amniocentesis is best carried out between the 12th and 16th weeks of pregnancy. A local anesthetic is given and a needle inserted into the uterine cavity. About 10-20ml of amniotic fluid is withdrawn and the cells in it studied for defects. There is probably a less than 1-in-2,000 risk to the fetus, though this may rise if it is carried out later. A growing number of fetal abnormalities can now be detected, including Down's syndrome and spina bifida (see D65). Those who might want the test are:

a) women who have already given birth to a defective child;

b) women carrying a serious disorder;

c) women aged over 40, since they have approximately a 1-in-50 chance of delivering a child with congenital abnormalities.

D53 Thalidomide

Widely prescribed as a nonaddictive tranquilizer, thalidomide was taken by thousands of pregnant women in the late 1950s. As a result, some 8,000 seriously malformed children were born, and thalidomide turned into a tragedy.

Thalidomide was synthesized in West Germany in 1956. It had been tested, on animals and humans, and was manufactured under the name of Contergan. As a sleeping pill and tranquilizer, especially recommended for pregnant women (it eased morning sickness), it became popular and was sold in Britain (as Distaval), various European countries, Canada, Australia, New Zealand, and Japan. In the USA it was judged unsafe and was not sold. By 1959 seriously deformed babies were delivered in Germany. They were suffering from phocomelia — a rare condition in which the hands, feet, or both start immediately from the main joint like seal flippers. By 1961 it was obvious that thalidomide was responsible, and it was withdrawn in every country.

The thalidomide disaster tragically demonstrated the dangers of taking drugs during pregnancy. Most of them cross the placenta and, as was shown, the effects can be disastrous.

D54

D54 Inherited Disorders

The chromosomes that the fetus inherits from its parents carry many thousands of "genes," or units of genetic information. These decide the characteristics and activities of every cell in the body: some cells respond to some genes, some to others. Inherited defects arise in two ways. First, if any of the parents' genes are faulty, the relevant body cells may not respond in a desirable way ("gene abnormality"). Second, even if all the genes are healthy, the chromosomes may have been muddled or broken in the original pairing of ovum and sperm ("chromosome abnormality").

GENE ABNORMALITIES

There are several examples.

a) Sickle cell anemia. The red blood cells are abnormally shaped and so are destroyed by the body.

b) Phenylketonuria (PKU). Failure to produce one enzyme causes inability to process a vital amino acid contained in milk. Severe mental subnormality results unless a special diet is followed from birth.

c) "Wilson's disease." Defective metabolism of copper results in deposits of excess copper in the brain, liver, and eyes. Unless treated it leads to mental derangement and cirrhosis of the liver.

Some gene abnormalities show up if just one parent has the faulty gene, others only if both parents have it.

SEX-LINKED GENE ABNORMALITIES

This special category includes hemophilia, red-green color

Patterns of inheritance of a
sex-linked gene abnormality

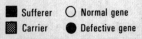

Father suffers
All girls are carriers
No boys suffer or carry

Risks in Pregnancy

blindness, and two forms of muscular dystrophy. The faulty gene responsible is carried on the X sex chromosome (see A02) — for this has other functions apart from determining sex. So in a woman the disorder does not usually show up, as her other X chromosome usually supplies a healthy gene: the healthy gene is "dominant." But in a man, there is no other X chromosome, only a Y chromosome, with no gene responsible for the defective function; and so the disorder appears.

The diagram shows the effects of this process of inheritance: a woman who does not herself show signs of the disorder can pass it on, so her sons may suffer and daughters carry it.

If a woman is found to be such a "carrier," there is risk not only to her own subsequent children, but also to those of her female relatives on the maternal side — because they may also have inherited the defective gene.

If no previous family history is found after a careful check, it is likely to be an isolated mutation — in either mother or child. If in the mother, she can still pass it on to subsequent children.

CHROMOSOME ABNORMALITIES

There are two types. First, those involving the X and Y sex chromosomes — so that the fetus, instead of having XX or XY chromosomes, has XXX, XXY, XYY, or X alone. All are linked with disorders — mostly involving abnormal genitals. Second, those involving other chromosomes; eg Down's syndrome (mongolism), where an extra chromosome results in physical and mental abnormalities.

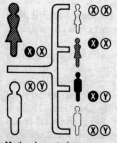

Mother is a carrier
Half girls likely to carry
Half boys likely to suffer; none carry

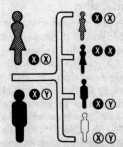

Mother is a carrier   Father suffers
Half girls likely to suffer; half to carry
Half boys likely to suffer; none carry

D55-56

D55 Malnutrition

Malnutrition in the mother during pregnancy can seriously affect the fetus. It may even die from undernourishment — revealed in autopsy not only by low weight, but also by stunting of each individual organ and low cytoplasm content of the body cells. More usually, the baby is born alive but underweight — and low birthweight carries with it increased risk of cerebral palsy, epilepsy, autism, blindness, deafness, mental subnormality, and neonatal death. Some sources estimate that a third of all long-term childhood handicaps are associated with low birthweight. In England, in 1973, babies weighing under $5\frac{1}{2}$lb (2.5kg) at birth accounted for 7.1% of births, but for 60% of stillbirths and deaths under 1 month.

Low birthweight is not totally due to malnutrition, but it is a major factor. In Guatemala, a nutritional program reduced

MINIMUM RECOMMENDED DIET

1pt milk, or $\frac{1}{2}$pt and 2oz (57g) of cheese

A portion of meat or fish, or an egg

A portion of root or raw green vegetable

Fruit, orange juice, and/or potato

Whole-wheat bread

1pt of water

D56 Infection

The amniotic sac protects the fetus against most bacteria. But virus infections in the mother's bloodstream cross the placenta and sometimes cause damage.

RUBELLA (German measles) in a woman in early pregnancy can cause fetal death or fetal deformities such as deafness, blindness, brain damage, and retarded growth. Rubella in the first 3 months of pregnancy causes defects in up to 50% of babies, and is often considered grounds for abortion. There is also slight risk in the 4th and 5th months. But if the mother has previously had the illness, or a vaccine against it, she is unlikely to contract an infection strong enough to spread to the fetus. (Vaccination cannot be given during pregnancy, as live vaccine is used.)

Risks in Pregnancy

low birthweight from 20% to 5.1% of births. This is below that of many industrialized countries, so it is not just in "developing" countries that there is room for nutritional improvement. But careful nutrition must begin before the 20th week of pregnancy. Any later improvement in diet has only limited effect.

MINIMUM DIET

Ideally, a pregnant woman should follow the normal daily food guide (H32), increasing Calorie intake and weight as suggested in D15 and H18. But many women find that their appetite in pregnancy is small or unpredictable; and poverty may be a factor. At the very least, whole-wheat bread and milk are preferable to tea or coffee and cookies. But if at all possible the minimum diet shown below should be followed each day. (Cold food may be more easily faced than heated food.)

Liver or oily fish once a week

White fish once a week

Bran to avoid constipation

CMV (CYTOMEGALO VIRUS) is spread between adults by close personal or sexual contact. It is found on the cervixes of up to 25% of pregnant women, usually without noticeable symptoms. It can cause low birthweight, prematurity, deafness, and mental retardation if it infects the fetus. No vaccine is available. But only when it is contracted for the first time during pregnancy is it usually strong enough to infect the fetus; and only 1 infected baby in 10 suffers permanent damage.

SEXUAL INFECTIONS Syphilis in the mother can cause death, deformity, or disease in the fetus, unless the mother is treated before the 16th week of pregnancy. (For the effects of gonorrhea, see L30.)

OTHER INFECTIONS Mumps, chickenpox, and fevers (as in influenza) are sometimes suspected of causing deformities.

D57-58

D57 Smoking in Pregnancy

As well as affecting a woman's own health, smoking may affect the health of an unborn baby. It is widely accepted that there is a connection between smoking and complications in pregnancy, and studies have shown that smoking while pregnant results in a lighter baby and an increase in perinatal mortality. Effects of smoking in pregnancy have also been found to persist into childhood. Probably the dangers are most severe if smoking continues after the first 3 months, and not all effects have been totally proven. Unlike many factors affecting her child's health, it is the mother's own decision whether or not she will smoke.

INCREASE IN SMOKING

Despite the possible ill effects of smoking while pregnant, a study of 18,631 pregnant women in Cardiff, UK, shows that smoking in pregnancy has become more common. In 1964 only 4% of Cardiff pregnant women smoked 20 or more cigarettes a day, compared with 15% in 1970.

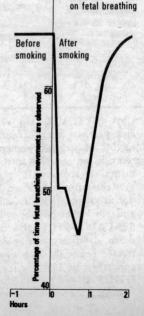

Effect of smoking on fetal breathing

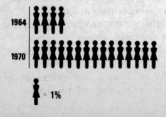

Percentage of pregnant women smoking 20+ cigarettes a day (Cardiff UK survey)

1964

1970

= 1%

Smoking in Pregnancy

SMOKING AND FETAL HEALTH

Fetal breathing movements are a direct measure of fetal health and well-being. Smoking has been shown to reduce the incidence of fetal breathing movements and must therefore be considered damaging to fetal health. A study of 18 normal pregnant women has shown that two cigarettes smoked consecutively produce a dramatic reduction in fetal breathing movements. The diagram on the previous page shows the percentage of time that fetal breathing movements could be observed during a test period.

D58 Birthweight

Statistics suggest that women who smoke when pregnant tend to produce lighter babies than nonsmoking mothers.

A study in Cardiff, UK, showed that the average birthweights of babies born to mothers who smoked in pregnancy was 5lb 14½oz (2.70kg), compared with 6lb 4½oz (2.83kg) for nonsmoking mothers.

Only 4% of the live babies born to nonsmoking mothers in Cardiff weighed less than 5lb 8oz (2.5kg), compared with over twice that percentage born to mothers smoking at least 20 cigarettes a day when pregnant.

A study made in California included the smoking habits of both parents. It showed that babies weighing less than 5lb 8oz (2.5kg) at birth were most common when both parents were smokers.

The diagram shows the difference in average birthweights of babies born (a) to nonsmokers (2870g) and (b) to smokers (2700g).

Percentage of babies who weigh less than 2.5kg at birth

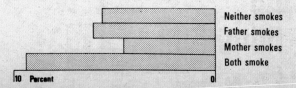

Neither smokes
Father smokes
Mother smokes
Both smoke

10 Percent   0

D59-61

D59 Perinatal Mortality

The relationship between smoking and unsuccessful pregnancy (miscarriage, stillbirth, neonatal death) is not yet completely clear. In findings at Cardiff, UK (a), the rate of stillbirth and neonatal death with mothers smoking over 20 cigarettes a day was 3.8%, with nonsmoking mothers only 2.5%. But in a California study (b), smokers' babies had a lower mortality rate than nonsmokers'. (This study, though, only considered babies born live and with birthweight under 5½ lb – 2.5kg.) However, a study at Sheffield, UK, clearly showed that, among women of similar blood pressure, smokers' pregnancies were much more likely to be unsuccessful (c). The confusing factor pinpointed was that smoking is also associated with low blood pressure (which favors successful pregnancy). But why there is this association is unknown. Does low blood pressure favor smoking, or smoking favor low blood pressure? Both seem unlikely.

Smoking and unsuccessful pregnancy

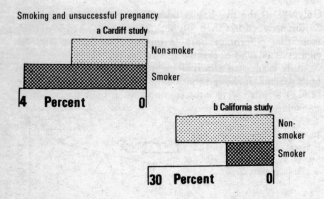

a Cardiff study
Nonsmoker
Smoker
4 **Percent** 0

b California study
Non-smoker
Smoker
30 **Percent** 0

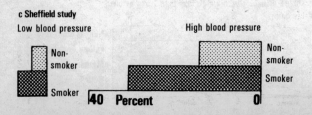

c Sheffield study
Low blood pressure
Nonsmoker
Smoker

High blood pressure
Non-smoker
Smoker
40 **Percent** 0

Smoking in Pregnancy

D60 Fetal Malformation

Although there is no firm evidence that smoking is associated with fetal malformation, findings at Cardiff suggest that there may in fact be such a link.

The incidence of congenital heart disease among babies born to women who smoked during pregnancy was 0.73% compared with 0.47% among babies born to nonsmokers. Hare lip and cleft palate were also found slightly more often among babies born to women who smoked.

Percentage of babies with congenital heart disease

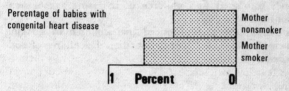

D61 Postnatal Development

Babies born to women who smoked while pregnant have been shown to grow more rapidly than babies born to nonsmokers. The difference in average weekly growth rates is most marked from birth to six weeks. But over a year the difference in growth between smokers' and nonsmokers' babies is negligible. So, in the end, nonsmokers' babies tend to preserve any size advantage they had at birth.

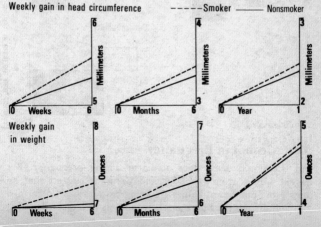

D62-63

D62 Long-term Effects

The diagrams below are based on a survey taken in the UK of 17,000 children whose progress had been followed from birth. They compare the mental abilities of 11-year-old children of mothers who smoked during pregnancy with those of non-smoking mothers.

Children of mothers who smoked up to 9 cigarettes daily were some 5-5½ months behind in school progress, and those of mothers who smoked 10+ cigarettes daily were 5½-7 months behind, compared with children of the same age of non-smoking mothers.

In addition, the survey noticed that children of smoking mothers tend to be 0.5-1cm shorter than the children of non-smokers.

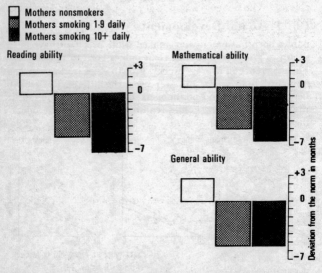

□ Mothers nonsmokers
▨ Mothers smoking 1-9 daily
■ Mothers smoking 10+ daily

Reading ability

Mathematical ability

General ability

Deviation from the norm in months

D63 Alcohol in Pregnancy

An occasional drink does no harm during pregnancy. But recent studies from the USA and Germany suggest that an increasing number of babies are being born seriously deformed or mentally retarded because their mothers have been drinking

Smoking, Alcohol, Drugs in Pregnancy

heavily during pregnancy. It has even been claimed that 1 in 3 women who drink heavily must expect their child to be mentally or physically defective. But so far evidence is mainly from actual alcoholics. The diagrams below are based on a US study of 23 children born to chronically alcoholic mothers. They were compared with children of nonalcoholic mothers and matched for socioeconomic group, race, maternal age, etc.

a Mortality rates. The diagram shows mortality rates among the newborn babies: 17% of those born to alcoholic mothers died within 1 week as opposed to 2% of those born to non-alcoholic mothers.

b Growth deficiencies. The diagram compares birthweight, length, and head circumference of both sets of infants. Comparisons were based on a measurement of normality that generally only 3% of the overall baby population fails to achieve. In the survey, 13% to 32% of the children of alcoholic mothers failed to reach the measurement.

c IQ performance. At the age of 7, 44% of the children born to alcoholic mothers had an IQ of 70 or under.

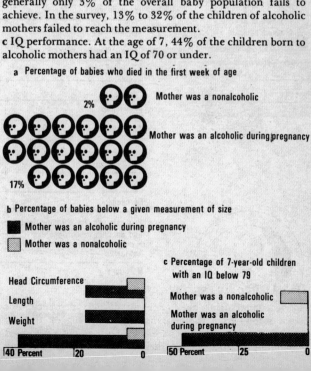

a Percentage of babies who died in the first week of age

2% — Mother was a nonalcoholic

Mother was an alcoholic during pregnancy

17%

b Percentage of babies below a given measurement of size

■ Mother was an alcoholic during pregnancy

▨ Mother was a nonalcoholic

Head Circumference
Length
Weight

40 Percent   20   0

c Percentage of 7-year-old children with an IQ below 79

Mother was a nonalcoholic

Mother was an alcoholic during pregnancy

50 Percent   25   0

D64

D64 Drugs and Placenta Crossing

Most doctors today recommend that women avoid all drugs during pregnancy unless they are absolutely essential for the mother's well-being. The fetus maintains its hold on life through the umbilical cord and the work of the placenta (see D09). Oxygen and nutrients pass from the mother's circulation into that of the fetus via the placenta and umbilicus, and carbon dioxide and other waste products pass back the same way.

DRUGS
Caffeine (in coffee) Tannic acid (in tea)
Sleeping pills
Tranquilizers
LSD and other psychedelics
Cocaine; Amphetamines
Heroin; Morphine
Aspirin
Phenacetin
Antibiotics a) Streptomycin, gentamycin b) Sulphonamides (long-term) c) Tetracycline
Antihistamines
Cortisone
Progesterone (for hormone deficiency and possible miscarriage)
Antithyroid
Marijuana

The diagram shows some of the drugs that cross the placenta and what the effects on the fetus might be.

Smoking, Alcohol, Drugs
in Pregnancy

As a result, most substances in the mother's bloodstream will reach the fetus. In the case of drugs, recent studies show that, as with thalidomide, effects on the fetus can be disastrous. This is particularly true during the first 3 months when the fetal organs are forming.

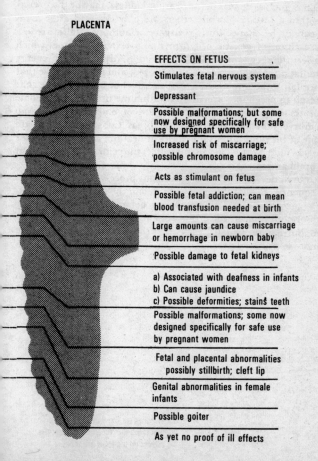

PLACENTA

EFFECTS ON FETUS

Stimulates fetal nervous system

Depressant

Possible malformations; but some now designed specifically for safe use by pregnant women

Increased risk of miscarriage; possible chromosome damage

Acts as stimulant on fetus

Possible fetal addiction; can mean blood transfusion needed at birth

Large amounts can cause miscarriage or hemorrhage in newborn baby

Possible damage to fetal kidneys

a) Associated with deafness in infants
b) Can cause jaundice
c) Possible deformities; stains teeth

Possible malformations; some now designed specifically for safe use by pregnant women

Fetal and placental abnormalities possibly stillbirth; cleft lip

Genital abnormalities in female infants

Possible goiter

As yet no proof of ill effects

D65

D65 Defects at Birth

These are anatomical defects present at birth. Thirty live births in every 1,000 have some kind of congenital malformation. They may be so severe that life is not possible, eg anencephaly, or they may be so trivial that life is not interfered with, eg an extra finger. Many, but not all defects are obvious at birth. Some, such as defects in the heart or kidneys, may be discovered within a few days, while others are only detected after many years or by chance during surgery or autopsy. Malformations are either of genetic origin or due to external factors which affect the pregnant woman, eg infection, drugs, or high-energy radiation. Most ova are never fertilized, and many of those that are fail to be implanted in the uterus; but 20% of those that result in pregnancy are aborted within the first 12 weeks. Some of these spontaneous abortions are of empty sacs with no embryo, others are of defective embryos. Congenital defects are one of the most important causes of death in the first and later weeks after birth. They mainly affect the central nervous system (brain and spinal cord).

Embryo development is a continuous process following a strict sequence. The initiation of each step in the process depends on the successful completion of the one before. Any interruption or disorganization of these processes at any time may result in a malformation. Usually, the earlier the interruption occurs, the more severe the defect.

Defects at Birth

DEFECT	RATE*	DESCRIPTION

* Rate per 10,000 live births

The most common anatomical defects in the newborn baby

Double ureter	300	Two ureters from one kidney. Usually without symptoms or significance. Very occasionally, obstructed urine flow, causing infection. Genetic. Surgery if necessary.
Male inguinal hernia	80	Hernia in the groin, between the muscles of abdomen and thigh. Developmental. Surgery needed.
Mental subnormality (except mongolism)	17	Varying degrees of defect from a variety of different causes.
Spina bifida, often with hydrocephalus	10	Spina bifida - defect leaving spinal cord exposed; hydrocephalus - obstruction in skull causing collection of cerebro-spinal fluid under pressure. Genetic, or result of antenatal injury or infection. Surgery to prevent paralysis or death.
Anencephaly	6	Absence of brain and top part of skull. Replaced by fibrous tissue. Invariably fatal. More common with very young or old mothers.
Cleft lip and palate	5	Lip and palate not fused. Difficult breathing, feeding, and speaking. Partly genetic. Associated with thalidomide, rubella. Plastic surgery required.
Down's syndrome (mongolism)	3.5	Rate rises to 200 if mother is over 40. Caused by extra chromosome (see D54). Characterized by mental retardation, heart defects, Mongoloid features, protruding tongue.
Coeliac disease	2.5	Disorder of unknown cause, producing inability to assimilate some foods. Chronic diarrhea and malnutrition. Treatment dietary. Recovery usual, but slow.

D66

D66 Death at Birth

MATERNAL MORTALITY

Medical advances have made childbirth safer today than ever before. A hundred years ago abnormal presentation, protracted deliveries, hemorrhage, and puerperal fever resulted in a mortality rate of up to 250 per 1,000 live births in hospitals; the rate for home deliveries was, however, much lower. Developments in antiseptic and operative techniques have controlled puerperal fever and helped overcome complications of pregnancy and birth.

Today the main causes of maternal death are: illegal abortion and miscarriage (35%); ectopic pregnancy (15%); hemorrhage (usually postpartum) (15%); toxemia (10%); and traumatic labor (10%). Other deaths mainly result from maternal disease (eg heart and lung complications).

FETAL MORTALITY

Though much higher than the maternal death rate, the fetal death rate has also fallen dramatically over the last 100 years. This is due to improved techniques, and better care and diet during pregnancy. Most stillbirths are due to prematurity (see D37), placental insufficiency, and congenital defects.

INFANT MORTALITY

The infant period covers the first year of life. One hundred years ago, 200 infants in every 1,000 died. Since then the rate has fallen to 23 per 1,000 live births. This is mainly due to improved antenatal and postnatal care, better delivery techniques, and advances in medical understanding. Congenital defects are the largest cause of death; and rhesus incompatability (D12), diabetes, eclampsia, and heart disease can also be fatal.

Maternal and Infant Mortality

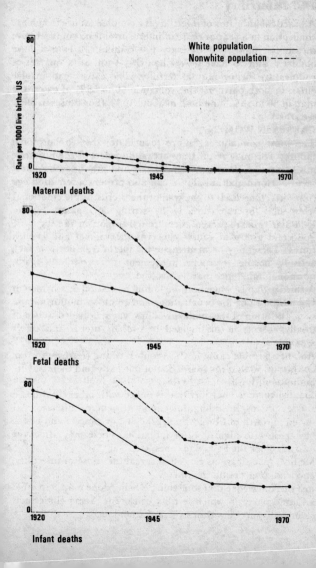

White population ⎯⎯⎯⎯
Nonwhite population ⎯ ⎯ ⎯

Rate per 1000 live births US

1920　　1945　　1970

Maternal deaths

1920　　1945　　1970

Fetal deaths

1920　　1945　　1970

Infant deaths

D67

D67 Infertility

A practical indicator of infertility is a couple's failure to achieve conception in a year or more of intercourse, if no contraceptive measure is used. Out of every 100 couples, 10 cannot have children, and 15 have fewer than they wish. So a quarter of couples are below normal fertility. The causes can involve either or both partners: the woman in 50 to 55% of cases, the man in 30 to 35%, and both in about 15%. (For causes in men, see D77.)

CAUSES IN WOMEN

The most common is failure to ovulate, due to hormonal failure. This may result from actual disorders of the hormone mechanism, or from emotional stress and other psychological factors. Hormonal imbalance can also prevent a fertilized egg from attaching itself to the wall of the uterus, while emotional stress may operate directly by setting up spasms in the Fallopian tubes to prevent them from transporting the egg.

A second group of causes concerns the vaginal and cervical fluids. These may be inadequate for sperm transport, or even actively hostile to sperm movement or survival. (Again, hormonal imbalance may be involved.)

A third group is congenital, including possession of a hymen or vagina too tight for penetration, and common malformations such as: fusion of the small vulval lips; vagina divided in two or totally absent; uterus divided in two; or uterus and cervix absent.

Another possible cause in this group is tilting (retroversion) of the uterus, so that the sperm do not normally find their way in; but most authorities dismiss this.

Finally, there is infertility that is linked with other disorders in the sex organs, including: infection with venereal disease, cystitis, etc; growth of fibroids, polyps, cysts, or cancer; and effects of exposure to high doses of radiation. These may affect the ovaries, block the Fallopian tubes, etc.

Medical investigations can often reveal the cause of infertility, and lead to successful treatment.

Just the knowledge that something is being done may help build an atmosphere in which fertility can occur. Some clinics now claim 65% success within 4 years of attendance.

Infertility

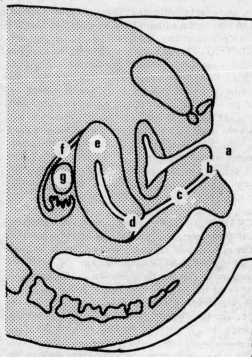

a Labia
b Hymen
c Vagina
d Cervix
e Uterus
f Fallopian tubes
g Ovary

The diagram shows possible faults
in the female genitals:
a small labia fused;
b hymen too strong;
c vagina narrowed or divided;
d cervical mucus unreceptive;
e uterus tilted or divided;
f Fallopian tubes blocked by
  infection;
g ovaries failing to produce eggs.

D68

D68 Investigations

Diagnosis may prove simple. But if necessary a woman's doctor may refer her to a team of specialists using advanced techniques of investigation and treatment.

POSTCOITAL TEST This is usually made 6-18 hours after intercourse, and as near as possible to the day of ovulation. A mucus specimen is taken from the cervix. Microscopic study of this shows the quantity and quality of the sperm present — which depend on both the material originally ejaculated and the condition of the cervical mucus. The mucus should be most receptive to sperm at ovulation, but hormonal imbalance may distort this. Also, infertility sometimes results from incompatability between mucus and sperm.

SCRAPING The health of, and hormonal influence upon, the uterus lining can be tested by dilation and curettage (see L09). The resulting stretching of the cervix helps sperm penetration, and so may itself aid fertility.

SALPINGOGRAPHY is X raying of the uterus and Fallopian tubes to reveal their internal condition, by introducing into them an X ray-opaque oily or water-soluble dye. It is done before ovulation to avoid possible ovum damage. Again, sometimes the procedure itself helps: the dye unsticks adhering tube walls, and pregnancy follows.

GAS TEST (INSUFFLATION) Carbon dioxide is blown through the Fallopian tubes, revealing and sometimes even clearing blockage. But it gives no detailed information, and some consider it outmoded.

UTEROSCOPY is use of a periscope instrument to give an internal view of the uterus via the vagina.

LAPAROSCOPY gives a good external view of uterus, tubes, and ovaries, without a large abdominal incision. Carbon dioxide gas is blown through a hollow needle into the abdominal cavity. This distends the abdominal wall, and allows a clear view of the reproductive organs through a laparoscope introduced through a tiny abdominal slit.

Various specialists may be involved.

a SURGICAL GYNECOLOGIST specializing in investigating and operating on the female reproductive organs.

b MEDICAL GYNECOLOGIST advising on nonsurgical treatments.

Infertility

c HISTOLOGIST analyzing tissue samples taken by surgical gynecologist from ovaries, uterus lining, etc.

d RADIOLOGIST interpreting X rays of (for example) the Fallopian tubes.

e ENDOCRINOLOGIST looking for disturbances in the hormones of the endocrine system.

f BIOCHEMIST providing the endocrinologist with precise measurements of hormone levels.

g PSYCHIATRIST to help overcome psychological barriers to pregnancy.

h GENETICIST assessing risks of inherited abnormality, and advising abortion if necessary.

i UROLOGIST specializing in disorders involving the urinary tract.

j ANDROLOGIST specializing in investigating the male reproductive system.

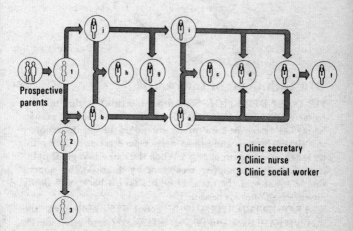

1 Clinic secretary
2 Clinic nurse
3 Clinic social worker

The diagram shows working relationships within the medical team.

D69 Timing of Intercourse

Chances of conception may be improved by concentrating intercourse on the woman's fertile phase of each month. If the charts that she keeps show that she has regular 28-day periods, her fertile phase will usually lie between days 11 and 16. With irregular cycles of between 27 and 35 days, chances of pregnancy improve if intercourse occurs on five alternate days, starting with the 13th day of the cycle. (Intercourse on all the fertile days would exhaust the man's sperm output.)

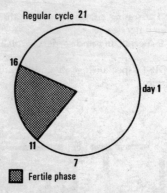

Regular cycle **21**

16

day 1

11

7

Fertile phase

D70 Techniques of Intercourse

FULL PENETRATION Sometimes infertility is due to poor coital connection. When obesity is the cause, if the woman hooks her knees over the man's shoulders during intercourse, this flexes the hips and allows deeper penetration. (Care must be taken in case pain occurs.) When the cause is vaginal tightness, then (perhaps after treatment by dilation) the woman should squat over the man, as he lies on his back, and slowly lower herself onto his penis.

RETROVERTED UTERUS In about 10% of women, the uterus is tilted back and the cervix forward (retroverted uterus, see L05). The typical position of intercourse may then not bring the semen into contact with the cervix. Most have no difficulty in becoming pregnant despite this. Fertility is helped in such cases though, if the woman uses a face-down position (lying or kneeling), with the man entering her from behind. The lying position should make the pool of semen bathe the cervix — but may cause cystitis if the penis bruises the woman's bladder. Instead, the woman can change from a kneeling position to a lying one after intercourse ends.

AFTER INTERCOURSE Fertility in any woman is usually improved if the woman remains fairly still for at least half an hour after intercourse ends.

Full penetration positions

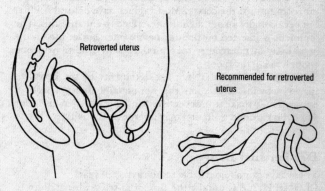

Retroverted uterus

Recommended for retroverted uterus

D71 Treating Infection

The cervix is often affected by infections involving vaginal discharge. The cause of some of these is unknown (see L15), but some are due to venereal disease or other diagnosable infection, or to foreign bodies such as forgotten tampons or contraceptive devices. Treatment usually involves a course of pessaries, or sometimes antibiotics. (Occasionally the cervix is cauterized under anesthetic, to burn away chronically infected tissue.) Infection may impair fertility. Risk of spreading infection may also prevent investigation.

D72-73

D72 Improving Receptivity

Mechanical devices and ointments may be useful for improving the sperm receptivity of various parts of the woman's genitals.

DILATION of the vagina with glass dilators or with the fingers helps in many cases where vaginal tightness prevents successful penetration.

DOUCHING Making the cervical mucus more alkaline may improve the chances of the cervix taking up viable sperm. The woman sits in the bath and douches the upper part of the vagina with warm water containing bicarbonate of soda. For this purpose she uses a douche can equipped with tube and nozzle. This method should only be used when a postcoital test has shown that it is appropriate.

VAGINAL ACIDITY Although alkaline cervical mucus can be desirable, it also sometimes helps if the mucus of the vagina itself is made more acid: vaginal acidity seems to make sperm move up toward the cervix. Most vaginas have natural acidity, but occasionally an ointment is prescribed to enhance this. The ointment is inserted on the day before intercourse; use on the actual day of intercourse may produce acid conditions strong enough to kill the sperm.

SYNTHETIC HORMONES The receptivity of the cervix to sperm depends largely on the hormonal balance. Lack of estrogen may make it unreceptive. Synthetic estrogen given for 4 or 5 days around ovulation may improve receptivity.

D73 Fertility Drugs

These have given remarkable results in recent years.

CLOMIPHENE is usually the first drug tried when failure to ovulate is suspected. Just how it works is unclear. (In fact, it was originally tested as a contraceptive, and found to have the reverse effect.) The woman may need no more than a single 5-tablet course taken during one menstrual cycle; with luck, ovulation follows less than two weeks after. If no pregnancy occurs after a month, a second course may be tried, and so on — with intervals — up to six courses. About 30% of those given the drug conceive. Only one ovum is released at a time, so multiple pregnancies are unlikely (twins occur in about 7% of cases). Ovarian cysts are a possible side effect; otherwise the drug seems harmless.

Infertility

PERGONAL is more controversial. It is an extract of FSH and LH hormones obtained from menopausal women. (FSH and LH stimulate the ovaries to produce estrogen and progesterone, the hormones that prepare the uterus for pregnancy: see A10.) Patients receive the drug by injection under closely controlled hospital conditions. Good supervision should yield no more than one or two ova; miscalculation may produce either none or a large number. Most unwanted multiple births due to fertility drugs stem from Pergonal, and such births carry increased risks to mother and babies alike.

HYPOTHALAMIC RELEASING FACTORS are substances produced by the hypothalamus at the base of the brain. They stimulate the pituitary to produce FSH and LH (see A10). Such hypothalamic releasing factors are now made synthetically, and have cured infertility which was due to poor pituitary action.

ANTISPASMODICS do not promote ovulation: they are used simply to get existing ova to their destination by preventing the Fallopian tubes going into spasm. (In some women, such temporary spasms block ova transport.)

Cumulative success rates claimed for the main fertility drugs

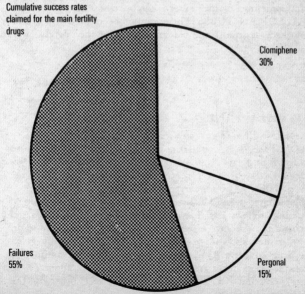

Clomiphene
30%

Pergonal
15%

Failures
55%

D74-76

D74 Operations for Fertility

A number of operations may be performed to improve fertility in appropriate cases.

VULVA Operations on the vulva include opening cysts and abscesses, and dividing the small lips of the vulva if these have fused.

HYMEN Where this is too thick and rigid to be stretched, it may be cut and stitched back.

VAGINA A narrow vagina may be widened and lined with a skin graft; and the longitudinal division that sometimes separates the two sides of the vagina can be removed.

CERVIX A badly torn cervix can be treated by plastic surgery. Repeated abortions between the 14th and 28th weeks are sometimes prevented by stitching the cervix. Dilation may aid sperm penetration.

UTERUS A backward-tilting (retroverted) uterus can be brought forward by inserting a special plastic pessary into the vagina, or by shortening the ligaments between uterus and groin. Fibroids can be cut away from the uterus wall. The wall that sometimes divides a uterus can be removed.

FALLOPIAN TUBES These cannot be cleared when totally blocked, as from some old infection. But the "petals" at the

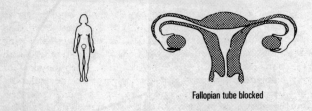

Fallopian tube blocked

Blocked section removed

Shortened tube rejoined

Infertility

ovarian ends of the tubes may need teasing out; and if the uterus end of a tube is blocked, this can be cut away and the shortened tube rejoined to the uterus.

Sometimes tubes are intact but hampered by bands of tissue that prevent them moving to collect the ovum from the ovary. These bands can be cut away.

OVARIES Cutting a wedge from the ovaries allows egg release, when this is blocked by certain ovarian cysts. Removal of other cysts also aids fertility. Probably a third of gynecological operations are for ovarian cysts.

D75 Psychiatric Help

This may be relevant. First, there are women in whom long-term failure to ovulate derives ultimately from psychological stress. These cases include those showing clear mental symptoms (eg severe depression), and those with no surface symptoms but nevertheless some underlying unhappiness or insecurity. Second, there are those men and women in whom long-term trauma interferes with the actual sexual act. Third, there are couples in whom the desire and struggle for fertility has itself given rise to mental tension, with emotional or physical consquences (eg male impotence).

D76 Artificial Insemination

This involves the artificial transference of semen onto the cervix — usually by syringing through a tube on 3 or 4 successive days around ovulation. After insemination the woman remains lying down for about half an hour. Artificial insemination (AI) with the partner's sperm (AIH) may be used when physical or psychological causes prevent normal intercourse or ejaculation; or when the man's sperm count is low, or the woman's cervical mucus is hostile to his sperm. AIH can be carried out in a clinic or (using special equipment) by the couple at home. AI using the sperm of an anonymous donor (AID) is much more common. It is used when the partner is totally infertile or when his chromosomes are known to carry hereditary disorders. The donor is carefully chosen to match the partner in appearance and to be free from disease.

The success rate from AID is about 66% within the first three months. Babies conceived by AI develop no differently, of course, from those conceived in the ordinary way.

D77

D77 Infertility in Men

Male infertility is of two kinds:

a) cases where there is no ejaculation (ie impotence: see N10);

b) cases where the quality of the ejaculate is poor — as shown by sperm concentration, shape, and mobility.

SPERM CONCENTRATION This depends not only on sperm production, but also on the amount of fluid — as shown by the total amount of semen. Both very small and very large amounts are unfavorable to fertility. A small amount suggests that sperm production is also low. It also fails to buffer the sperm against the acidity of the vaginal fluids. A large amount dilutes the semen too much, and makes it more likely to spill out of the vagina.

SPERM SHAPE The higher the number of abnormal forms, the less the likelihood of fertility. For example, fertility is probably impossible if the tapering shapes rise above 8 or 10%.

SPERM MOVEMENT The length of life of the sperm (as shown by their movement) is significant not only because they may need time before encountering an egg to fertilize. For some reason not yet understood, sperm also need to survive for some time in the female reproductive tract before they are capable of fertilizing an egg.

CAUSES OF MALE INFERTILITY Causes of poor sperm production can include:

a) heat around the testicles, due, for example, to tight underclothing, obesity, or working conditions;

b) factors of general vitality, such as poor health, inadequate nutrition, lack of exercise, excessive smoking and drinking, etc;

c) emotional stress; and

d) too prolonged sexual abstinence (this can increase the number of abnormal sperm).

More specialized factors (some of which can cause sterility) include:

a) some birth defects;

b) failure of the testes to descend before puberty;

c) some childhood diseases, and some other illnesses (eg mumps if it occurs in adulthood rather than childhood);

d) some hazards such as exposure to X rays, radioactivity, some chemicals and metals, gasoline fumes, and carbon monoxide; and

e) some genital disorders, such as varicocele and blocked ducts, and tuberculous infection of the prostate.

Infertility

AIDS TO FERTILITY

Many of these causes of infertility are treatable. But, more generally, we do not yet know of any substances that will improve male fertility. Severe lack of vitamins will impair fertility; but no special vitamin intake seems to raise the fertility level of a well-fed person. As for hormones, the pituitary hormones have only limited effect, while testosterone actually hinders sperm production — it is only useful where infertility is due to genital underdevelopment or impotence. However, there are techniques to aid fertility. One is the medical technique of artificial insemination (see D76). Another is a practical sexual technique. It seems that the second half of a man's ejaculate — the fluid from the seminal vesicles — is actually likely to harm the sperm, while that of the prostate, in the first half, protects it. So a couple can increase their chances of parenthood if the man withdraws from the vagina halfway through his ejaculation. (They should also abstain from further intercourse for 48 hours afterward.)

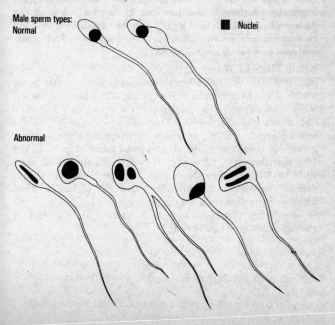

Male sperm types:
Normal

■ Nuclei

Abnormal

E01-03

E01 Abortion

Abortion — the deliberate termination of pregnancy — is a controversial and emotive issue. The decision to end a pregnancy is rarely easy. For most women, however, whether the pregnancy has resulted from lack, misuse, or failure of contraception, the problems of continuing with an unwanted pregnancy are generally greater than those of terminating it.

CONFIRMING PREGNANCY

A missed period is usually the first sign of pregnancy. Others may be feelings of sickness, revulsion against some foods, and frequent urination. Fourteen days after the first missed period, a urine test can confirm pregnancy. Although there are home-testing kits, these are not reliable, and a sample of early-morning urine in a clean container can be taken to a doctor, clinic, hospital, or pregnancy testing association. Results are often known within a few hours.

CHOOSING AN ABORTION

Once a woman has decided to have an abortion, time becomes important. Although abortions can be carried out until the 28th week (the fetus is then legally considered to have a separate existence), they are not often performed after the 12th week, and only very rarely after the 20th.

ABORTION LAWS

Abortion is the most widely used method of birth control in the world. It has been estimated that nearly 1 in 4 pregnancies are terminated either legally or illegally. There has been a gradual liberalization of abortion laws, and today well over 75% of the world's population live in countries where abortion is, to a greater or lesser extent, legal. Laws and facilities vary. In the US, abortion up to 12 weeks has been available "on request" since 1973; in Britain, abortion has been legal since 1967, but various socio-medical grounds must be presented, and ultimately the decision is not the woman's alone.

In only a few countries, such as Belgium and Indonesia, is abortion completely outlawed.

Methods of Abortion

E02 Endometrial Aspiration

Known also as interception, menstrual regulation, and menstrual suction, this is a preemptive abortion technique — meaning that it can be performed for up to 2 weeks after a period was due, ie before a pregnancy can be positively confirmed.

EQUIPMENT
This consists of a small, flexible plastic cannula (tube) about 4-5mm long attached to a suction source — usually an electrical or mechanical pump. A syringe may be used in very early pregnancy.

PROCEDURE
The cannula is passed through the cervix into the uterus, its small size making much dilation unnecessary. The endometrium, or lining of the uterus, is gently sucked out, and with it the fetal tissue. The process takes only a few minutes and local anesthetic is rarely needed. Interception, although not yet widely available, is generally performed in a clinic or doctor's office.

ADVANTAGES AND DISADVANTAGES
Interception is fast and there are apparently few risks — the flexible cannula reduces risk of damage to the uterus. Also, being carried out so early in pregnancy, emotional strain on a woman is lessened.

However, for the same reason, the method may be used unnecessarily, on a woman who is not pregnant; or, as the fetus is so tiny at this stage, there may be uncertainty about its complete removal.

MENSTRUAL EXTRACTION
In some women's self-help groups, the above process is used, not as an abortion technique, but as a means of avoiding menstrual discomfort by extracting the uterus lining in one quick operation. It is then given the different name of "menstrual extraction."

E03 Dilation and Evacuation (D & E)

Also called vacuum curettage, suction abortion, or STOP (suction termination of pregnancy), D & E is the most common method of abortion today. It is quick, easy to perform (it is increasingly carried out in clinics), and there is low risk of complication. Essentially the fetus is removed, by suction, from the uterus through a narrow tube inserted through the cervix. D & E is normally carried out between 7-12 weeks from the last menstrual period, after which time the fetus is too large for D & E to be performed safely.

PREPARATION
Very little preparation is needed. The woman's blood type is checked, and she should not eat for about 6 hours before the operation. Pubic hair need not be shaved. After an internal examination, the speculum is inserted and the patient given an anesthetic — local or general.

RECOVERY
The abortion takes about 10 minutes; the rest period afterward about 2-3 hours. When D & E is performed in the hospital, patients often stay in overnight. Recovery is fast, though strenuous activity should be avoided for a couple of

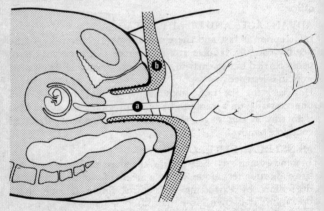

DILATION
The diagram shows the cervix being dilated. A series of polished metal dilators (a) are used, the largest being about the width of a finger. A speculum (b) holds the vaginal walls open.

Methods of Abortion

days. There is usually some bleeding, possibly with mild cramps, for up to 7 days. The normal period starts 4-6 weeks after the abortion. Most doctors advise that tampons and sexual intercourse should be avoided for 2-4 weeks to prevent possible infection.

DILATION AND CURETTAGE (D & C)

Before the development of suction abortion, D & C was the standard method used for pre-12th-week abortions. It is still a standard gynecological procedure (see L09), and is the only abortion technique used from the 12th to 15th weeks.

After dilating the cervix, the uterus contents are scraped away with a curette. D & C is more complicated to perform than D & E, is more painful, requires general anesthetic, and carries more risks of perforation and infection.

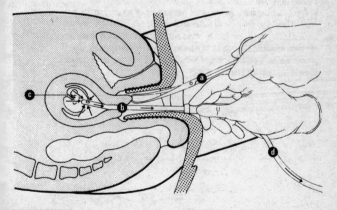

EVACUATION ONE
Once dilation is complete the cervix is held steady with a tentaculum (a). A vacurette or suction curette (b) is inserted into the uterus until it touches the fetus (c). The vacurette, which is about ⅓ in (8 mm) wide, has 2 side openings and is attached (d) by transparent plastic tubing to a suction machine or aspirator.

E03-04

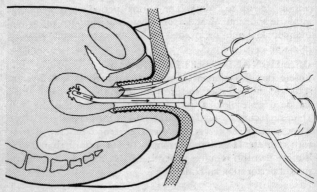

EVACUATION TWO

With the vacurette inside the uterus the suction machine is turned on. The fetal material breaks up and is gently suctioned through the tip of the vacurette into a vacuum bottle. The suction tube is moved around until the uterus is empty, and then removed. Aspiration takes about 2-5 minutes and afterwards the doctor usually scrapes the inside of the uterus (see below) to ensure that none of the fetus or placenta has been left behind.

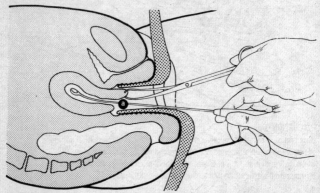

CURETTAGE

The diagram shows the uterus being scraped with a curette (a). When curettage only is used as an abortion technique, the cervix is first dilated as described above. A curette – a thin metal instrument with a spoonlike tip – is then inserted into the uterus. The fetus and placenta are scraped loose and are removed with forceps.

Methods of Abortion

E04 Induced-Labor Abortions

Currently, the usual technique for late abortion is to induce miscarriage. Being so similar to normal childbirth, this can be a much more distressing experience than earlier abortion methods. There is also more potential risk, eg hemorrhage, shock, infection, incomplete abortion. Therefore, late abortions are always carried out in a hospital, and are rare.

PROCEDURE

Under local anesthetic an amniocentesis (see D52) is performed. Amniotic fluid is withdrawn (a) and replaced (b) by a miscarriage-inducing agent, normally a concentrated saline (salt) solution. The fetus dies and in 6-48 hours the cervix dilates. Contractions occur, and the fetus and placenta are expelled. Recently, use has also been made of prostaglandins (naturally occurring hormones). These stimulate contractions of the womb, causing miscarriage more rapidly than saline solution. Also, despite side effects, prostaglandins are safer.

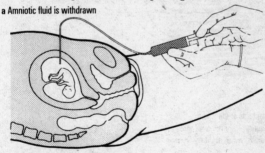

a Amniotic fluid is withdrawn

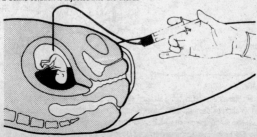

b Saline solution is injected into the uterus

E05-06

E05 Hysterotomy

Hysterotomy (not to be confused with hysterectomy — see L10) is a method of late abortion that is rarely used today. It is similar to a mini-Cesarian section (see D40), and involves major surgery and hospitalization.

Hysterotomy is the most complicated of all abortion techniques, and carries the highest risks. It is generally used only when a saline-solution abortion has failed. The resulting scar may rupture in a subsequent pregnancy.

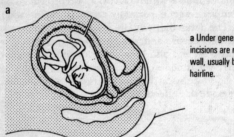

a Under general anesthetic, incisions are made in the abdominal wall, usually below the pubic hairline.

b The contents of the uterus — fetus and placenta — are removed through the incisions, which are then sewn up.

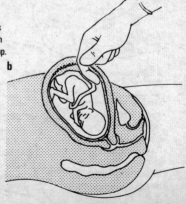

Methods of Abortion

E06 Illegal Abortions

The diagram shows some of the physical damage that can result from illegal abortions. "Back-street" and self-induced abortions are still common — worldwide they cause 30-50% of all maternal deaths from pregnancy and childbirth. Various techniques are used, most of them either unsuccessful or highly dangerous. Inserting objects or pumping fluid and air into the uterus are among the most common methods. They are often fatal. But there has always been a demand for abortion, legal or otherwise. One argument for complete legalization is to prevent catastrophes that result from crude, unhygienic abortions. Ironically, it was, in some part, for this reason that abortion was outlawed in the 19th century.

POSSIBLE PHYSICAL CONSEQUENCES OF ILLEGAL ABORTION

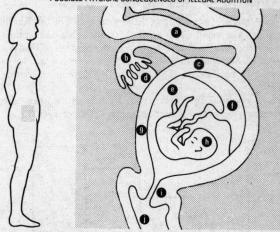

a Punctured intestine, possibly leading to peritonitis, septicemia, and intra-peritoneal hemorrhage
b Infection of Fallopian tubes
c Perforation into the peritoneal cavity
d Infection of the ovaries
e Intrauterine infection
f Perforation through placental site causing internal hemorrhage
g Blood clot (possibly infected) or air embolism (possibly lethal)
h Fetal malformation
i Laceration of cervix
j Laceration of vagina

Fo1-03

F01 The Menopause

The menopause (also called the climacteric, or change of life) marks the end of the reproductive part of a woman's life. Its chief outward sign is the cessation of the monthly flow of menstrual blood. Some women also experience a variety of symptoms due to change in hormonal balance. Parts of the body may begin to age noticeably, but most women should be able to remain physically, mentally, and sexually as active after the menopause as before it. Some see the menopause as a time of regret. For others, it represents a welcome release from unwanted biological demands on the body.

F02 Onset of the Menopause

The menopause begins at different ages in different individuals. The usual age is around 50, though a few women start the menopause in their 30s, while onset in others is delayed into the 50s. But about half of all women lose their capacity to bear children by the age of 50, and only 5% remain capable beyond 55.

The diagram shows the percentage of American women who have experienced a natural menopause by different ages.

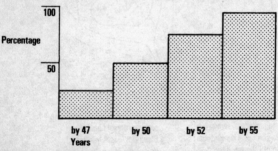

F03 Variations

There are many reasons for variation in the time of onset. Race is one factor. White women of northern European stock tend to reach the climacteric late if they entered puberty early, and early if they entered puberty late. With women of Mediter-

The Change of Life

Factors influencing the relative time of onset

	Early menopause		Late menopause	
Race	Black; southern European		White; northern European	
Living standard	Poor		Rich	
Motherhood	Non-childbearing		Childbearing	
Weight	Fat		Thin	
Puberty	Late puberty		Early puberty	
Surgery	Ovaries removed		Ovaries intact	
Heredity	Heredity may favor either early or late menopause			

ranean or colored origin, both puberty and menopause come relatively early. Then, too, women of some families cease menstruating early, others late, for their racial group. Thus heredity plays a part. At one time, climate also seemed to be implicated, though, in fact, it makes no difference. But a high living standard does tend to prolong a woman's reproductive life, while poor conditions shorten it. Childbirth is also relevant; if a woman has a child after she has passed 40, her menopause may be delayed. The menopause may be hastened in women who have never given birth.

ABNORMAL VARIATIONS
Some women experience exceptionally early menopause for no apparent reason. In the majority of cases, however, exceptionally early menopause occurs as a result of disease or medical treatment. Disease of the pituitary gland can trigger the event. So can medical irradiation of the ovaries, or their surgical removal.

F04 How the Change Occurs
BEFORE THE CHANGE
The top diagram opposite reminds us how ovary and uterus function in a normal 28-day menstrual cycle (see A19). FSH and LH hormones (produced by the pituitary gland at the base of the brain) stimulate one of the ovaries to release a ripened egg into the nearest Fallopian tube, so making that egg available for fertilization by male sperm. Meanwhile, the follicle inside which the egg has developed is producing hormones too, first estrogen and then also progesterone. These cause the lining of the uterus to thicken in preparation for implantation if the egg is fertilized. If the egg is not fertilized, the thickened lining breaks down, and the woman experiences her menstrual period.

THE CYCLE BREAKS DOWN
In middle age, the aging ovaries cease to respond to FSH and LH, though secretions of these increase. As a result:
 a) fewer follicles are formed, and fewer release eggs;
 b) estrogen and progesterone output from the ovaries falls off;
 c) the uterus lining ceases to thicken, and menstrual bleeding changes pattern and eventually stops; and
 d) uterus and ovaries start to shrink.
Once egg production has ceased entirely, the woman is infertile.

The Change of Life

AFTER THE CHANGE

Small quantities of FSH and LH are still produced by the adrenal glands. Some androgenic (male) hormones are produced by the ovaries.

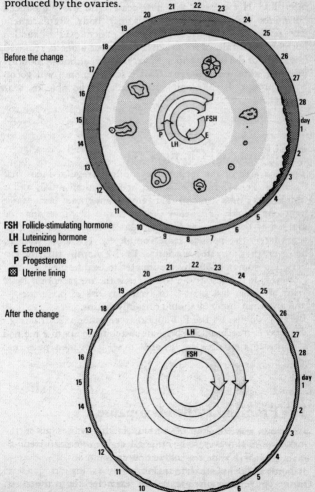

FSH Follicle-stimulating hormone
LH Luteinizing hormone
E Estrogen
P Progesterone
Uterine lining

F05-07

F05 Surgical Menopause

If a woman's ovaries have to be removed (see L14), she will undergo a "surgical menopause." The effects include infertility. Her periods will now cease, and ovary-produced hormones will stop circulating in her body. Replacement estrogen is often prescribed to ease the patient over the sudden hormone shortfall. More usually, the uterus alone is removed (see L10), or the uterus and one ovary. Then, although monthly bleeding stops, the woman's female sex hormones will go on being produced. (She will not, of course, be able to bear children.)

F06 Menstrual Changes

The first sign of the menopause is often irregular menstrual bleeding. Periods may be lighter, or later, than usual, and a woman may miss a month altogether. Sometimes periods are light one month and heavy the next; this heaviness may be marked if the period is late. Gradually, months or perhaps years later, the periods cease completely. (In some women, however, they may stop abruptly.) Twelve months after the last period, a woman of 50 plus is estimated to be infertile.

However, it is safest is she continues with contraception for 2 years after her last period, to avoid any risk of pregnancy — and a woman under 50 should certainly do this.

Because women on the Pill appear to continue menstruating, doctors often recommend periodic switching to another method of contraception after the age of 42 to see if the menopause has begun.

F07 Problems at the Menopause

In many women, loss of periods is the only sign of the menopause. However, some other effects are often experienced. HOT FLASHES, or flushes, are most common. These are a response of the hypothalamus gland to the falling estrogen level in the body. They often start as a warm feeling in the chest, moving to the neck and face, which color up. The disorder may

At the Menopause

spread to the rest of the body, perhaps with a prickling sensation. Sweating sometimes follows. Hot flashes can last up to 15 minutes and may occur several times a day, or they may be transient and infrequent. Some coincide with the due dates of periods. Hot flashes may start before periods stop and recur over 2 or 3 years. The worst types cause discomfort and depression, and "night sweats" may even break up sleep. In such cases, treatment with estrogen or the drug "Clomiphene" may be prescribed.

GENITAL SYMPTOMS

Hormonal change may cause itching in any part of the body, but especially in the genitals. Vaginal dryness is also typical (see F11 for the long-term aspects of this). In both cases, creams and ointments can be prescribed.

OTHER PHYSICAL PROBLEMS

Many physical symptoms have been blamed on the menopause, and some doctors talk of a "menopausal syndrome." Apart from symptoms already described, this might include: dizzy spells, headaches, and insomnia; fatigue and lack of energy; abdominal bloatedness; digestive troubles, including pain, flatulence, constipation, and/or diarrhea; and breathlessness and palpitations.

But all these symptoms can be very variable from day to day, and many women do not experience them at all (see F16). In fact, no direct link with the menopause has been proved. (Some, though, are sometimes signs of illness, so always check with a doctor.)

WEIGHT GAIN

At the menopause, appetite often becomes variable and may increase, while the body's energy needs fall. Obesity results unless food intake is controlled.

EMOTIONAL PROBLEMS

Moodiness is quite common, and sometimes also irritability, forgetfulness, anxiety, and depression. Causes may include:

a) possibly, the hormonal changes themselves — though no direct link has been proved;

b) the mental consequences of such physical symptoms as hot flashes, headaches, insomnia, etc; and

c) in some cases, such psychological factors as fears of aging or of an altered sex life, or maybe regret at unrealized motherhood.

F07-08

In the occasional serious case, tranquilizers and antidepressants will help. Hormone treatment may also be valuable.

If a woman starts to develop, or better still has always had, interests beyond her family and home, emotional problems at the menopause may be less likely, and less distressing if they do occur.

F08 At the Menopause

SIGNS AND SYMPTOMS	TREATMENT
a) Fatigue, headaches, dizzy spells, insomnia; moodiness, forgetfulness, irritability, difficulty in concentrating, anxiety, depression	a) Normally no treatment: symptoms eventually disappear. Short-term prescription of tranquilizers or anti-depressants in severe cases; possibly control by hormone therapy in very severe ones
b) Hot flashes and sweating	b) Control by hormone treatment in severe cases
c) Palpitation	c) None if only due to menopause
d) Breathlessness	d) None if only due to menopause
e) Tendency to gain weight	e) Diet control
f) Variable appetite, digestive troubles, abdominal bloating	f) None if only due to menopause
g) Ovaries stop producing eggs, and, therefore, estrogen	g) An irreversible change
h) Menstrual bleeding changes character and eventually stops	h) Normally no treatment needed. If bleeding occurs after the menopause, see a doctor
i) Vaginal dryness and itching	i) Use of creams and ointments, possibly hormonal. Also lubricant creams and jellies for intercourse

At the Menopause

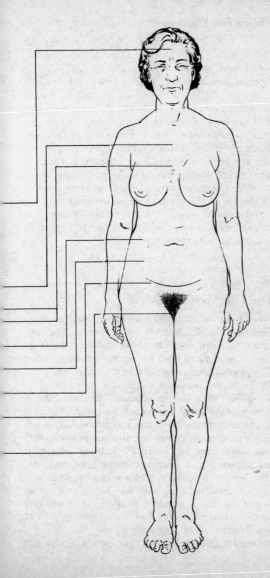

F09-11

F09 Checking for Cancer

Certain forms of cancer occur more often at or after the menopause than before. They are: cancers of the breast, stomach, lower bowel, uterus, and genitals. At this period in her life, a woman should be watchful for the warning signs described in section L41, and especially careful in noting changes in her breasts (see J04). She should also have a regular examination of the neck of the uterus, or cervix, including a "cervical smear" (also called a "Pap test": see L43). This test, which is painless and brief, involves taking a minute piece of tissue from the cervix, usually on a wooden spatula. From it, laboratory tests can tell whether cancer is likely to develop there or not. Over 80% of women operated on at an early stage of cancer of this sort (or of the breast) have no recurrence of the disease. For menopausal women, this examination also has another advantage, since it can reveal the nature and extent of any hormone lack and make treatment possible.

F10 Sex and the Menopause

One of the main factors often underlying menopausal gloom is a woman's fear that she will lose her attractiveness. She may feel that, because she can no longer bear children, she is no longer feminine. And the step from feeling unloveable to being embarrassed by physical expressions of love is a short one.

There is absolutely no reason, though, for lovemaking to stop at, during, or after the menopause. Occasionally, a woman does experience some temporary lessening of sexual desire during the menopause itself. But this is normally brief, and a postmenopausal woman has lost neither her sexuality nor, given reasonable care, her looks: all that has changed is her ability to conceive. Sexual desire is stimulated by the male, rather than the female, hormones, and a woman continues to have her share of these right through her life. Certainly no woman, however old she is, should feel ashamed of enjoying sexual intercourse. Indeed, many find that there is greater enjoyment now that the risk of pregnancy is past.

A menopausal woman should, however, get a doctor's advice as

After the Menopause

to when contraceptives can be safely abandoned. A doctor can also suggest how to deal with vaginal dryness — usually by use of a lubricant.

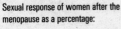

Sexual response of women after the menopause as a percentage:

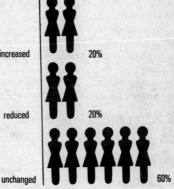

increased   20%

reduced   20%

unchanged   60%

F11 Postmenopausal Changes

Estrogen influences the growth and nourishment of breasts, uterus, vagina, smooth muscle, and skin. It also tends to protect women against circulatory diseases, and possibly against loss of calcium from the bones. Thus the fall in estrogen accompanying the menopause heralds aging changes in the body.

Estrogen loss largely explains why muscles lose tone and skin loses elasticity and becomes wrinkled. Deprived of estrogen, the breasts gradually flatten and droop. The womb and ovaries shrink, and the vaginal wall becomes thinner. The vagina is also likely to become drier and lose some of its natural protective acidity, making it more prone to infections. In addition, sexual intercourse may become difficult and even painful. The vulva atrophies. Tissues supporting the vagina and the muscles of the pelvic floor become less elastic and rather more flabby over the years. Prolapse of the uterus or vagina may follow (see L04); it is usually treatable without surgery.

Changes in secondary sexual characteristics include the loss of some pubic hair, and growth of hair on the upper lip and chin.

F11-12

More serious, the risk of heart attack increases, while obesity, if it occurs, increases the risk of arthritis. Finally, well after the menopause, calcium loss from the bones can produce a curve in the spine. Many of the problems are treatable (see F12).

NONOVARIAN ESTROGEN

Some women do not suffer hormone deficiency conditions as severely as others. These women make up for loss of ovarian estrogen by that produced in other parts of the body, probably including the liver. These women suffer few menopausal symptons, and they seem to avoid some of the aging and the disturbed sex life often linked with the menopause.

F12 After the Menopause

SIGNS	TREATMENT
a) Straggling hairs may begin to appear	a) Facial hair removed by electrolysis or depilatory waxes
b) Skin loses elasticity	b) Skin care and massage help skin tone; estrogen tablets are a possible treatment but mistrusted by some doctors
c) Bones lose calcium; spine eventually affected	c) Estrogen tablets may retard calcium loss from the bones; exercise and plenty of calcium in food is arguably a better prevention
d) Breasts eventually flatten and droop	d) Hormone therapy still questioned by some doctors; support sagging breasts with a well-fitting brassiere
e) Increased risk of circulatory disease	e) Circulatory disorders are best prevented by regular exercise and sensible diet
f) Ovaries and uterus shrink. Uterine muscle becomes fibrous.	f) No treatment needed. Exercise helps muscle tone
g) Vaginal wall grows thin and is liable to irritation (less so if intercourse continues)	g) Application of estrogen cream helps, and use of lubricants in intercourse
h) Vulval walls atrophy	h) Hormonal cream may help
i) Urinary infection and/or incontinence may occur	i) Drugs for infection; treatment of incontinence depends on cause
j) Pubic hair gets scantier	j) No treatment needed
k) Increased risk of arthritis	k) Arthritic pain is helped by anti-inflammatory drugs, such as aspirin. Surgery may be needed in severe cases.

After the Menopause

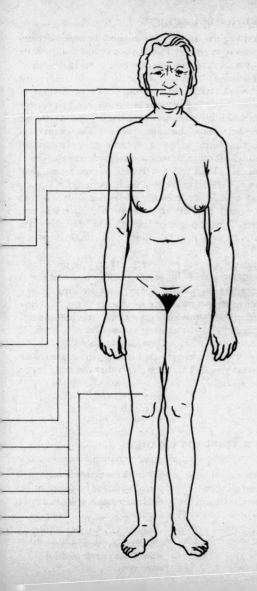

F13-14

F13 Hormone Replacement

Hot flashes and vaginal atrophy are treated by many doctors with prescriptions of estrogen. This, however, has usually been essentially short term: the aim being to cure specific disorders, and tide the woman over a difficult patch. Hormone replacement therapy (HRT) takes a longer view. According to supporters, menopausal women who are given estrogen for the rest of their lives will be protected from some types of disease and to some extent escape the aging process. The estrogen is prescribed in the form of pills, creams, and injections. Therapy of this type is much more controversial than the short-term treatment. It is most widely accepted to combat surgical menopause (see F05), very severe "hot flash" symptoms, and, in some cases, loss of calcium from the bones (see M04). It may also delay the onset of arthritis (though not cure it), and promote clearer skin and general well-being. Local cream application can certainly help maintain the vaginal tissue and vulva.

Beyond this, the usefulness of replacement therapy is uncertain. Moreover, estrogen intake in postmenopausal women may cause breast tenderness, gastric upsets, and swelling of the ankles; and, more important, there is some evidence of a link with blood thrombosis and with breast and uterine cancer. Certainly, estrogen helps any existing breast cancer to grow. It also may cause postmenopausal menstrual bleeding; this is significant simply because any such bleeding must always be investigated (usually by D & C) to establish that the cause is not uterine cancer.

F14 Do Men Have the Change?

Since men do not have women's equipment for childbearing, they cannot have a "change of life" in the way women know it Their hormonal decline is gradual. As shown in diagram (a) testosterone production in the typical male adult reaches a peak in early adulthood and declines into old age. Although the amount of testosterone produced by a man of 60 has dropped to the level of a preteens boy, it is usually adequate to allow sexual activity.

The Menopause Experience

A man's sexual functioning, however, does slow down naturally with the onset of old age. Semen production, erection, and ejaculation all take more time and more stimulation, while the need and ability for orgasm declines. Again, poor nutrition, general bodily decline, depression, and a hidden relief at being able to drop an activity which has caused anxiety may all play a part in reducing virility. But a healthy and fit man should nevertheless be capable of some sexual activity at any age. Diagram (b) shows that the percentage of men suffering from total impotence increases slightly through the middle years, and more rapidly into old age. But impotence is often caused by psychological rather than physical problems (see B31).

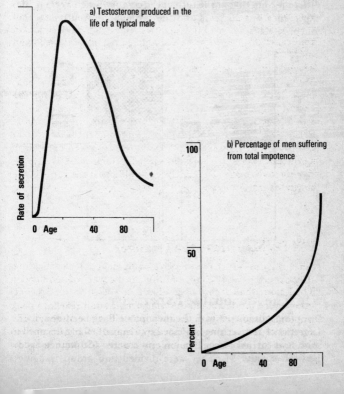

a) Testosterone produced in the life of a typical male

Rate of secretion

0 Age   40   80

b) Percentage of men suffering from total impotence

100

50

Percent

0 Age   40   80

F15-16

F15 Menopause and Life Expectancy

The menopause is a highly charged time for many women. It is associated with aging, but more significantly it is the time when a woman's reproductive abilities come to an end. Many women still seem to think of childbearing and homekeeping as their prime functions. Not surprisingly, therefore, their fears reveal an attitude that equates the menopause with the end of a woman's usefulness and productive life.

Nothing could be further from the truth. In the United States, just over 20% of the female population is over 55. Life expectancy for the average American woman is 76. With the menopause occurring around 50, these women may well have one-third of their lives to come. Their life situation is very different from that at the turn of the century, when average life expectancy was 50 years and the menopause occurred in the mid or late 40s.

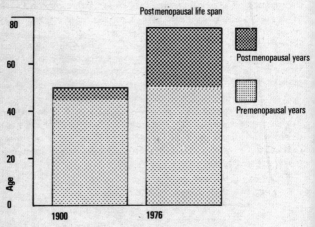

F16 The Menopause Experience

Symptoms associated with the menopause have been described in section F08. But they are not experienced by all women. A study was carried out in London and covered 638 women aged between 45 and 54. They were divided into groups ranging

The Menopause Experience

from those who were still menstruating to those whose periods had been over for 9 or more years.

The women were asked to report on 8 symptoms — hot flashes, night sweating, headaches, dizzy spells, palpitations, insomnia, depression, and weight gain. The results are shown in the diagram. Nearly half (49.8%) reported hot flashes, while 35-50% reported other symptoms. No symptoms were reported by 8.6%. Further investigation showed that, apart from hot flashes and night sweating, the occurrence of symptoms did not vary greatly from one group to another. Hot flashes, however, were reported by 75% of women whose periods had been over for 3-12 months as opposed to less than 30% of women whose periods had been over for 9 or more years.

DIRECT SYMPTOMS

The London survey and others seem to confirm that only hot flashes, night sweats and vaginal atrophy are directly linked to the menopause. The other commonly associated symptoms such as depression and insomnia are probably indirect and may result from physical discomfort or emotional upset.

Interestingly, an American sociologist, Pauline Bart, found that many of these emotional symptoms are more likely to be reported by premenopausal women and by adolescents than by postmenopausal women.

SEVERITY OF SYMPTOMS

In general, it seems that up to 90% of women may experience one or more menopausal "symptoms." Some experience great distress and discomfort. But it has been found that not more than 20% of women actually have symptoms severe enough to disrupt their lives.

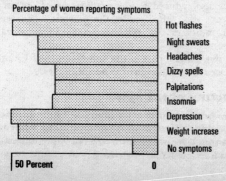

Percentage of women reporting symptoms

G01-03

G01 The Skin

The skin is the largest organ of the body. It covers an area of about 17sq ft (1.6sq m) in the average adult woman — compared with 20sq ft (1.9sq m) in the average man. It accounts for about 16% of the total body weight. Skin thickness over most of the body is about 1.2mm — compared with 0.5mm on the eyelids and 4-6mm on the palms and soles.

The skin is attached to the underlying tissues by elastic fibers, which give it relative flexibility to allow for free joint movement. In old age, the body bulk shrinks and the skin loses its elasticity, causing bagginess and wrinkles.

G02 Functions of the Skin

The skin is a versatile organ with a variety of essential functions. Most important, the skin protects the more delicate internal organs, acting as a barrier against physical damage, harmful sun rays, and bacterial infection.

The skin also acts as a sensory organ, being more richly supplied with nerve endings than any other part of the body. Sensations of touch, pain, heat, and cold from the skin provide the brain with a continuous flow of information about the body's surroundings.

Also very important is the skin's role in the regulation of body temperature: 85% of body heat loss is through the skin. During exposure to heat, blood vessels near the skin's surface dilate so that more blood flows near the surface to lose its heat. When it is cold, these blood vessels contract to reduce blood flow near the skin's surface.

Body heat is also reduced by the evaporation of perspiration (see G04) on the skin, while the chemical content of perspiration indicates the skin's function as an organ of excretion.

Finally, the skin plays a part in the manufacture of Vitamin D in sunlight (see H10), and even of some antibodies.

G03 Structure of the Skin

The skin consists of two distinct layers — the epidermis, or outer layer, and the dermis, or inner layer. The epidermis is covered by a thin layer of keratin — the horny protein material also found in hair and nails.

Skin

Deep in the dermis, just above the subcutaneous fatty layer, lie the sweat glands which secrete sweat through ducts, or pores, to the surface of the skin.

Also found in the dermis are nerves, and the blood capillaries which nourish the epidermal cells. Hairs are produced by specialized epidermal cells and grow from hair follicles which extend down into the dermal layer. Each hair has its own erector muscle, and a sebaceous gland which secretes grease, or sebum, to keep the skin supple.

Cross section of the skin

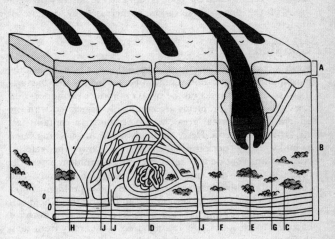

A Epidermis
B Dermis
C Subcutaneous fat
D Sweat gland
E Hair follicle
F Hair shaft
G Erector muscle
H Nerve
J Blood capillaries

G04-07

G04 Perspiration

Perspiration is a term used to describe the fluid produced by the sweat glands (sweat), and also the process during which this fluid is produced.

Sweat contains over 99% water, together with small amounts of salts, urea, and other waste products. An average person produces about 1½ pints of sweat a day in temperate conditions. The process of perspiration helps keep body temperature down because heat is lost when sweat evaporates. Some sweating, however, occurs when the body is cool and the skin dry. In some areas of the body, perspiration is increased by exercise or anxiety.

G05 Body Odor

Fresh perspiration produces very little smell in a healthy person. Stale perspiration results in body odor because bacteria that live on the skin act on the sweat to produce substances that smell. Body odor problems are commonly associated with the underarm and genital areas, where perspiration contains fats attractive to bacteria. Here, too, body shape and clothing cause a build up of perspiration by slowing down the rate of evaporation. Foot odor is another common problem caused by perspiring into a constricted area. Regular washing and changes of clothing help counteract body odor problems. Most people also use a deodorant and/or antiperspirant. Chemicals in deodorants and some soaps slow down the growth of bacteria. With soaps, any lasting effect comes only from soap that remains in the pores after washing. Deodorants are more effective because they dry on the skin and can be concentrated where needed. Antiperspirants reduce perspiration in areas where they are applied, although perspiration over the body as a whole is not reduced. They work by blocking the pores, or by swelling the surrounding area to shrink the pore size. Manufactured sprays, sticks, roll-ons and creams usually contain both deodorant and antiperspirant.

G06 Skin Color

A person's skin color is due partly to color pigments found in the skin cells, and partly to the presence of tiny blood vessels near the surface of the skin.

Skin

Most important of the pigments that color the skin is melanin — a brown pigment present in skin cells known as melanoblasts.

The melanoblasts of dark-skinned people contain more melanin granules than those of people with fairer skins. The concentration of melanin in an individual's skin is largely determined by heredity — but can be considerably modified by exposure to sunlight (see G07). There are a few individuals whose bodies contain no melanin pigment at all. Known as albinos, these people have white hair, light-colored eyes, and a pale skin tinted pink by blood vessels.

G07 Skin and Sun

Exposure to the ultraviolet rays of the sun produces an increased concentration of melanin (see G06) in the skin. In fair-skinned people this increase in melanin produces freckles and tanning.

Freckles are brown spots formed by patches of melanin. A suntan results from a more even increase in the skin's melanin content. Many people believe that they look more attractive when they have a suntan — and lying in the sun is a popular holiday pastime. Certainly the sun often produces an improvement in skin conditions such as acne (see G13), and sunbathing can produce feelings of relaxation and general well-being. If you are unused to the sun or have a very fair skin, it is essential to sunbathe with moderation.

Painful sunburn — or even sunstroke — may be the price of overzealous exposure to the sun's rays. Gradual building up of sunbathing time and the use of protective oils and creams are simple precautions that are well worth the trouble.

▓ Sunburn danger areas

G08-12

G08 Birthmarks

Birthmarks are various types of skin blemish present at birth. They include strawberry marks, port wine stains, vitiligo, and liver spots.

Strawberry marks are red, slightly raised and spongy areas of skin containing enlarged blood vessels. They are usually fairly small and often disappear without treatment. If a strawberry mark persists, it may be shrunk by injections or removed surgically.

Port wine stains are dark red, flat areas of skin containing enlarged blood vessels. They tend to be extensive and often occur on the neck and face. Surgical removal may not be recommended because of the risk of unsightly scarring. Various treatments have been developed by dermatologists to make the mark less noticeable, and special cosmetics provide satisfactory concealment.

Vitiligo can be present at birth. It is a condition in which an area of skin always remains white whatever the color of the skin around it. It can be concealed, but there is no treatment.

Liver spots are dark patches of skin resembling large freckles. They are caused by concentrations of the brown pigment, melanin.

G09 Moles

Moles are raised brown skin blemishes comprising a mass of cells with a high concentration of melanin. They are sometimes present at birth or may develop later — pregnancy often causes an increase in their size or number. Some moles have a growth of hair which should not be plucked because of the risk of infection. If removal of a mole is considered, it is important to consult your doctor. Most moles are harmless, but occasionally a mole may become malignant. Medical advice should always be sought if a mole changes character and enlarges, ulcerates, or bleeds.

G10 Dermatitis (Eczema)

Dermatitis is a general term for inflammation of the skin. It is usually caused by exposure to a particular substance, but may also be of nervous origin.

Some substances usually have an irritative effect on the skin: others affect only those people who are hypersensitive, or

Skin

"allergic," to them. Frequent culprits include cosmetics, paints, detergents, insecticides, metals, textiles, rubber, and some plants.

After contact with the offending substance, the blood vessels dilate and become porous. This allows fluid from the cells to collect in the skin and form blisters, which eventually burst. Later, the fluid dries out and the area becomes encrusted. The skin thickens around the sores and flakes off in scales. There is a serious risk of infection if the affected area is scratched or left untreated.

Recurrence can be prevented by identifying the condition's cause and then avoiding or protecting against the substance responsible.

G11 Hives

Hives is a common allergic reaction characterized by painful, irritating skin wheals. Also called nettle rash, its medical name is urticaria. It is most commonly caused by an allergy to a particular type of food — citrus fruits, shellfish, wheat products, and chocolate can all be troublemakers. Other causes include antibiotics, dust, pollen, and emotional stress.

An allergy produces hives because sensitive skin tissues react by releasing the chemical histamine, which dilates the blood vessels. This increases the flow of fluid to the skin, and produces wheals. The condition is not usually serious, and relief may be obtained by applying soothing lotions. Medical attention must be sought, however, if large swellings that may affect breathing occur in the area of the mouth and throat.

G12 Boils

Boils are painful, pus-filled lumps caused by bacterial infection of a hair follicle, a sebaceous or sweat gland, a cut, or some other break in the skin. They occur most commonly around sites of friction with clothing, such as the neck or wrists, and may be an indication that a person is run down. Only after the dead skin that forms the boil's core has been released will the boil disappear. Most boils require no more than a protective dressing. A doctor should be consulted if a boil is particularly painful, if several boils occur, or if the sufferer is very young or very old.

G13-18

G13 Acne

Acne is an infection of the sebaceous glands resulting in pimples, blackheads, whiteheads, and sometimes boils and cysts. It characteristically develops in adolescence, when the sebaceous glands become more active. Face, neck, shoulders, chest, and back may all be affected. Most cases clear up if attention is paid to diet, hygiene, and choice of cosmetics. Treatments include lotions and creams to reduce the spread of infection, make the skin peel, and unblock the pores. Antibiotics may be needed in severe cases. Exposure to sunlight or ultraviolet rays can also help make the skin peel, and through tanning, hide the spots.

G14 Blackheads and Whiteheads

A blackhead or whitehead appears when a skin pore becomes blocked by dust, dirt, or sebum. The waxy plug that blocks the pore is called a comedo. This forms a blackhead when it is exposed to the air: oxidation turns the head of the comedo black. If it is not open to the air, a whitehead is formed. A pore may be cleaned by gently pressing out its contents, but unless this is done soon after the plug is formed the spot is probably best left to take its own course. When cleaning out pores, it is important to avoid damaging the skin or spreading infection. A preliminary wash with warm water will loosen the plugs.

G15 Psoriasis

Psoriasis is a chronic skin complaint characterized by red spots and patches covered with loose, silvery scales. The skin of the elbows, forearms, knees, legs, and scalp is most usually affected. The condition results from large-scale production of an abnormal type of keratin. It takes 28 days for normal skin to produce a mature keratin cell, but only 4 days for a person with psoriasis. The cause is unknown, but there may be a genetic link. Psoriasis is not infectious and does not affect general health. The condition comes and goes intermittently but there is no cure. Various types of treatment bring some relief.

G16 Warts

Warts are small benign tumors of the skin. As well as the type common on the hands, plantar warts (see G97) are common on

Skin

the feet, and moist warts occur on the genitals (L36). Many vanish without treatment — otherwise they can be "frozen" or removed chemically.

G17 Bruises

Bruises develop when small blood vessels under the skin are ruptured. Blood seeps into the surrounding tissue to give the bruise its color — usually bluish or blackish at first, often changing through purple and green to yellow as the blood cells are broken down and their constituents reabsorbed.

Cold, wet compresses speed healing and ease pain, but even without treatment most bruises disappear after about a week. A severe bruise that remains painful may be a sign that a bone is broken.

G18 How a Cut Heals

1 If the skin is cut, the process of healing begins at once. Blood vessels contract to stop the flow of blood and prevent the entry of bacteria. Then, clotting substances from the blood vessels form fine threads which knit together the sides of the wound.

2 During the first day, white blood cells enter the wound to break down and later absorb any foreign particles. At the same time the epidermal cells begin to multiply.

3 By the second day, a scab has formed over the wound. Beneath the scab, epidermal cells on each side of the wound join up to form a continuous layer.

4 About one week later, the scab comes away, revealing the new epidermis.

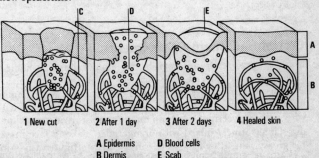

1 New cut   2 After 1 day   3 After 2 days   4 Healed skin

A Epidermis   **D** Blood cells
B Dermis   **E** Scab
C Blood vessels

G19-22

G19 Skin Type

Before embarking on a program of skin care, it is important to identify your skin type.

NORMAL SKIN is smooth, without any enlarged pores or flaking cells. Pimples and blemishes are rarely troublesome.

OILY SKIN is coarse in texture, with open pores around the nose and on the chin. A tissue held against the face will be slightly greasy when it is removed. Oily skin is very prone to pimples and even acne.

DRY SKIN is flaky in texture, and it tends to become lined early in life. It may become sore and red in cold weather, but pimples are rare.

G20 Choosing Cosmetics

To maintain healthy, blemish-free skin, and to stave off wrinkles, it is a good idea to follow a 3-part skin care plan involving cleansing, toning, and moisturizing. (This procedure varies with skin type, but details are given in G22.)

Special hypoallergenic products made without perfume are useful for hypersensitive skins.

It is unnecessary to spend a lot of money on skin care and make-up products, though it is probably wise to avoid highly perfumed preparations or heavy, sticky creams, and to concentrate on simpler preparations containing natural ingredients rather than chemicals.

G21 Home Beauty Treatments

Many beauty preparations can be made quite simply at home. Cucumber slices placed over each eye will refresh tired eyes. Pounded cucumber flesh mixed with milk makes a good toning lotion for normal or oily skin. Mashed avocado flesh mixed with a little glycerine or lanolin makes a moisturizing mask for dry skin. Oatmeal mixed with orange juice makes a face mask for greasy skin. Raw egg white can be used to tighten the skin and to iron out temporarily any tiny wrinkles. Rosewater diluted with mineral water makes a good toning lotion for dry skin.

Skin

G22 Skin Care

Details are given below of a 3-point skin care plan for each different skin type.

NORMAL SKIN
CLEANSE every night with a light cleansing cream. Remove the cream with a tissue and repeat. Wash with mild unperfumed soap in the morning (or use cream again).
TONE with a mild skin tonic after cleansing. Apply to the face with cotton balls.
MOISTURIZE morning and night using a liquid moisturizing lotion. Apply with the fingertips. Women over 25 may want to dab on a cream around the eyes.

OILY SKIN
CLEANSE with a medicated liquid cleanser at least twice a day. Pay particular attention to the extra-oily parts: chin, forehead, sides of nose. Remove the cleanser with a tissue and repeat. If the skin is blemished, medicated soap and water can be used after the cleanser.
MOISTURIZE once a day with a light liquid moisturizer.

DRY SKIN
CLEANSE with a rich cream night and morning. Massage the cream in thoroughly, and remove with a tissue. Repeat. If you like to wash your face, use a mild, creamy soap, of a special creamy face-wash product.
TONE with a gentle toner, preferably a rosewater-based product (see G21 for details of a homemade toner).
MOISTURIZE in the morning with a light cream and at night with a rich, heavier cream.

G23-24

G23 Using Make-up

Make-up can accentuate the face's good points and disguise its bad ones.
Always choose a basic foundation which suits your skin type and matches its natural color.

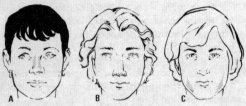

Make-up tricks for:
A Broad nose   E Round chin
B Long nose   F Broad forehead
C Broad jaw   ▨ Darker shade
D Wide cheeks

G24 Plastic Surgery

Plastic surgery is used to correct or improve minor disfigurements which are either congenital or caused by illness or injury.
The branch of plastic surgery which alters facial characteristics considered aging or disfiguring is often called cosmetic surgery.
Cosmetic surgery on the face can be used to remove the deep folds of skin or fat found as a double chin, sagging cheeks, or bags beneath the eyes.

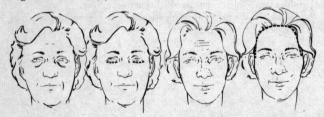

Bags under the eyes can be removed by making small tucks in the skin of the lower eyelids.

Forehead lines and wrinkles can be smoothed away by making a tuck just inside the hairline.

Skin

By the skillful use of a darker shade of foundation or a blusher on top of the basic foundation, you can make the shape of your face look different.

The illustrations suggest simple make-up tricks that can help you do this.

An incision is made, generally along the line of a fold. The flap of skin is pulled taut, fat removed if necessary, and the remainder stitched back into place.

Cosmetic surgery can also be used to rid the face of wrinkles.

These techniques are sometimes known as facelifts.

All cosmetic surgery is very costly and it can be a long time before all evidence of surgery has finally vanished. For many women, however, cosmetic surgery is invaluable, for it can relieve extreme anxiety and restore undermined confidence.

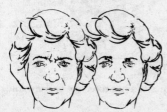 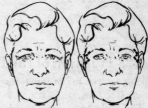

Wrinkles between the eyes can be smoothed out by tucks made just beneath the eyebrows.

"Crow's feet" at the corner of the eyes can be removed by making tucks inside the hairline at the temples.

G25-30

G25 Hair

Hair is found over the whole surface of the human body except the palms of the hands, soles of the feet, and parts of the genitals.

There are three types of hair: scalp hair, body hair, and sexual hair. Scalp hair resembles the body hair of other mammals. Human body hair is usually fine and light in color. Sexual hair develops around the genitals, the armpits, and (in men) the face. Its growth is dependent on the male sex hormone testosterone produced by both sexes at puberty.

G26 Hair Root

Each hair, properly called hair shaft, grows from its own individual follicle, and each follicle has its own sebaceous (oil) gland and tiny muscle.
Capillaries supply nutrients from the bloodstream.

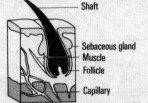

Shaft

Sebaceous gland
Muscle
Follicle

Capillary

G27 Hair Shaft

A cross section through the hair shaft shows a hollow core (medulla) surrounded by an outer cortex, and covered by a thin coating of keratin — a sheet of horny cells which overlap one another. This coating is called the cuticle.

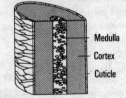

Medulla

Cortex

Cuticle

G28 Function of the Hair

Hair has two major functions: it acts as a protective barrier, and it acts to conserve heat.

The eyelashes protect the eyes, and the hairs in the nose and ears prevent the entry of foreign bodies. The eyebrows prevent sweat from dripping into the eyes.

Air trapped between hairs on the body insulates the skin and reduces heat loss. In the cold, or in danger, a tiny erector muscle attached to each hair follicle contracts to make the hair stand on end. The resulting "goose flesh" means that more air can be trapped, reducing even further the heat loss. Hair on the head is a particularly effective insulation.

Besides fulfilling these roles, hair is often considered an attractive bodily feature, and it can play a part in sexual attraction.

G29 Growth of the Hair

Hair on the scalp grows at the rate of about $\frac{1}{2}$in (1.25cm) per month. (This means that the end of a hair measuring 18in —45cm—is about 3 years old!)

The root is the only live part of the hair: it grows and pushes the dead shaft out above the skin. Hair growth is cyclical with a growth phase followed by a rest phase in which the hair is loosened. The loosened hair is then pushed out by a new hair growing in its place. In this way, up to 100 hairs are lost each day from a normal head of hair.

THICKNESS OF GROWTH

The thickness of the growth of the hair depends on the number of hair follicles. The follicles are established before birth and no new ones are formed later in life. The thickness of individual hairs is influenced by hereditary factors.

G30 Straight or Curly

The degree of curliness of the hair depends on the shape of the follicle from which it grows.

Straight hair grows from a more or less round follicle and is round in cross section. This hair shape is characteristic of Mongoloids.

Curly hair is oval in cross section. It grows from a very curved follicle which forces the growing hair into curls. This hair shape is characteristic of Negroes.

Wavy hair is kidney-shaped in cross section. The extent of the curl depends on the curve of the follicle. This hair shape is characteristic of Caucasians.

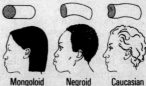

Mongoloid   Negroid   Caucasian

G31-34

G31 Hair Care

a) Wash your hair regularly. For normal hair, this means every 5-7 days, but if you have oily hair (caused by overactive sebaceous glands), you will need to wash it more often. Remember, however, that washing can actually stimulate the glands through rubbing the scalp. Also, the detergent in the shampoo can strip the hair of its natural oil and cause the glands to work overtime to replace it.

b) Always choose a mild shampoo. Lots of lather feels good, but it is caused by detergents. Use an appropriate shampoo for your hair type: lemon-based for oily hair and cream for dry hair.

c) Stick to a sensible diet (see H32).

d) Choose a good quality brush and comb. Sharp teeth or bristles can damage the structure of the hair.

e) Unclean brushes and combs spread infection and bacteria. Keep them clean and do not lend them to anyone else.

f) Do not tug at tangles as this will break your hair. Take a small strand at a time and beginning near the end, comb downward. Continue, working toward the scalp, gently easing out the tangles as you go. Take special care when the hair is wet; it is more prone to pulling and splitting in this state.

g) Rubber bands should be avoided because they break the hair. There are special fabric-covered rubber bands for holding hair.

h) Do not sleep in rollers. Again, they will cause the hair to split or break.

i) Be careful to wind your hair carefully around rollers. Hastily rolled hair causes knots when the rollers are removed.

j) Remember that the condition of your hair reflects your state of health and general well-being. A balanced diet, plenty of sleep, and regular trimming will do more to make your hair look good than anything else.

G32 Hair Color

White hair
Cortex contains
transparent cells

Normal hair
Cortex contains
pigment cells

Hair

The color of the hair is decided by heredity.

Special pigment cells at the base of the hair follicle give a hair its color. These cells inject colored granules of black, brown, or yellow into the hair.

If the cells receive no pigment, the cortex of each hair becomes transparent and the hair appears white.

"Gray" hair is the result of a mixture of dark and white hairs.

G33 Diet

Protein, vitamins of the B complex, and certain minerals are all essential for strong, healthy hair. The best sources of protein are meat, fish, milk, cheese, and eggs. Vitamin B is obtained from liver and from brewer's yeast — easily available in tablet form.

Iron, copper, and iodine are probably the most important minerals for healthy hair. Iron and copper are readily available in everyday foods like meat and green vegetables, and iodine is present in fish and shellfish. Women with oily hair should avoid fried and fatty foods, and concentrate on meat, fresh fish, salads, fruits, vegetables, eggs, and cheese. They should also drink plenty of water. Women with dry hair should include vegetable oils in their diet.

G34 Scalp Massage

Direction of massage

Massaging the scalp with the tips of the fingers increases the blood flow to the massaged area. This stimulates the follicles and can aid hair growth. It also means that the scalp is kept more healthy, with a greater supply of nutrients and speedier removal of waste products.

In scalp massage, it is important that the fingers do not slide over the scalp. This exerts pressure on the hair and can damage it. Massage can go from the neck up to the crown, and then again from the temples back to the crown, thus covering the whole scalp.

G35-39

G35 Sudden Hair Growth

This is usually due to a hormonal imbalance and can occur when the Pill is first taken or is left off; during pregnancy; or during the menopause.

Tufts of hair on either side of the chin or a fine down on the upper lip may appear.

Very often these will disappear once hormonal balance restores itself. However, if the growth is unusually marked and distressing, other hormones can sometimes be given to help adjust the balance — although the treatment of hormonal imbalance is a very complex and delicate process.

G36 Hair Lice

Two species of lice affect humans: Phthirus pubis, found in pubic hair (see Sexual infections, L36); and Pediculus humanus, found in the hair on the head. The latter can be acquired not only by contact with an infected person, but also via objects such as combs and hats.

The infestation causes severe itching. It is most easily diagnosed by examining the scalp for the tiny eggs ("nits") attached to the hair shafts. The lice themselves are more difficult to find. Suitable treatment should be obtained from a doctor or pharmacist: it will include a special shampoo and often a scalp emulsion.

G37 Dandruff

There are two kinds of dandruff. The first, affecting about 60% of the population to a mild degree, takes the form of fine, dry scales which fall from the scalp. The second kind, which is rarer, takes the form of thick, greasy scales adhering to the scalp.

The cause of both types is unknown, and there is no real cure for dandruff, but there are things that can be done to control it.

Washing the hair with ordinary shampoo may not help, in which case a medicated shampoo can be used instead. These shampoos are designed to remove the scales and delay the recurrence of dandruff. Some have a simple antiseptic, and others contain stronger chemicals. The most effective contain zinc pyrothionate, "ZP11."

However, if you do have difficulty in controlling dandruff, it

Hair

may be caused by a skin disorder or some other condition that a doctor should treat.

G38 Losing Your Hair

A number of hairs are lost from the scalp every day. These are usually replaced by new head hairs, but if they are replaced by fine, downy hairs of the kind found on the face or arms, a thinning of the general growth of head hair results.

Only in very exceptional cases do women lose all their hair, though many notice a general thinning, particularly as they grow older. This condition is known as diffuse alopecia and is caused by an increase of male sex hormones in the body. If this hormonal imbalance is corrected, the full head of hair is usually restored.

Stress can also cause hair loss because it interferes with the production of the hormones that stimulate hair growth. When the period of stress is over, normal hair growth is resumed.

After childbirth, many women notice an acute loss of hair. This too is a hormonal problem, but the hair soon returns to normal.

G39 Coping with Hair Loss

There are several ways of coping with hair loss.

TRICHOLOGICAL TREATMENTS

Several clinics now offer a variety of different treatments for the scalp disorders that cause hair loss. These treatments can include: creams, lotions, massage, shampoos, and ultraviolet and infrared radiation.

Courses of these treatments are expensive; but there are no good medical grounds for them. In fact, there is a risk of wrong diagnosis, and inappropriate treatment being given for a condition that could be dealt with by a doctor.

TRANSPLANTS

This is a recent technique. Hair follicles are removed surgically from parts of the head where growth is abundant (often the nape of the neck) and implanted in the bald areas. This treatment is costly and takes considerable time, but there is no guarantee that the hairs will grow in their new location.

WIGS AND HAIRPIECES

The hairpiece is built from a base shaped to the bald area. Hair is attached to the base and cut to match the rest of the hair. The hairpiece is fixed to the scalp with strips of double-sided tape.

HAIR WEAVING

Also known as hair linking or hair extension, hair weaving can take two different forms.

In the first, a hairpiece is made in the usual way and then attached to the scalp by stitching the side of it to the normal hair.

In the second, threads are strung across the bald area and pieces of hair, sewn together in clumps, woven directly into this.

G40 Permanent Waves

A "perm" or "permanent" is a 2-stage chemical process which causes each hair to alter the chain of the cells in its cortex. (The process is not literally permanent as the artificially created waves grow out as the hair grows.)

After washing, the first solution is applied to the wet hair. This is an alkaline-based solution designed to soften the hair by breaking the chain of the cells. The hair is then wound around small curlers and the second solution applied. This is an oxidizing lotion that halts the softening process and causes the cells to coalesce again, but this time under the stress of the roller which gives the hair its "permanent" wave. The hair is then rinsed and wound around larger rollers for drying.

Some women are allergic to the chemicals involved, so it is important to make a test curl first to check for hypersensitivity. Dyed or bleached hair is particularly sensitive to the chemicals, and it is essential to leave an interval of about 4 weeks between a "permanent" and a change of hair color.

Hair

G41 Hair Removal

Superfluous hair can be removed in several ways. The different methods suitable for different parts of the body are shown below.

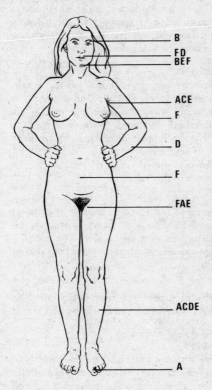

A Shaving:
armpits
pubic hair
legs
toes
B Plucking:
eyebrows
chin
C Waxing:
armpits
legs
D Bleaching:
upper lip
arms
legs
E Depilatory creams:
chin
armpits
pubic hair
legs
F Electrolysis:
upper lip
chin
breasts
abdomen
pubic hair

G42-43

G42 Changing Your Hair Color

The color of your hair can be changed by the application of chemical or natural colorants. The color change can be permanent (not literally, because the effects grow out as the hair grows), semipermanent, or temporary. Although a change of hair color can give your whole appearance a "lift," too drastic a color change will not suit your natural coloring. Try on a wig in your chosen color before making the decision.

PERMANENT COLORANTS
The application of a permanent colorant is a job for a hairdresser. A chemical compound of peroxide and ammonia is applied to the hair to "burn" away the color pigment. When the bleach has been rinsed off, the hair is porous and ready to receive the new color. The dye is applied, and it is this synthetic pigment that gives hair its new color.
As the hair grows, the new growth near the scalp must be retouched to match the rest of the hair.

SEMIPERMANENT COLORANTS
These colorants, designed to last through about 6 shampoos, can be applied at home. They do not contain bleach, and the chemicals simply coat the hair shaft with color. The use of a semipermanent colorant can also add body or bounce to thin or lank hair.

COLOR RINSES
The effect of a rinse is only temporary. It simply colors the hair superficially rather like a watercolor paint, and washes out at the next shampoo.

NATURAL COLORANTS
Henna, mixed to a paste with hot water and applied directly to the hair, will dye hair a reddish color. An infusion of camomile, used as a rinse after shampooing, may lighten mousy colored hair.

G43 The Eyeball

THE CONJUNCTIVA is the membrane covering the front of the eyeball and the inside of the eyelids. It has a rich supply of blood vessels and is extremely sensitive.

Eyes

THE CORNEA is the clear part of the eyeball which lets in the light.

THE IRIS controls the amount of light entering the eyeball. By contracting, it reduces the size of the pupil (the hole through which the light enters). It is the iris which gives the eye its "color."

THE LENS has a firm center, surrounded by a softer substance contained in a fibrous capsule. By being stretched or thickened, it focuses light on the back of the eyeball.

THE SUSPENSORY LIGAMENTS are attached at one end to the lens and at the other to the ciliary body. They hold the lens in place.

THE CILIARY BODY. The muscles of the ciliary body control the shape of the lens. If they contract, the lens is stretched, and light rays from long distances are focused on the retina (are "accommodated"). If they relax, the lens thickens, and close objects are accommodated. Both the lens and the iris are under the control of the autonomic nervous system and cannot be controlled at will.

THE ANTERIOR CHAMBER lies in front of the lens and is filled with a watery fluid called the aqueous humor.

THE SCLERA or sclerotic coat is a layer of dense white tissue. It completely surrounds the eyeball, except where the optic nerve enters at the rear, and where it is modified at the front to form the transparent cornea. The sclera forms the "whites" of the eyes.

THE CHOROID tissue lies beneath more than two-thirds of the sclera. It is colored brown or black and contains blood vessels. The ciliary body and the retina are formed from the choroid. Its color absorbs excess light within the eyeball, making for clearer vision.

THE RETINA is a thin layer of light-sensitive cells which lines the inside of the eyeball. It has a rich blood supply.

THE FOVEA lies on the visual axis of the eyeball. It is a small depression in the retina, at which vision is sharpest. It contains only "cone" cells (see G48).

THE OPTIC NERVE is a direct extension of the brain. It enters the eyeball at the rear. The head of the optic nerve is called the optic disk. It forms a blind spot in the vision, as there are no light-sensitive cells there. We are sometimes aware of this blind spot as a black dot at one corner of our vision.

G43-44

THE VITREOUS BODY occupies the space behind the lens. It is a transparent jelly-like substance that fills out the eyeball, giving it its shape. It contains small specks which are often seen when looking at white surfaces.

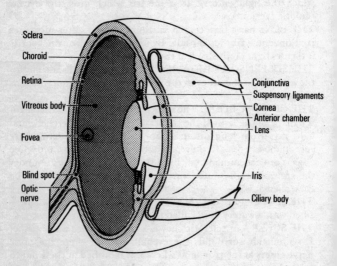

G44 Protective Structures

The eyes — the organs of sight — lie in deep hollows in the skull, on either side of the nose, and are protected in various ways.

THE EYEBROWS prevent moisture and solid particles from running down into the eye from above.

THE EYELIDS are folds of skin which, when closed, cover and protect the eyes. The inner membrane of each eyelid is a continuation of the "conjunctiva" which covers the front of the eyeball.

THE EYELASHES are hairs that protrude from the eyelids. They prevent foreign bodies from entering the eye, and trigger off the protective blinking mechanism when touched unexpectedly.

Eyes

THE LACRIMAL GLANDS produce a watery, salty fluid that cleans the front of the eyeball. It also lubricates the movement of the eyelid over the eyeball. When stimulated by strong emotion or irritants, the glands produce excess fluid.

THE LACRIMAL DUCTS drain the fluid from the eyeballs into the lacrimal sacs which lead into the nasal passage. When the ducts cannot clear the fluid fast enough, it overflows and runs down the face as tears.

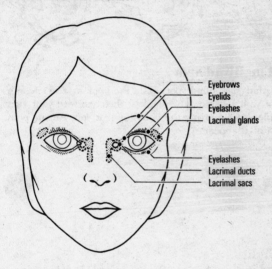

Eyebrows
Eyelids
Eyelashes
Lacrimal glands

Eyelashes
Lacrimal ducts
Lacrimal sacs

BLINKING is a protective action of the eyelids which spreads the lacrimal fluid over, and cleans, the front of the eyeball. Blinking is controlled by the brain. It occurs every 2 to 10 seconds, and the rate increases under stress, in dusty surroundings, or when tired, and decreases during periods of concentration.

G45-48

G45 Eye Movement

Movement of the eyeball is controlled by six muscles attached to the outside of the sclera.

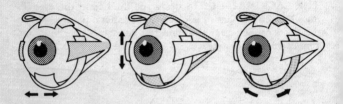

G46 The Blind Spot

How to find your blind spot. Hold the book at arm's length, and shut your left eye. Then look at the cross with your right eye, while slowly moving the book towards you. At one point the dot will disappear.

G47 Sight

When the light rays from an object enter the eye, they are bent ("refracted") by the cornea and the lens (and to a lesser extent by the aqueous humor and vitreous body). Because of this refraction, the rays are focused on the retina (though the image is upside down). The action of light on the cells of the retina triggers off an impulse which travels down the optic nerve to the visual centers of the brain. Here the impulses are interpreted and "seen" as colors and shapes the right way up.

Eyes

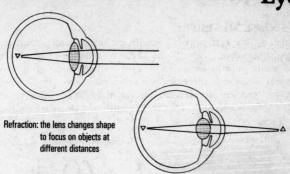

Refraction: the lens changes shape
to focus on objects at
different distances

G48 The Retina

There are two types of light-sensitive cells in the retina. They are classified by shape: rods and cones. They are connected by nerve fibers to the optic nerve.

RODS

There are about 125 million rods in each eyeball. They are sensitive to low intensity light, and are used mainly in night vision. They are not sensitive to color, and therefore give only a monochrome image (black, white, and shades of gray). They are less than one four-hundredth of an inch in length and one-thousandth of an inch thick. The rods contain a purple pigment called rhodopsin. Light bleaches the rod as the pigment breaks down. This sets off electrical charges in the rods, which are transmitted down the optic nerve to the brain in the form of nervous impulses.

CONES

These are shorter and thicker, for most of their length, than the rods. They are used for high intensity light, such as daylight, and give color vision.

The actual process of color vision is not known, but it is thought that there are three different classes of cones, each containing a different pigment. Each pigment would be sensitive to a different color: blue, green, or red. Other colors would be combinations of these. It is thought that the nerve messages are produced by bleaching, as in the rods.

G48-51

RESPONSE TO LIGHT
When a light-cell pigment has been broken down, and an impulse has been passed, the pigment must re-form before another impulse is possible. This takes about one-eighth of a second. The eye is therefore like a cinema screen. It does not give a continual picture, but successive "stills" at intervals of one-eighth of a second. They seem continuous because they run together.

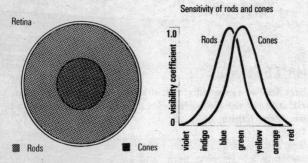

Retina

Sensitivity of rods and cones

Rods

Cones

Rods   Cones

G49 Transfer of Images
The nerves from the left sides of the two retinas travel to one side of the brain, those from the right sides to the other side of the brain.

a Eyeball
b Nerve
c Brain

G50 Composite Images
Each eye sees a slightly different view of the same object. The images received in the two visual centers (at the rear of the cerebral hemispheres) are composite images from both eyes, mixed 50:50. The further away the object is, the less the discrepancy between the two views. This, plus the amount of tension needed to focus and the amount of blurring, forms the

Eyes

basis of judgment of distance.

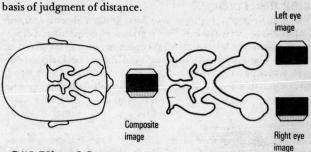

Left eye image

Composite image

Right eye image

G51 Visual Scope

THE FIELD OF VISION is the area that can be seen by an eye without moving it. The size of the field varies with different colors. White has the largest, then yellow, blue, red, and green.
THE RANGE OF MOVEMENT of the eyeball, with the head still, is also limited. The human eyeball can tilt 35⁰ up, 50⁰

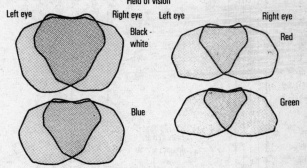

Field of vision

Left eye   Right eye   Left eye   Right eye

Black white   Red

Blue   Green

down, 50⁰ in (ie toward the other eye), and 45⁰ out. The greater angle available when turning in allows an eye to focus on an object that is just within the other eye's outer range.
THE AREA OF VISION is the total range through which a creature can see without moving head or body. It is determined by: the position of the eyes in the head; the shape of the head; the eyes' range of movement; and, at the edge, by the eyes' field of vision.

G52-54

G52 Perception

The ability to perceive objects, colors, and distances is learned by experience. To the newborn child, the images received are meaningless and confused. It takes time to learn to use the eyes and correlate past with present information to bring about recognition.

This dependence of perception on the brain's judgments can be shown by presenting the eye with trick pictures; ones that allow alternative interpretations, or that give evidence that seems contradictory (a). Our perception will then shift or struggle between the alternative interpretations. The same process can be observed when waking up in unfamiliar surroundings — a series of alternative pictures flashes through the brain, as it tries to make familiar sense of the data it is receiving. In other cases, though, the brain accepts deceptive information unquestioningly (b).

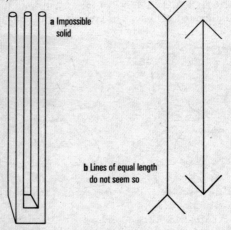

a Impossible solid

b Lines of equal length do not seem so

G53 Eye Care

INJURIES to the eye and the immediately surrounding area should receive expert medical attention. Infection is a danger even if there is no significant damage. The eyes are tough but vital, and should be treated with care.

SMALL FOREIGN BODIES that get stuck in the eye can usually be removed by blinking. If this fails, then pull the upper

Eyes

lid outward and downward over the lower lid. When the upper lid is released, the particle may be dislodged. A particle can also be removed with the corner of a clean handkerchief or by blowing it toward the edge. If none of this succeeds, get help and if necessary medical attention.

BLACK EYES are bruises of the eyelids and tissues around the eyes. They can be treated by applying a cold compress. If a black eye appears after a blow elsewhere on the head, see a doctor.

A **STYE** is an inflammation of the sebaceous gland around an eyelash, and is caused by bacterial infection. It is most often found in young people. A large part of the eyelid may become affected. To treat a stye, remove the relevant eyelash and bathe the eye with hot water. Antibiotics should only be used in extreme cases.

CONJUNCTIVITIS is inflammation of the conjunctiva. It can be caused by infection or irritation. If due to bacterial or viral infection, it needs the appropriate antibiotic eyedrops; if due to irritation, the irritant (eg an ingrown eyelash) is removed. Bathing the eye with warm water and lotions is soothing and is all that is needed in mild cases. Bandages or pads encourage the growth of bacteria, but dark glasses or eyeshades protect the eye from light and wind. Conjunctivitis is not very serious in itself (except for the trachoma form found in the tropics), but can sometimes cause serious complications such as ulceration of the cornea.

G54 Corrective Lenses

Spectacles (or contact lenses) are used because of faulty focusing in the eye. The artificial lens corrects the work of the defective part of the eye.

NEARSIGHTEDNESS (myopia) is due to the refractive power of the eye being too strong (eg the lens may be too thick) or to the eyeball being too long. In both cases, the light rays are focused in front of the retina, giving a blurred image. Concave corrective lenses are needed to focus on distant objects.

FARSIGHTEDNESS (hypermetropia) is due to the eye's refractive power being too weak or the eyeball too short. The light rays are focused behind the retina, again giving a blurred

G54-56

image. Convex corrective lenses are needed for close work such as reading.

ASTIGMATISM means that the cornea does not curve correctly, and the person cannot focus on both vertical and horizontal objects at the same time. A special spectacle lens is needed, that only affects the light rays on one of these planes. Alternatively, a hard contact lens can be used, as the fluid layer between eye and lens compensates for the cornea.

PRESBYOPIA occurs in old age (see M13).

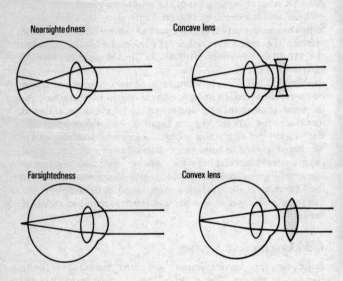

Nearsightedness

Concave lens

Farsightedness

Convex lens

G55 Contact Lenses

Contact lenses are thin round disks of plastic that rest directly on the surface of the eye. They are increasingly used instead of spectacles, as they do not affect the appearance, often give better vision, and counteract many year-to-year changes in the eyesight. However, not everyone can wear contact lenses successfully, and some people find that they can wear them for only part of the day.

Eyes

They also require more care because of their smallness and fragility, and because of the effect a damaged, dirty lens can have on the eye. They need to be cleaned and stored in special fluid when out of the eye, and it is wise to insure them against destruction or loss.

TYPES OF LENS

Contact lenses can be "hard" or "soft." Hard lenses are either "scleral" lenses — covering the whole of the visible part of the eye — or "corneal" lenses, which rest on the center of the eye, floating on a film of tear fluid.

Corneal lenses are the most popular of all contact lenses, but scleral lenses are useful for very active sports. Soft lenses differ because they absorb water from the tear fluid.

COMPARING HARD AND SOFT LENSES

Soft lenses are immediately more comfortable, easier to get used to, can generally be worn for longer periods, can be left off for several days and then worn again without discomfort, can be alternated more easily with spectacles, and can be worn with less discomfort in dirty atmospheres.

Hard lenses are much less easy to damage, much cheaper, last perhaps 6 to 8 years (compared with 2 to 3 years for soft lenses with routine wear and tear, and often under a year as damage occurs), are more suitable for the majority of eye prescriptions, often give clearer vision, are easier to keep free from bacteria, and are much easier for the optician to adjust if difficulty arises.

G56 Blindness

OBSTRUCTION OF LIGHT

When areas of the naturally transparent part of the eye become opaque, light rays are prevented from reaching the retina. Opacity of the cornea can be caused by corneal ulcers, or by keratitis, ie inflammation of the cornea. Opacity of the lens is commonly caused by its becoming hard — "forming a cataract." Cataracts most often occur with aging, but can also be caused by wounds, heat, radiation, and electric shock.

DISEASES AFFECTING THE RETINA

These are often caused by diseases elsewhere in the body, especially those involving the blood supply.

G56-57

a) Retinitis is inflammation of the retina with consequent loss of vision. It is associated with diabetes, leukemia, kidney disorders, and syphilis.

b) Retinopathy covers any disease of the retina that is not inflammatory. It is usually caused by degeneration of the blood vessels, impairing the retina's structure and function. It can be due to high blood pressure, diabetes, kidney disorders, and atherosclerosis.

c) Detachment of the retina. Primary detachment occurs if damage to the retina allows fluid from the vitreous body to leak through and lift the retina from the choroid. Treatment is possible. Secondary detachment occurs if the retina is pushed away from the choroid and damaged by underlying tumors, bleeding, or retinal disease. No treatment is possible.

d) Glaucoma (M13) can occur in old age.

e) Choroiditis is inflammation of the choroid due to infection (especially syphilis) or allergy. The effects depend on the size and position of the inflammation: the nearer the fovea, the greater the vision loss. The inflammation can be treated, but damaged vision is seldom improved.

Declining field of vision in a case of progressive blindness in both eyes

Left eye
showing declining field of vision

Right eye

G57 The Ear

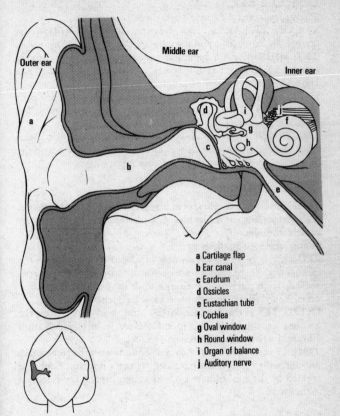

Outer ear

Middle ear

Inner ear

a Cartilage flap
b Ear canal
c Eardrum
d Ossicles
e Eustachian tube
f Cochlea
g Oval window
h Round window
i Organ of balance
j Auditory nerve

G58-62

G58 The Ear

The structures of the ear fall into three groups.

THE OUTER EAR includes: the external flap of cartilage (the "pinna" or "auricle"); and the ear canal (the "meatus").

THE MIDDLE EAR includes: the eardrum (the "tympanic membrane"); three small bones called the "ossicles," and known individually as the hammer ("malleus"), anvil ("incus"), and stirrup ("stapes"); and the eustachian tube, which opens into the back of the throat, and keeps the air pressure in the middle ear equal to that outside.

THE INNER EAR includes: the cochlea, a spiral filled with fluid and containing the "organ of corti"; the oval window; the round window; and the organs of balance.

G59 Sound

When a solid object vibrates in air, it passes on this vibration to the surrounding air molecules. Sound waves are the vibrations of air molecules.

Sound has three qualities:

PITCH, the highness or lowness of a sound, depends on the "frequency" of the sound waves, ie the number of vibrations per second. High pitched (piercing) sounds have a high frequency. Low pitched (deep) sounds have a low frequency.

INTENSITY is the loudness of a sound, and depends on the amount of energy in the sound waves, ie how widely they vibrate. Intensity is measured in "decibels."

TIMBRE is the quality of a sound. Sounds with the same pitch and intensity can be distinguished by their timbre. Timbre is created by the subordinate tones that accompany the pitch, or main sound.

G60 Hearing

THE OUTER EAR Sound waves are collected by the pinna and funneled into the ear canal.

THE MIDDLE EAR The eardrum vibrates in time with the sound waves. This vibration is passed on along the three ossicles to the oval window. The lever action of the ossicles increases the strength of the vibration. This allows the vibration to be passed from the air of the outer and middle ear to the fluid of the inner ear.

THE INNER EAR The vibration of the oval window makes

Ears

the fluid in the cochlea vibrate. The pressure changes in the fluid are picked up by specialized cells in the organ of corti. This organ converts the vibrations into nerve impulses, which pass along the auditory nerve to the brain. Meanwhile, the vibrations pass on through the cochlea and back to the round window, where they are lost in the air of the middle ear and eustachian tube.

G61 Sensitivity

LOUDNESS The human ear can hear sounds ranging in loudness from 10 decibels to 140 decibels (though the loudness becomes painful after 100 decibels). On the decibel scale, a ten-unit increase means 10 times the loudness. Therefore, the quietest sound the human ear can hear is one 10 million millionth the loudness of the loudest.

PITCH Different frequencies stimulate different parts of the organ of corti. That is why we can distinguish one sound from another. The human ear can hear sounds ranging in pitch from 20 cycles per second (low) to 20,000 cycles per second (high).

Frequencies above this are called ultrasounds, and can be heard by some animals but not humans.

DIRECTION The slight distance between the ears means that there are minute differences in their perception of a given sound. The brain interprets these differences to tell from which direction the sound came. But if a sound comes from directly behind or in front of the listener, both ears receive the same message, and the listener must turn his head before he can pinpoint the location.

DECLINE in hearing often progresses with age (see M12).

G62 Balance

The organ of balance is in the inner ear next to the cochlea. It consists of three U-shaped tubes ("semicircular canals"), at right angles to each other. They are filled with fluid, which is set in motion when the person moves. Hairs at the base of each canal sense this movement and send messages to the brain, which are interpreted and used to maintain the person's balance. The organ also contains two other structures, the saccule and the utricle. These have specialized cells which are sensitive to gravity, and so keep a check on the body's position.

G63-66

G63 Ear Care

THE OUTER EAR should be kept clean at all times, to prevent wax and bacteria from collecting in the ear canal and damaging the eardrum.

To examine the outer ear, a beam of light from a flashlight is shone down the ear canal.

THE INNER EAR is tested by using a tuning fork. The fork should be heard clearly when it is held in front of the ear. If the tuning fork is heard more clearly when placed on the bone behind the ear, then: either the outer ear is blocked with wax; or, if not, the middle ear is faulty, since sound vibrations are being heard better through the skull. If hearing is still poor when the fork is placed on the bone behind the ear, it is the inner ear or the auditory nerves that are at fault.

SYRINGING of the outer ear cleans it, and washes out obstructions such as wax or foreign bodies. A large glass or metal syringe is used — one with a blunt point not more than 1in (2.5cm) long, so it cannot hurt the eardrum. The syringe is filled with warmish water, containing, if necessary, an antiseptic and/or wax dissolving agent. The fluid is directed along the upper wall of the canal, and flows out along the lower.

G64 Symptoms of Disorder

DEAFNESS can be temporary or permanent, caused by obstruction or disease.

EARACHE is usually caused by infection and inflammation in the ear.

In the outer ear this can occur through physical damage, boils, or eczema (a skin disorder).

Large wax deposits can also cause earaches.

Germs from throat infections may spread up the eustachian tube and cause inflammation of the middle ear (especially in children). This is common after tonsilitis, measles, flu, or head colds, and can be very painful.

Earache can also arise without any ear disorder, because of disturbances affecting the nerves it shares with other parts of the head. Tonsilitis, bad teeth, swollen glands, and neuralgia can all cause earache in this way.

RINGING IN THE EARS ("tinnitus") is usually associated with

Ears

earache in the middle ear and/or high blood pressure. It is also caused by certain ear diseases.

GIDDINESS or vertigo can be caused by infections of the inner ear that affect the organs of balance.

DISCHARGES can come from boils or other infections.

G65 Sites of Disorder

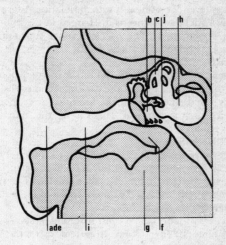

a Blockage
b Ringing
c Vertigo
d Discharge
e Otitis externa

f Otitis media
g Mastoiditis
h Ménière's disease
i Fungus
j Otosclerosis

G66 Ear Disorders

OTITIS EXTERNA

This is infection and inflammation of the outer ear, due to physical damage, allergy, boils, or spread of inflammation from the middle ear. There is itching and often a discharge, which may cause temporary deafness if it blocks the ear canal. Treatment is by antiseptic syringing and use of soothing lotions. Hot poultices and aspirin may relieve the pain.

OTITIS MEDIA

This is middle-ear infection, usually due to bacteria arriving via the eustachian tube. The eardrum becomes red and swollen, and may perforate. Pressure and pain increase as pus fills the middle ear. There is often temporary deafness and ringing, and sometimes fever. Treatment is with antibiotics. A form of otitis in which a sticky substance is discharged in the middle ear is common in children. The ossicles cannot function, and in severe cases permanent deafness results.

MASTOIDITIS

Middle-ear infections can spread to the mastoid bone — the part of the skull just behind the ear. Infection swells the bone painfully, and the patient is feverish. Treatment is by antibiotics or the surgical removal of the infected bone (mastoidectomy).

MENIERE'S DISEASE

This affects the inner ear, and results in too much fluid in the labyrinths. Its cause is not known. It tends to occur in middle age, usually affecting more men than women. The symptoms are attacks of giddiness and sickness, followed by deafness with accompanying ringing in the ears.

Treatment is with drugs and control of fluid intake — not more than 2½ pints (1.2 liters) a day. In extreme cases, the labyrinths or their nervous connections are destroyed.

FUNGUS INFECTIONS

Fungus infections can occur in the outer ear. They are more common in tropical climates. There is persistent irritation and discharge, which is treated with antibiotics and antiseptic cleansing of the ear canal.

G67 Deafnesss

TYPES OF DEAFNESS

"Conductive deafness" refers to any failure in the parts of the ear which gather and pass on sound waves, eg blockage of the ear canal, eardrum damage, ossicle damage, etc.

"Perceptive deafness" refers to any failure in: that part of the ear which translates the sound waves into nerve impulses (the cochlea); or in the auditory nerves which transmit the impulses

Ears

to the brain; or in the auditory centers of the brain which receive the message. Perceptive deafness may not mean that the person can perceive no sound. It may be that sound is received, but so scrambled as to be unintelligible.

CAUSES OF DEAFNESS

a) Disease. Some disorders can end in deafness (see G66).

b) Noise-induced. Any exposure to extremely loud noise, or continued exposure to moderately loud noise, can damage the eardrum and middle ear, causing hearing decline and eventual deafness. The main victims are those who work in very noisy surroundings, and also the fans — and performers — of loud popular music.

c) Congenital deafness. Deformities at birth range from complete absence of the ears to minute mistakes in the internal structure. The latter can often be cured surgically. Congenital deafness can be due to heredity (genetic defects). It can also result from certain infections in the mother in the first few months of pregnancy, including German measles, flu, and syphilis. If there is anything in your child's response to sounds that gives rise to worry, consult your doctor.

d) Otosclerosis. This is a condition in which the stirrup becomes fixed within the oval window, due to deposits of new bone. About one person in every 250 suffers from this, and it is more common in women than men. Surgical treatment may give improvement, but there is no way of halting the process responsible (though it may stop spontaneously).

G68 Hearing Aids

Hearing aids work by amplifying sound. If the amplification is loud enough, it can overcome the blockage or damage that causes conductive deafness, and allow the sound to reach the inner ear. Amplification also seems to help in many cases of perceptive deafness. However, sometimes the aid does not allow speech to be distinguished: it only makes the person more aware of unintelligible noise.

The performance of a hearing aid depends on:

a) the frequency response. Normal speech usually lies between 500 and 2,000 cycles per second;

b) the degree of amplification;

c) the maximum amount of sound that the aid can deliver.

G68-7¹

Too much sound can make speech unintelligible, and/or damage the ear mechanisms. One problem with hearing aids is "acoustic feedback." This is the reamplification of sound vibrations that have already passed into the ear but have partly leaked out again.

INSERT RECEIVERS are the most common type of aid. They are molded to fit into the ear canal and form a perfect seal. No sound escapes, there is little or no acoustic feedback, and background noise is at a minimum. They can also be very small and, if transistorized, need no wires or attachments. A high degree of amplification is possible.

FLAT RECEIVERS fit against the external ear cartilage, and are kept in place by a metal band. They are usually used only if there is a continuous discharge from the ear, or if there has been a serious mastoid operation. Because of the bad contact, many sounds escape, and acoustic feedback produces much background noise.

BONE CONDUCTORS amplify the sound waves and send them through the bone of the head, not the air passages of the ear. They are uncomfortable and not very efficient, and are usually only used where some ear condition rules out an insert receiver.

G69 The Nose

The outer nose consists of tissue and cartilage supported at the top by the nasal bones. The nasal cavity beneath is divided into two (left and right) by a wall of bone and cartilage called the nasal septum.

The nose has two functions — it is an opening to the respiratory system, and it houses the organs of the sense of smell (the olfactory system). The olfactory system consists of tiny hairlike nerve endings in the roof of the nasal cavity which detect odorous molecules in the air, and transfer signals to the brain via olfactory bulbs and a set of nerve fibers called the olfactory tract.

Nose and Mouth

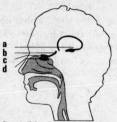

a Brain center for smell
b Olfactory tract
c Olfactory bulbs
d Olfactory hairs

G70 Sense of Smell

The sense of smell is one of the keenest of all the human senses. (It can, for instance, distinguish more odors than the ear can distinguish sounds.) It is a vital part of the taste process — people who have lost their sense of smell cannot taste the full flavor of foods.

The precise mechanism of smell remains a mystery. Similarly, attempts to classify different odors have mostly been unsuccessful. A recent theory proposes four categories — fragrant, burnt, acid, and rancid — and suggests that every smell is a blend of these four basic odors.

G71 Disorders

COMMON COLD is an infectious disease of the respiratory system caused by viruses. It results in a running nose, reduced sense of smell, and sometimes a cough.

HAY FEVER is an allergic reaction which causes the mucous membranes in the nose and eyes to become swollen and irritated. It may also cause a watery discharge or sneezing. Antihistamine drugs are often prescribed to give relief.

NOSE BLEEDS are usually caused by the rupture of a blood vessel inside the nose. The bleeding may be the result of a blow, violent exercise, or exposure to high altitudes, or may be a sign of high blood pressure. It can usually be relieved by pinching together the nostrils; severe or persistent bleeding needs medical attention.

POLYPS are benign tumors in the nasal passages which cause a permanently stuffy nose. Often the result of frequent colds, they are easily removed by simple surgery.

RHINITIS is inflammation of the nose's mucous membranes caused by colds or hay fever.

G72 Sinuses

Sinuses are air cavities in the skull which open into the nasal passages. Inflammation of the sinuses is called sinusitis, and symptoms include headaches and pain in the cheekbones. Drugs are used to treat most cases, and minor surgery can improve more severe ones.

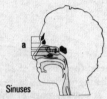

a Sinuses

G73 Cosmetic Surgery

Surgery can correct the bridge line, shorten the nose, build up a depressed nose, straighten a crooked one, or alter the shape of the tip. All involve shaving back or implanting extra bone or cartilage. The incisions are made inside the nose, and the new shape takes about 6 months to settle. Though cosmetic surgery of this kind is often performed at the whim of the patient, in many cases it relieves very real distress.

G74 The Mouth

The mouth is the entrance to the digestive system and one opening of the respiratory system. It is completely surrounded by muscle except for the hard palate and lower jaw which are rigid. Behind the hard palate is the soft palate from which hangs the uvula, a projection of muscle tissue important in speech. On either side at the back of the mouth are the tonsils — oval masses of lymphoid tissue. The cavity is lined with mucous membrane. The mucus it secretes, along with saliva from the salivary glands, cleanses the mouth and keeps it lubricated.

Nose and Mouth

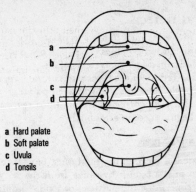

a Hard palate
b Soft palate
c Uvula
d Tonsils

G75 Disorders

Very few serious disorders affect the mouth. A mixture of saliva, mucus, and secretions from the tonsils keep it moist and mostly germ-free. Any injuries to the mouth seem to clear up more quickly than they do elsewhere, and there is considerable resistance to infection. The most common minor disorders are ulcers, cold sores, and thrush.

ULCERS are inflamed sores in the mouth's mucous membrane, usually caused by a scratch or similar injury. Most people suffer occasionally from small ulcers of this type (aphthous ulcers) which usually heal on their own, but mouth ulcers can also be signs of diseases such as diphtheria, leukemia, and cancer.

COLD SORES (HERPES SIMPLEX) are small inflamed blisters that appear around the mouth. They are usually the result of a virus which many people carry around in their bodies all their lives. An eruption can be triggered by another infection, or by exposure to very hot or very cold weather.

THRUSH (MONILIASIS) is an infection of the mucous membrane in the mouth, caused by a yeastlike fungus. It produces white patches inside the cheeks, but it can usually be treated by antifungicides.

G76 Congenital Defects

CLEFT PALATE In the unborn baby, the palate develops in two halves which fuse. In some babies the palate has not fused completely. This condition is known as cleft palate.

HARELIP This is the failure of the three parts of the upper lip to join — a congenital defect associated with cleft palate.

Both defects can usually be corrected by plastic surgery in a series of operations beginning soon after birth.

G77 The Taste Process

Before it can be tasted, a piece of dry food must be moistened and partly dissolved in the mouth by saliva from the salivary glands. The saliva, containing the particles of food, stimulates the taste buds on the tongue. Different areas of the tongue register different tastes (see below). The taste buds send signals to the brain which interprets these signals as tastes.

The sense of smell is also part of the taste process. The odors of food enter the nasal cavity and stimulate the olfactory system (see G69). This greatly heightens the sensation of taste.

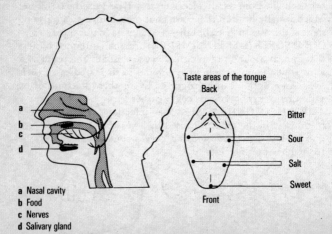

Taste areas of the tongue
Back

Bitter
Sour
Salt
Sweet

Front

a Nasal cavity
b Food
c Nerves
d Salivary gland

Teeth

G78 Teeth

Teeth are hard structures set in bony sockets in the upper and lower jaws. Their main function is to chew and prepare food for swallowing. They also help in the articulation of sounds in speech. In humans there are three main types of teeth.

INCISORS are sharp, chisellike teeth at the front of the mouth, used for cutting into food.

CANINES are round, pointed teeth at the corners of the mouth, used for tearing and gripping food.

MOLARS AND PREMOLARS are square teeth with small cusps, which grind food at the sides of the mouth.

A tooth consists of two parts: the root, which is embedded in the jaw; and the crown, which projects out of the jaw. Where the root and crown meet is called the neck. Each tooth is made up of enamel, dentine, pulp, and cementum.

ENAMEL is the hardest tissue in the body, and it protects the sensitive crown of the tooth.

DENTINE is a slightly elastic material which forms the bulk of the tooth under the enamel. It is sensitive to heat and chemicals.

PULP is the soft tissue inside the dentine, and contains nerves and blood vessels, which enter the root of the tooth by a small canal.

CEMENTUM is a thin layer of material which covers the root of the tooth and protects the underlying dentine. It also helps attach fibers from the gum to the tooth.

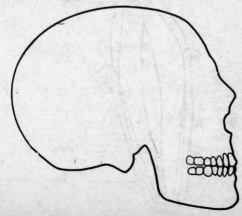

G78-79

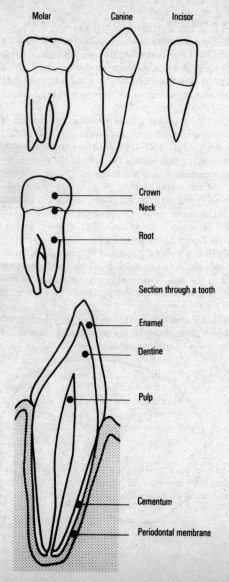

Molar   Canine   Incisor

Crown

Neck

Root

Section through a tooth

Enamel

Dentine

Pulp

Cementum

Periodontal membrane

Teeth

G79 The Teeth We're Given

In humans there are two successive sets of teeth. The primary or "milk" set arrive 6 to 24 months after birth. Later, they gradually fall out, from the age of 6 on, as the permanent teeth appear. Most of these are out by the age of 13, but the 3rd molar or "wisdom tooth" can erupt as late as the age of 25, or never.

Human teeth do not keep growing, but reach a certain size and then stop. Also, when the permanent teeth fall out, they are not replaced by a new set. But in some animals, such as the rabbit, the incisors keep growing, as they are worn down by use, while the shark grows set after set of teeth — to its great advantage!

AGE OF APPEARANCE

These are average figures only: actual dates vary greatly from child to child.

PRIMARY TEETH

Central incisors	6 to 8 months	1
Lateral incisors	9 to 11 months	2
Eye teeth	18 to 20 months	4
First molars	14 to 17 months	3
Second molars	24 to 26 months	5

ADULT TEETH

Central incisors	7 to 8 years	2
Lateral incisors	8 to 9 years	3
Canines	12 to 14 years	6
First premolars	10 to 12 years	4
Second premolars	10 to 12 years	5
First molars	6 to 7 years	1
Second molars	12 to 16 years	7
Third molars	17 to 21 years	8

The end numbers list the typical order of appearance.

The final number of adult teeth is between 28 and 32 — depending on how many of the wisdom teeth appear.

Sequence of appearance of adult teeth (upper jaw)

Primary teeth

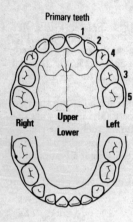

Looking into the mouth

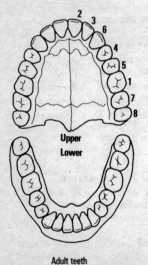

Adult teeth

Upper

Lower

Right Upper Left

5 years

8 years

10 years

11 years

13 years

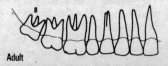

Adult

Teeth

G80 Dental Disorders

Tooth decay is the most universal of human diseases. It especially afflicts those who eat a highly refined diet which is overcooked, soft, sweet, and sticky.

Bacteria in the mouth change carbohydrates in the food into acids strong enough to attack tooth enamel. Gradually the enamel is broken down, and bacteria invade the dentine, forming a "cavity." The pulp reacts by forming secondary dentine to wall off the bacteria, but without treatment the pulp becomes inflamed and painful (toothache).

The infection may then pass down the root and cause an "abscess" — a painful collection of pus under pressure, affecting the gum and face tissues.

PERIODONTAL DISEASE

This is a general term for disorders in the supporting structures of teeth: the gums, cementum, and other tissues. The commonest cause is overconsumption of soft food, which cannot stimulate and harden the gums. Other causes include sharp food which scratches the gums, inefficient brushing, badly contoured fillings, ill-fitting dentures, irregular teeth, and teeth deposits. General factors, such as vitamin deficiencies, blood disorders, and drug use, may also be involved.

Periodontal diseases can be painless but, if allowed to progress, the gum may become detached from the tooth. The socket enlarges, securing fibers are destroyed, and the tooth loosens. Many teeth can be lost in this way.

Painful periodontal disorders include abscesses in the gum and "periocoronitis." The latter is inflammation around an erupting tooth (usually the "wisdom tooth"), caused by irritation, food stagnation, pressure, or infection. It may accompany swollen lymph glands.

G81 Dental Treatment

The dentist's intricate work has to be carried out in the confined, dark, wet, and sensitive environment of the mouth.

FILLING CAVITIES

Tooth decay is dealt with by drilling out the decayed matter and filling up the resulting cavity. All decayed and weakened areas must be removed; otherwise decay will continue beneath the filling. Also the cavity must be shaped so that the filling will stay in securely and withstand pressure from chewing. High-speed electric drills are now usual, and so is the use of injected local anesthetic to make the procedure painless.

A lining of chemical cement is put in the prepared cavity to protect the pulp from heat and chemicals. The filling, placed on top of this, is usually an amalgam of silver, tin, copper, zinc alloy, and mercury. Alternatively, translucent silicate cement is used, for its natural appearance — but, since it can wear away, this cannot be used on grinding surfaces.

When the filling has hardened, it is shaped, and any excess trimmed off.

OTHER RESTORATIVE WORK

Some other replacement work can be prepared outside the mouth, and then cemented into place.

Inlays are cast gold fillings, shaped to fit a cavity in the crown of a tooth. A wax impression of the cavity is made and the resulting mold filled with molten gold. Crowns are extensive coverings to the crown of a tooth, made of porcelain or gold. The whole of the enamel of the tooth is removed, an impression made, and the crown made from a model.

PULP AND ROOT CANAL TREATMENT

If the pulp or root canal is decayed, normal fillings are complicated. Part or all of the pulp may have to be removed. The root canal is sterilized and a silver pin sealed in place to fill it. The pulp cavity is then filled in.

EXTRACTION

Teeth need to be removed if they are irretrievably decayed, or so broken that they cannot be repaired, or if new teeth are erupting and have no room.

Forceps are used. They grip the tooth at the neck, while the blades of the forceps are inserted under the gum. The tooth is then moved repeatedly to enlarge the socket, and finally can be pulled out. Local or general anesthetic, by injection or gas, usually makes extraction painless.

TREATMENT OF GUM DISORDERS

Acute conditions are treated by pus drainage, antiseptic mouthwashes, antibiotics, and tooth extraction if necessary. Surgery may be needed to cut away the diseased gum. Long-term treatment aims at eliminating as many causative factors as possible, by improving oral hygiene, diet, and general health.

Teeth

G82 Orthodontics

This is the branch of dentistry concerned with preventing and correcting irregularities of the teeth, eg variations in the number of teeth and abnormalities in their shape, size, position, and spacing. All these can cause defects in eating, swallowing, speech, and breathing.

Malocclusion is the typical example. This means that the teeth are not in the normal position when the jaws are closed, relative to those in the opposite jaw. Teeth may stick out or in, or there may be spaces between the biting surfaces due to uneven growth of the teeth or jaws.

Irregularities may be caused by: bottlefeeding and thumb sucking; loss of teeth, nonappearance of teeth, and appearance of extra teeth; birth injuries and heredity; and disease and poor health.

TREATMENT

Treatment may be long-term, but it is needed if the health, function, and esthetic appearance of the mouth are to be preserved. Methods include:

elimination of bad habits such as thumb sucking;

practice of exercises to strengthen certain muscles and improve mouth movements;

relief of overcrowded teeth by extraction;

surgery on the soft tissues or bones to recontour the jaws.

But the commonest technique is to attach "braces" or similar appliances to the teeth, to apply continual pressure and so make them shift position. The braces, made of steel bands, wires, springs, or bands of elastic, may have to be worn for up to 2 years or more. They are not attractive, and, if cemented in position, can make cleaning the teeth difficult. They are also more effective in the young than in older people.

G83 False Teeth

Ideally, false teeth ("dentures") should preserve normal chewing and biting, clear speech, and facial appearance.

TYPES OF DENTURES

These include full sets, partial dentures, and immediate dentures. For the construction of a full set, all the teeth are removed, and the healed bony ridge acts as a base. Impressions of both jaws are made in warm wax, and these give the basic patterns from which the dentures are made up.

With partial dentures, the new teeth are attached to surviving natural ones to keep them anchored. Where the anchoring teeth are not immediately alongside, they are linked to the false teeth by a bridge.

With immediate dentures, the false teeth are prepared before the teeth being lost have been removed. After extraction, the empty sockets are immediately covered with the new dentures, and healing takes place beneath. A new set is then needed after about 6 months, as the ridge where teeth have been extracted shrinks.

USING DENTURES

Dentures can be uncomfortable. To avoid gum soreness, new dentures should at first be used only with soft food chewed in small amounts.

If soreness does occur, the dentist should be consulted. The dentures should not be left out of the mouth for more than a day or two, or the remaining natural teeth may begin to shift position.

False teeth should be brushed after every meal, and detachable dentures should be soaked overnight in water containing salt or a denture cleaner.

The wearer can regain her usual ease of speech by practicing reading aloud.

G84 New Teeth for Old

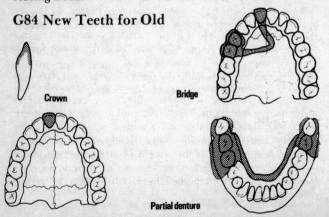

Crown

Bridge

Partial denture

Teeth

G85 Preventing Dental Trouble

DIET

At any age, the ideal diet for dental health should be:
well balanced and adequate, so general health is maintained;
chewable enough to stimulate the gums;
and low in sugar content.

The balance and adequacy of the diet is especially important in the case of expectant mothers and growing children, so that strong teeth form.

ORAL HYGIENE

Teeth should be cleaned at least twice a day: after breakfast and last thing at night. But it is better if they are cleaned after every meal. Cleaning polishes the teeth and removes stains and food debris.

Methods of cleaning vary from culture to culture. The toothbrush can be used ineffectively, and even cause damage (electric toothbrushes tend to be better). The value of toothpaste is doubtful, and it can give a misleading "clean feeling." Brushing with salt stimulates the gums and cleans just as effectively.

"Dental floss," or toothpicks of soft wood, are valuable for dislodging food between the teeth. Highly effective techniques used elsewhere include the fibrous chewing stick used in Africa, and the Moslem tradition of rubbing the teeth and gums with a towel.

DENTAL INSPECTIONS

Regular visits to the dentist about every 6 months catch disease in its early stages and so avoid drastic measures in the future.

FLUORIDE

Fluoride is a tasteless, odorless, colorless chemical, which, if added to drinking water in small amounts, reduces tooth decay in children by 60%. (Excessive amounts can cause the enamel to become mottled.) In the US, 60 million people now drink water with fluoride added, and 7 million others drink water naturally contains fluoride. Some toothpastes also contain fluoride, and tablets can be bought to add to unfluoridated water. So far, no ill effects of the use of fluoride in these quantities have been established, but it only benefits the teeth of children under 14.

G86-87

G86 The Breast

The adult female breast, or mammary gland, consists of 15-25 lobes that are separated by fibrous tissue, rather like the segments of an orange. Each lobe resembles a tree and is embedded in fat.

After childbirth, milk produced in the alveoli of each lobe (the "leaves" of each "tree") travels along small ducts into the main "trunk" or milk duct. This duct is enlarged to form a reservoir just below the areola — the dark ring visible around the nipple. A narrow continuation of the duct links this reservoir with the nipple's surface. Each of the breast's 15-25 lobes has its own opening on the nipple.

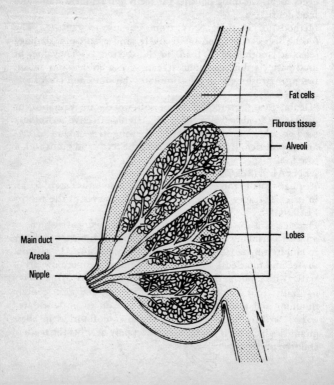

Fat cells

Fibrous tissue

Alveoli

Lobes

Main duct

Areola

Nipple

Breasts

G87 Breastfeeding

Breast milk is sterile and better suited to most human babies than cow's milk. Breastfeeding also helps to establish the important physical contact between mother and baby.

MILK SECRETION by the breast begins just before childbirth as estrogen and progesterone output from the ovaries decreases. The reduction of the level of these hormones in the bloodstream affects the hypothalamus which then causes the pituitary to produce prolactin. It is this hormone that sparks off milk secretion in the breasts.

The first substance secreted is not milk but colostrum — a thick, yellow liquid rich in antibodies (as the milk itself is). These antibodies give the newborn baby protection against disease and infection for up to 6 months.

MILK YIELD starts only about 3 days after childbirth. The flow is set off by the baby sucking the nipple (1). This sends nerve impulses (2) to the hypothalamus, which releases oxytocin that travels via nerve fibers (3) to the pituitary. From there, oxytocin flows through the bloodstream (4) to the breasts, causing the alveoli to contract and force liquid through the ducts to the nipples. Milk flow usually starts about 30 seconds after suckling begins. For discussion of breastfeeding of babies, see D50.

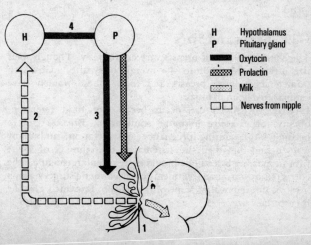

H	Hypothalamus
P	Pituitary gland
	Oxytocin
	Prolactin
	Milk
	Nerves from nipple

G88-90

G88 Changes in the Breast

The breasts undergo great changes during a woman's life.

BEFORE PUBERTY

The breast is simply a nipple projecting from a pink area — the areola.

PUBERTY

By the 11th year, the areola bulges, the nipple still projecting from it. Secretion of the hormones estrogen and progesterone stimulates breast development. The milk ducts develop from the nipple inward and fat accumulates around them, so that by the age of 16 or so, the breasts are prominent.

IN PREGNANCY

Early indicators of pregnancy often include swollen areolae, breast tenderness, and a marbled appearance produced by prominent veins in the breast. In the first 3 months, changes in blood supply and growth of milk ducts and alveoli enlarge the breast by 20-25%. Toward the end of pregnancy, breasts are about ⅓ larger than normal. Breastfeeding triggers further development but the breasts resume their former shape once breastfeeding ceases.

IN LATER LIFE

Around the menopause, breasts begin to droop and become less firm, as fibrous tissue slackens and milk ducts and alveoli shrink.

G89 Shapes and Sizes

The shape and size of breasts vary enormously. Though their size often corresponds to the overall body size, many slim women have large breasts and many obese women have comparatively small breasts.

LARGE BREASTS can occur because of fluid retention, obesity, or excessive hormone stimulation. Breasts tend to become larger during pregnancy and lactation, and many women find that their breasts enlarge after the age of 35. A firm supporting bra will help, and extreme enlargement can be corrected by hormone treatment, or by cosmetic surgery which involves the removal of some of the pads of fat which give the breasts their size.

Breasts

SMALL BREASTS can occur because of too little hormone stimulation or just because the woman is slim. Underdevelopment at puberty can occasionally be helped by rubbing estrogen creams into the breasts, but these creams enlarge only the ducts and not the pads of fat. Cosmetic surgery can also help. Surgeons can insert silicone, or bags filled with fluid, between the breasts and the pectoral muscles — though the breasts do sometimes become infected later as a result. For most women who are anxious about their small breasts, however, a padded bra, upright posture, and perhaps exercises to strengthen the underlying pectoral muscles are all that is necessary.

IS A BRA NECESSARY? The need for a bra has been overemphasized, but women who are in late pregnancy or breast-feeding are generally advised to wear one to avoid stretching supporting tissues.

ABNORMAL NIPPLES Naturally inverted nipples are a developmental fault that makes breastfeeding difficult. (But inversion of previously normal nipples may be a sign of breast cancer — see L44.) Extra nipples sometimes occur — usually in the armpits.

G90 Sexual Response

Sexual stimulation affects the breasts in several ways. The nipples become erect and enlarged, then intermittently soft and pliable. Increased blood supply to the breasts causes their temporary enlargement by as much as 25%, especially in younger women who have not suckled. Also the areolae swell often, in younger women, sufficiently to engulf the base of the nipples. (In women over 50, this swelling is less marked, and may occur in one breast only.)

Finally, in many younger women, a pink flush mottles the breasts just before orgasm.

After orgasm, first the flush, then the areola swelling, soon vanish. But nipple erection may persist for hours, especially in older women or in those who have not had full release of sexual tension.

G91 Hands

THE HAND is remarkable for its flexibility. In particular, the thumb's ability to move in opposition to the fingers enables the hand to grasp objects and perform other delicate tasks. The hand contains 3 important sets of bones: carpals in the wrist, metacarpals in the hand itself, and phalanges in the fingers.

Movements of the fingers are controlled by tendons attached to the muscles in the forearm. The hand is very strong — even a tiny baby can exert a very powerful grip.

HAND CARE

The following points will help to keep the hands in good condition.

a) Do not wash hands more than necessary — soap removes some of the oils that keep the skin pliable.

b) Use hand cream when necessary to prevent dryness and redness, eg if hands have constantly been in water, and in cold weather.

c) Wear rubber gloves for all heavy jobs and for washing dishes.

d) Avoid direct contact with detergents and scouring products — an allergic reaction (contact dermatitis—see G10) may result.

e) Do not expose hands to extremes of temperature. Exposure to extreme cold, for example, causes chilblains.

HAND PROBLEMS

Only a few serious disorders affect the hands.

RHEUMATOID ARTHRITIS is probably the most severe of the common diseases affecting the hands. The lining of the finger joints becomes inflamed, causing the joints themselves to swell painfully. Treatment varies, but medical advice should be sought as early as possible. (See also Osteoarthritis M19.)

SWOLLEN FINGERS are often a symptom of heart disease, and need immediate medical attention.

WARTS often appear on the hands and are a particular problem in childhood (see G16).

WHITLOWS, or felons, are areas of inflamed tissue surrounding the nail. Pus often develops, and a poultice may be used to draw it out, and antiseptic creams applied to prevent the spread of infection. Alternatively a whitlow may be lanced by the doctor.

Hands and Nails

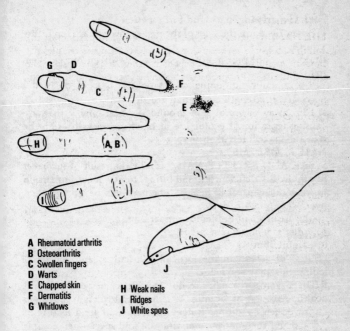

A Rheumatoid arthritis
B Osteoarthritis
C Swollen fingers
D Warts
E Chapped skin
F Dermatitis
G Whitlows

H Weak nails
I Ridges
J White spots

G92 Nails

A NAIL consists of a small plate of dead cells. The horny, visible portion is made up of keratin — the substance found in skin and hair. The nail grows from a bed, or matrix, which is protected by a fold of skin at the base. The white crescent at the base of the nail is the visible part of the nail bed. The nail rests on soft tissues which contain blood vessels to nourish the matrix.

Nails grow about 1½in (3.8cm) per year, though the rate varies with the individual.

NAIL CARE

Nails are easily damaged, and it can be a long time before the damage grows out. To keep the nails in good condition, several points may be helpful.

a) Never use a steel file; it will tear the delicate keratin layers. Instead, use an emery board.

b) Always file from each side of the nail toward the center —

never use a sawing, back-and-forth motion.

c) Never file down the sides of the nail as this will weaken future growth.

d) Do not shape your nails to a point as this will encourage them to break.

e) Use a nail-conditioning cream on the base of the nail if necessary, to strengthen new nail growth.

f) Clip away pieces of skin around the nail only if they are causing irritation. Regular use of hand cream will soften the skin and make it less likely to split.

NAIL PROBLEMS

WEAK AND BRITTLE NAILS can be the result of incorrect filing, dietary deficiencies, nail biting, too frequent immersion in water, or general ill health. The nails can be strengthened by:

a) the use of a nail-hardening preparation;

b) a diet rich in calcium (see H32);

c) careful filing.

"Doses" of gelatin in the form of jello cubes, and courses of iodine pills, may also help.

RIDGES across the nail are due to a deficiency caused by ill health. A course of vitamin A, iodine, and calcium may help improve their condition. Ridges down the nail are a feature of old age and rheumatism, but vitamins and special nail creams can alleviate this condition.

WHITE SPOTS are common on weak nails and are usually caused by injury. This causes the nail cells to separate and allows air to filter between them. Overacidity may also be a cause of white spots.

NAIL BITING

This common problem often begins in childhood, perhaps caused by stress of some kind, whether from a nervous disposition or a specific outside cause. It then develops into a habit difficult to break. Biting off the nail leaves it weak and rough, and the irritation caused by the ragged edge will encourage further biting.

Use of evil-tasting chemical preparations painted on the nails is an effective means of discouraging nail biting; but it is also a good idea to try to pinpoint and remove any causes of stress. Adults anxious to break the habit may find it helpful to concentrate on allowing one nail at a time to grow longer.

Legs and Feet

G93 The Leg

The leg contains 3 important bones — the femur (thighbone) in the upper leg, and the tibia (shinbone) and fibula in the lower leg.

The upper femur meets the hip in a ball and socket joint (which allows free movement). The lower femur and upper tibia meet at the knee joint, a hinge joint (allowing movement in one direction only). Here cartilage forms buffers between these bones, and the front and base of the lower femur abuts the synovial membrane — a sac filled with lubricating fluid. The patella (kneecap) covers and protects the knee joint.

The thigh muscles are used to bend the knee, while the lower leg muscles move the feet and toes. The sciatic nerve — the longest and thickest in the body — provides the nervous system for most of the leg. Blood feeds into the thigh through the femoral artery, and back toward the heart through two systems of veins, one deep, one superficial.

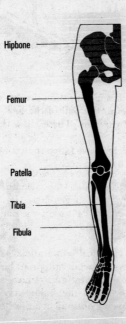

Hipbone

Femur

Patella

Tibia

Fibula

G94-98

G94 The Foot

Each foot is comprised of 26 bones with 33 joints, linked by more than 100 ligaments. Muscles, tendons, and ligaments keep the foot in different positions.
There are 3 sets of foot bones:
a 7 tarsal or ankle bones forming the ankle and the rear of the instep, and jointed for foot rotation;
b 5 metatarsal or instep bones forming the front of the instep; and
c 14 phalangeal or toe bones   3 for each small toe and 2 for the big toe.

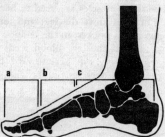

Bones in the foot

a Phalanges
b Metatarsals
c Tarsals

G95 Arches

The normal foot has 2 important arches, one running lengthwise from the heel to the ball of the foot, the second running across the ball of the foot. These allow the spring needed for walking.
In flat feet, the arches have fallen so that weight is borne on the sole as well as the ball and heel.

Print of
normal arch

Print of
fallen arch

Legs and Feet

G96 Athlete's Foot

This is a common disorder, best avoided by keeping the foot clean, dry, and cool, and avoiding contact with infected people and with changing room floors. It is caused by a fungus infection, and first appears in the toe clefts. There may be splits and flaking, or pieces of dead white skin.

Treatment involves rubbing away the dead skin, applying a mixture of water and medicinal alcohol, and using a special dusting powder. A fungicidal ointment may be prescribed by the doctor. The feet should be exposed to the air as much as possible, and panty hose should be clean every day.

G97 Common Foot Disorders

CALLUSES are areas of skin hardened to form protection for parts that suffer pressure or friction. To clear them, soak the foot in warm water and remove the callus by rubbing with an emery board.

CORNS are a type of callus usually caused by ill-fitting shoes. They have a cone-shaped core which causes pain when it presses on nerve endings. Corn pads may relieve pain but removal should be left to a chiropodist.

PLANTAR WARTS, or verrucas, are the result of a virus infection, and are often contracted at swimming pools. The warts grow into the skin and cause pain. Verrucas should be treated by a doctor.

G98 Disorders of the Leg

DISLOCATED HIP Hip dislocation may be present at birth or occur later. It causes a lurching gait, backache in middle age, and sometimes osteoarthritis (see M19). Treatment varies with age, and may involve an operation.

DISLOCATED KNEE Slipping of the kneecap to the side may result from an injury, or the tendency may be present from birth. Doctors may recommend rest, or sometimes an operation.

HOUSEMAID'S KNEE Kneeling on hard surfaces for long periods may inflame the fluid-filled sac (bursa) that lies in front of the kneecap. Tissues at the knee joint swell, become tender, and make knee-bending painful. Poulticing or minor surgery may be needed.

G98-100

WATER ON THE KNEE This is a collection of fluid beneath the kneecap. It may be due to infection, rheumatoid arthritis, or to a blow or strain. Rest usually brings recovery.

RHEUMATOID ARTHRITIS Hips, knees, ankles, and feet can be badly affected. Painful joint swelling is sometimes followed by joint erosion and dislocation. Cortisone treatment is used, and hip and knee joints are sometimes replaced with metal or plastic devices. (Also see M19.)

SCIATICA Inflammation of the sciatic nerve produces a form of neuritis called sciatica. A slipped disk in the spine may press on a nerve, producing intense pain in the leg and lower back. Bed rest, heat applied to the painful area, physiotherapy, and special exercises may bring relief.

VARICOSE VEINS are swollen veins in the legs, which stand out above the surface and can be acutely painful. Their exposed position also makes them vulnerable to bleeding and ulceration.

Varicose veins develop if the valves in the leg veins fail to prevent the backflow of blood. They are more likely in occupations involving long periods of standing — and also where there is a swelling of the abdomen, as in obesity, chronic constipation, and pregnancy. This last is why 1 in 2 women over 40 suffer from varicose veins, but only 1 in 4 men of the same age. Possible treatments include: wearing pressure bandages and resting with the leg raised; courses of injections; and surgical tying or removal of the varicose veins.

THROMBOPHLEBITIS A blood clot in a deep vein produces deep pain and a swollen ankle. A blood clot in a superficial vein produces tenderness and a red, cordlike formation beneath the skin. The patient may feel ill and have a high temperature. Medical aid must be sought. Treatments include anticoagulants, supportive stockings, and resting the leg.

Legs and Feet

G99 Bunions and Hammer Toes

A BUNION is a hard swelling at the base of the big toe. Ill-fitting shoes cause the big toe to bend in, forcing out the base of the toe in a bony outgrowth. A fluid-filled sac (bursa) may develop between the outgrowth and the skin.

A HAMMER TOE is a toe bent up at the middle joint, where it presses on the shoe and causes a corn.

Both these conditions can improve with exercise, manipulation, or well-fitting shoes, but severe cases may need surgery.

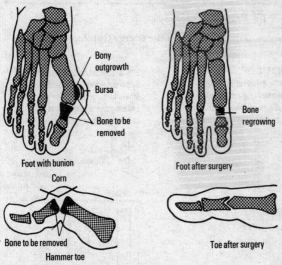

Bony outgrowth

Bursa

Bone to be removed

Foot with bunion

Bone regrowing

Foot after surgery

Corn

Bone to be removed

Hammer toe

Toe after surgery

G100 Foot Care

a) Wash feet at least once a day. Soaking in cold salt water or diluted cider vinegar refreshes the feet in hot weather.

b) Dust the feet daily with a special foot powder to avoid friction, to help dry out the feet, and to prevent odor.

c) Cut toenails straight across and not in at the edges.

d) Wear clean panty hose every day.

e) Keep the feet free of corns and calluses (see G97).

f) Wear comfortable, well-fitting shoes. Very high or very flat heels on shoes can force the body into an unnatural position and cause considerable discomfort.

H01-02

H01 Life and Energy

All living things need sources of energy and material, because all life uses up energy and material: in movement, repair, and growth, and just in the internal processes of maintaining its own existence.

Where living things find these sources is what governs their primary division into animals and plants. Most plants survive on inorganic (ie nonliving) material — chemicals drawn from the soil and the air, and then processed within them in the

H02 The Food Chain

This series of diagrams shows the energy transferred in the food chain.

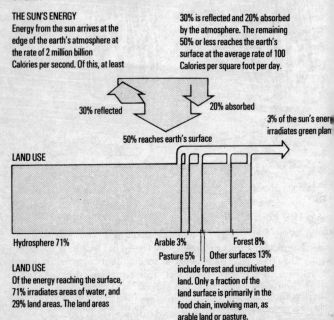

THE SUN'S ENERGY
Energy from the sun arrives at the edge of the earth's atmosphere at the rate of 2 million billion Calories per second. Of this, at least 30% is reflected and 20% absorbed by the atmosphere. The remaining 50% or less reaches the earth's surface at the average rate of 100 Calories per square foot per day.

30% reflected

20% absorbed

3% of the sun's energy irradiates green plant

50% reaches earth's surface

LAND USE

Hydrosphere 71%

Arable 3%
Pasture 5%

Forest 8%
Other surfaces 13%

LAND USE
Of the energy reaching the surface, 71% irradiates areas of water, and 29% land areas. The land areas include forest and uncultivated land. Only a fraction of the land surface is primarily in the food chain, involving man, as arable land or pasture.

Life and Energy

presence of sunlight. They can build up complex substances out of simple ones. Animals cannot make food in this fashion. They must get it ready-made by eating plants or other animals. For them, food is the source of chemical energy and material. From the already complex substances in food, they break down the chemicals that they need.

So the synthesis of food from plants begins a chain of energy transference: energy and matter are passed on, thereafter, because one life form consumes another.

PLANTS

In all, only about 3% of the sunlight actually irradi⸱ ⸱s green plants on the land surface or algae in the sea. The land plants include cereals, grasses, root crops, and vegetables and fruit.

HUMAN SOURCES OF ENERGY

The chain reaches us in the form of food grains, livestock products, root crops, vegetables and fruits, fats and oils, sugar, and fish.

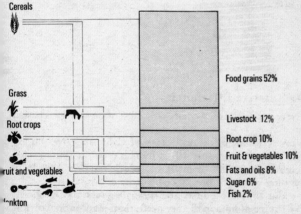

Plants	Energy conversion	Human sources of energy

Cereals

Grass

Root crops

uit and vegetables

⸱nkton

Food grains 52%

Livestock 12%

Root crop 10%

Fruit & vegetables 10%

Fats and oils 8%

Sugar 6%

Fish 2%

ENERGY CONVERSION

The plants convert about 1% of the energy reaching them into chemical energy. Some of this is stored. In the food chain, the plants are consumed, and about 10% of the plants' stored energy is stored by the animal that eats them. Similarly, when the animal is eaten, about 10% of its stored energy is stored by the eater.

H03-04

H03 Metabolic Turnover

. . . showing the daily input and output of a 135lb (61kg) woman in a closed environment.

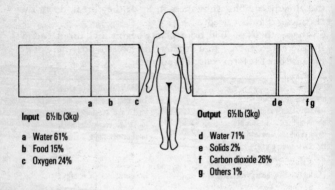

Input 6½lb (3kg)

a Water 61%
b Food 15%
c Oxygen 24%

Output 6½lb (3kg)

d Water 71%
e Solids 2%
f Carbon dioxide 26%
g Others 1%

H04 Relative Efficiencies

At every step in the food chain, only 10% of the energy is passed on.

Professor Hardin of the University of California gives an example of this: to produce 1lb of human requires 10lb of bass, which requires 100lb of minnows, which requires 1,000lb of water flies, which requires 10,000lb of algae.

Meat and animal products are usually a much more concentrated source of human dietary needs than plant products. But the process of their production is far more inefficient, as there are more steps in the chain.

Opposite we compare energy loss in a potato crop and in beef cattle production. With potatoes, about 30% of the trapped sunlight energy becomes usable food energy for humans; with beef, only 4%. In fact, an acre of land can produce, in a year, almost 9 times as much potato protein as beef protein.

Life and Energy

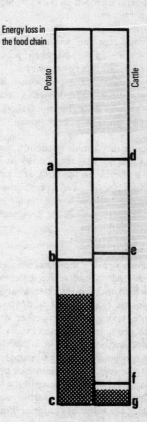

Energy loss in the food chain

POTATO
a Plant metabolic loss 37%
b Farming loss 24%
c Available for processing 39%
   Available after processing 30%

CATTLE
d Plant metabolic loss 34%
e Farming and feeding loss 25%
f Animal metabolic loss 35%
g Available for processing 6%
   Available after processing 4%

Available after processing

H05-07

H05 What Food Is

Food is anything that has a chemical composition which can provide the body with:

a) material from which it can produce heat, activity, and other forms of energy;

b) material that can be used in the growth, maintenance, repair, and reproduction of the body; and/or

c) substances to regulate these processes of energy production, growth, repair, reproduction, etc.

Not everything we eat or drink is food. Flavorings such as pepper are not utilized by the body. Tea affects the nervous system and is a drug, but not a food. (But alcohol, though it is a drug, also provides energy, and so falls within the definition of food.)

Bran performs a useful function as a laxative, but again is not food as it is not absorbed by the body. The constituents of food that are of value to the body are: proteins, carbohydrates, fats, vitamins, minerals, and water. Energy uses carbohydrates, fats, and proteins. Growth and repair use proteins, minerals, and water. Control of body processes uses proteins, minerals, vitamins, and water.

H06 Calories

The constituents in food that help growth and repair cannot all be measured on one scale: different constituents do different jobs, which are not interchangeable. The same applies to the constituents that control body processes. It is no good, for example, trying to add together vitamin A units and calcium units to get so many "control units." That is like trying to add cows and washing machines. But the constituents that provide energy can be measured on a single scale and added together. For, in the end, all of them can be measured in terms of the amount of heat they produce in the body.

The basic unit for measuring any energy (including heat output) is the scientist's calorie. This is defined as the amount of energy needed to raise the temperature of 1cc of water by 1°Centigrade. The measure used in talking about food and human energy needs is a thousand times larger than this: the kilocalorie, or Calorie (which should be — but is not always — written with a capital "C").

For example, a typical number of Calories for a woman to use

What Food Provides

up in a day is about 2,500. So this is the amount of energy her food must supply, unless she is to run down her stored reserves. Protein, fat, and carbohydrate are all sources of energy (though protein is more vital as a source of other things). One ounce of protein produces over 113 Calories in the human body, one ounce of carbohydrate the same, and one ounce of fat 225 Calories. (An ounce of alcohol — rich in the carbohydrates that we call sugars — produces 180 Calories.) Actual foods range in calorific value from, for example, 105 Calories to the pound (tomatoes) to 4,200 Calories to the pound (lard).

H07 Proteins

Protein is the basic ingredient of the living organism. There is no substitute for protein, for it is the only constituent of food which contains nitrogen — essential for the growth and repair of the body. Proteins, in fact, provide raw materials for the body's tissues and fluids. They also have certain specialized functions. They help to maintain the chemical fluid balance in the brain, spine, and intestine, and they aid the transport of food and drugs.

Proteins are very complex substances made from a number of chemicals called amino acids. About 20 different kinds of amino acid are found in protein food, and the thousands of different ways these can be linked up produce the many types of protein that exist in food. A single protein molecule can contain as many as 500 amino acid units linked together.

The two main sources of protein are from animals, in the form of meat, fish, eggs, and dairy produce, and from plants in the form of nuts, peas and beans, grains and grain products (such as bread, especially wholemeal), and in small quantities in many tubers and vegetables.

Most animal proteins contain all the essential amino acids that humans need, and so are called complete proteins. But vegetable proteins are all, individually, more or less incomplete. They can carry out some individual jobs in the body, but cannot fulfill the vital task of cell repair and growth unless combined together, or with animal protein.

Most proteins are insoluble in water. Some are soluble — such as casein (milk) and albumen (egg white) — but become insoluble when heated or beaten.

Ho8-09
H08 Carbohydrates

Carbohydrates provide our main source of energy for immediate use. Energy is used up even during sleep, to keep body organs functioning. Carbohydrates play a vital role in the proper functioning of the internal organs and the central nervous system, and in heart and muscle contraction. Our bodies cannot manufacture carbohydrates, so we get them from plants, or from animals that feed on plants. Plants synthesize carbohydrates out of the reaction of sunlight on water and carbon dioxide. This is called photosynthesis, and it occurs in the green leaves of plants.

All carbohydrates are made up from carbon, hydrogen, and oxygen. The end product of these three elements is first sugar and then starch, which is stored in plants for future use.

There are several different kinds of carbohydrates.

SUGAR

This is one kind, of which there are various types:

Glucose is the form in which fuel is transported in the body (though, eaten, it gives energy no more quickly than other sugars).

Fructose comes from most fruits and from honey. It can also be made out of sugar cane. Glucose converts to fructose during the process of the release of energy in the body.

Sucrose is a chemical combination of fructose and glucose and occurs naturally in sugar beet and sugar cane. It is also present in fruit and in carrots. Sucrose forms the common household sugar, which is available in various grades and crystal sizes due to different refinement processes.

Lactose occurs naturally in human's and cow's milk and is not as sweet as sucrose. It is a combination of glucose and galactose.

Maltose is derived from malt and is also produced naturally from starch when grain germinates.

STARCH

This forms the largest part of the carbohydrate in our food. It is the stored food in plant seeds, intended for use in maintaining the growing plant until it is able to feed itself by photosynthesis. Unripe fruit contains starch which converts to sugar as the fruit ripens. Starch is composed of complex chains linked together with glucose units. Starch is indigestible unless it is cooked, when the starch granules swell and burst.

GLYCOGEN

Glycogen is similar to starch, and it serves the same purpose in

What Food Provides

animals as starch does in plants, ie it stores fuel — in this case in the liver and muscles. It is not found in most meat as it breaks down into glucose after the animal is killed, but horse meat and oysters do retain it.

OTHER FORMS

Cellulose is the compound produced in plants to give themselves rigidity and strength. It is fibrous, and indigestible to most animals except some insects (but does function as roughage).

Pectin is present in apples, other fruits, and turnips. It has no direct food value but has the property of making jam set.

Sources of useful carbohydrates include bread, potatoes, rice, wheat, sugar, honey, vegetables, fruit, jam, liver, milk, eggs, and cheese.

H09 Fats

Fat is the most concentrated source of energy. Also, when stored in the body as a layer of fat beneath the skin and around organs, it provides insulation and protection for body structures. Finally, certain fats carry the fat-soluble vitamins (A, D, E, and K).

Fat contains the same three elements as carbohydrates — carbon, hydrogen, and oxygen, but combined in a different way. Chemically, fat is a combination of fatty acids and glycerine. At normal temperatures, fat can be solid as in animals or liquid as in vegetable and fish oil. But all fat can be made liquid by heating and solid by cooling.

Fat is not soluble in water, though it is in alcohol, ether and chloroform. But by chemical treatment with alkalis, fat can be broken down into its separate units, and then can be mixed with water. This is the process by which fats are digested in the body. Mineral oils such as Vaseline and paraffin cannot be broken down in this way and are therefore not digestible by the body and of no value as food.

Fat in the diet falls into three categories. Sources such as butter, lard, margarine, and oils are added to recipes in a recognizable and measurable form. Other sources, such as the fat found in meat, fish, eggs, etc, are not so readily measurable, and vary with the quality of the source, the time of year, and so on. In addition, when fat is added as a cooking medium, it finds its way into the outer layer of the food, increasing its fat content.

H10

H10 Vitamins

Vitamins are certain substances found in food in minute amounts. They are needed for the regulation of chemical processes inside the body, and through this have an important role in growth and development and in protection against illness and disease. The presence of vitamins in the diet is essential, as most of them cannot be made by the body.

The role of vitamins in nutrition was only discovered in the present century, but there are now known to be about 40, of which 12 or more are essential in the diet. Because of the haphazard process of their discovery, they originally formed a jumbled list of alphabetic names (A, B_1, B_6, etc). But now their chemical structures have been identified, chemical names are often used for many of them. Identification has also meant that some can now be made artificially.

Chemically, in fact, they are proving to be a mixed bag — only sharing the characteristic of being complex substances needed by the body in tiny amounts. For example, the body only needs one ounce of thiamin in its lifetime — despite the vital importance of that ounce. Above an average day-to-day requirement, increased amounts of a vitamin do no further good, and in some cases are actually harmful.

Vitamins in the diet can be divided into two classes: those soluble in fat (vitamins A, D, E, and K), and those soluble in water (vitamin C and the B vitamin complex).

VITAMIN A is found in halibut and cod liver oil, milk, butter, and eggs. It is destroyed by cooking and sunlight.

It plays a role in the formation of bone and of the enamel and dentine in teeth. It is also responsible for the ability to see in dim light.

VITAMIN D is found in eggs, milk, butter, and fish liver oils. It is also synthesized in the skin during exposure to sunlight.

It plays a part in the digestive absorption of some minerals, such as calcium and phosphorus. It is also necessary for retaining calcium in bones.

VITAMIN E is found in wheat germ, oil, lettuce, spinach, watercress, etc. There is no definite evidence that it is essential to humans, but it does help in the healing of skin wounds, and may also be connected with fertility.

VITAMIN K is found mainly in green plants such as spinach, cabbage, and kale. But it is also synthesized in the gut by the

What Food Provides

action of bacteria. It is a necessary factor in the blood-clotting mechanism, as it is needed for the production of prothrombin.

VITAMIN C is found in fresh fruit and vegetables, especially lemons, oranges, tomatoes, and watercress. Human milk also contains vitamin C. This vitamin is easily destroyed by cooking, especially if the food has been chopped up.

One of its most important functions in the body is to control the formation of dentine, cartilage and bone. It also helps the formation of red blood cells, and the correct healing of wounds and broken bones. There is no conclusive evidence that vitamin C prevents colds.

VITAMIN B is in fact a complex of 15 different substances, but they are classed together because they occur together in the same types of food, such as yeast and wheat germ. Unlike the other vitamins, at least some vitamins of the B group are found in all living plants and animals.

The following are the most important B vitamins.

THIAMIN forms the part of the enzyme system essential for the breakdown of carbohydrates and the nutrition of nerve cells.

RIBOFLAVIN acts with thiamin and nicotinic acid in the oxidation of carbohydrates. It is also important for the growth of the fetus, and is thought to play a part in the mechanism of vision.

PYRIDOXINE (B_6) helps the breakdown of protein into amino acids and is necessary for the formation of blood cells. However, sufficient pyridoxine is produced in the intestine.

PANTOTHENIC ACID probably plays a part in the detoxification of drugs and the formation of chemicals that pass nerve impulses along the nerves.

NIACIN is needed for healthy skin and nerves and food digestion.

FOLIC ACID is an antianemic factor found in green leaves and in liver and kidneys. It is especially important during pregnancy, to prevent anemia.

COBALAMIN (B_{12}) is the only vitamin containing a metal, cobalt. It is found in a high concentration in the liver and is essential for the formation of red blood cells. Unlike the other B complex vitamins, it has no vegetable source.

H11-12

H11 Minerals

Minerals, like vitamins, do not supply any heat or energy, but play a vital role in the regulation of body fluids and the balance of chemicals.

MACRONUTRIENTS

These are the minerals needed by the body in comparatively large quantities.

CALCIUM is found in milk, cheese, fish, some green vegetables, and in "hard" drinking water. It is necessary for the proper formation of bones and teeth; also for the functioning of muscles and clotting of the blood. During growth, calcium is constantly being laid down in bones and simultaneously withdrawn into the bloodstream for use elsewhere. The body of an adult normally contains $2-3\frac{1}{2}$lb of calcium of which at least 99% is present in the bones.

PHOSPHORUS is found in animal organs such as brains, kidneys, and liver. Dairy produce such as cheese is also rich in phosphorus.

It is important for energy transfer. Its function in the body is closely linked with that of calcium.

SODIUM AND CHLORINE occur together in the familiar form of common salt, and also in animal protein. Both are vital for life: they maintain water balance and distribution, osmotic pressure, acid-base balance and muscular functioning. The amount taken in a normal diet is usually more than enough, but in hot weather much may be lost in sweat.

POTASSIUM is related in function to sodium and chlorine. It is found mainly in meat, fish, vegetables, chocolate, and dried fruit.

SULFUR occurs in certain amino acids, especially in animal proteins. Sulfur in the body is found especially in insulin, which regulates the level of sugar in the blood and in the human hair.

MAGNESIUM occurs in nuts, beans, cereals, dark green vegetables, seafood, and chocolate. Its function is similar to calcium.

MICRONUTRIENTS

These are the minerals needed by the body in much smaller quantities.

IRON is found in fish, liver, eggs, black pudding, beans, green vegetables, and oatmeal. The body of a healthy adult contains about 4g of iron — roughly the amount of a 3in nail.

What Food Provides

Iron is an essential part of red (hemoglobin) blood cells, which enable the blood to take up oxygen from the lungs and carry it to all cells in the body.

IODINE is important for the healthy functioning of the thyroid gland. It occurs in seafish, shellfish, iodized table salt, and vegetables grown on soil naturally containing iodine.

FLUORINE is found naturally in seafish, some "hard" drinking water, and china tea. It is also added to the water artificially in some localities. Traces of fluorine are present in bones, teeth, skin and thyroid gland. One known function is that it helps prevent tooth decay.

OTHER MICRONUTRIENTS are zinc, selenium, manganese, copper, molybdenum, cobalt, and chromium.

TRACE ELEMENTS

These are found in the body in tiny amounts, but their function, if any, is not yet known. They include strontium, bromine, vanadium, gold, silver, nickel, tin, aluminum, bismuth, arsenic, and boron.

H12 Water

Water is not really a food, but it is an essential part of all tissues. Our bodies are composed of about $\frac{2}{3}$ water. It acts as a form of transport: the blood, which is mainly water, carries food in its basic forms to the tissues and takes away waste products to be excreted. Chemically, water is a simple compound of oxygen and hydrogen, but is never found pure as it contains traces of minerals, dissolved gases, and solids. The amount of these depends on the water's source.

As well as in liquid form, water is also found in most solid food. Since it is constantly being lost in sweat, urine, and breathing out, it must be replaced every day or dehydration of the body will occur. However, the body's need for water at any time is very accurately registered by the degree of thirst.

H13

H13 The Digestive System

The digestive tract forms a tube over 30ft long, beginning in the mouth and ending in the anus. Between these it includes the esophagus (gullet), stomach, small intestine and large intestine.

In the mouth, food is chewed into smaller pieces, mixed with saliva, and formed into a rounded ball ("bolus").

On swallowing, the bolus passes down the esophagus into the stomach.

The stomach varies in shape and size according to its contents. Its maximum capacity is about $2\frac{1}{2}$ pints. Here food is churned into even smaller pieces, and mixed with gastric juices, including hydrochloric acid. Fat is melted by the heat.

From the stomach, food passes into the small intestine. In the first 12in of this (the duodenum), the food is mixed with pancreatic and intestinal juices and with bile from the gall bladder. Then here, and in the remaining 21ft of small intestine, most of the useful elements in food are absorbed through the intestinal walls into the blood and lymph streams.

In the 6ft-long large intestine, water is absorbed into the body, turning the waste products into a soft solid (feces): a mixture of indigestible remnants, unabsorbed water, and millions of bacteria. Finally, the feces pass out of the body via the anus.

Food takes from 15 hours upward to pass through the whole system. It usually stays in the stomach 3 to 5 hours, the small intestine $4\frac{1}{2}$ hours, and the large intestine (where the sequence of meals may get jumbled) 5 to 25 hours or more.

Digestion and Absorption

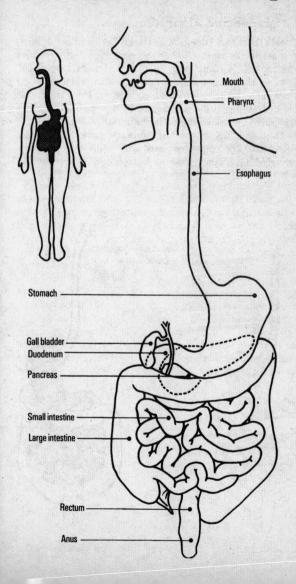

Mouth

Pharynx

Esophagus

Stomach

Gall bladder

Duodenum

Pancreas

Small intestine

Large intestine

Rectum

Anus

H14

H14 Digestion and Absorption

CARBOHYDRATES Digestion of starch begins in the mouth. It continues in the stomach, but the stomach usually empties itself before this is completed. In the duodenum, pancreatic juices break the carbohydrates down into monosaccharides, which are then absorbed into the bloodstream. But some forms of carbohydrate (eg cellulose) cannot be digested, while some sugars begin to be absorbed even in the mouth.

FATS Digestion begins in the stomach, where naturally emulsified fats are converted into fatty acids and glycerol. (Unconverted fat causes food to be retained longer in the stomach.)

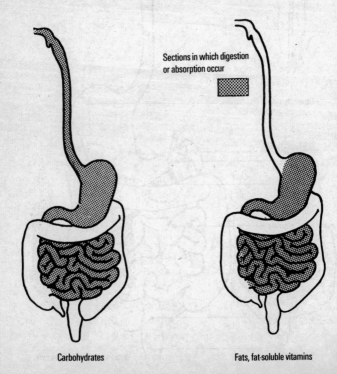

Sections in which digestion or absorption occur

Carbohydrates

Fats, fat-soluble vitamins

Digestion and Absorption

In the small intestine, bile emulsifies the unemulsified fats, and pancreatic juice converts them into fatty acids. These are absorbed into the lymph vessels (70%) or the bloodstream (30%). Fat-soluble vitamins are absorbed at the same time.

PROTEINS Digestion begins in the stomach, where proteins are broken down into peptones. In the small intestine, the pancreatic and intestinal juices break the peptones down into amino acids. The amino acids are absorbed into the bloodstream.

WATER is absorbed in the large intestine, into the lymph vessels and bloodstream. It is not digested before absorption.

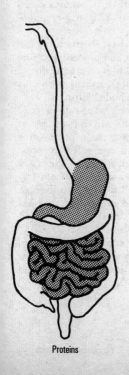

Proteins   Water, water soluble vitamins

H15

H15 Food Intake

What people eat varies enormously. For many people in tropical countries, a typical day's food is based on rice and a little vegetable — totaling perhaps 1,600 Calories, and containing only tiny amounts of necessary proteins, vitamins, and minerals. Yet in industrial countries, the daily diet of a food lover may total over 3,500 Calories, and supply in all respects about twice the body's needs.

Even taking national averages, great differences remain. In Ghana, on a diet mainly of roots, cereals, and vegetables, the average total daily intake is perhaps 2,000 Calories, including 1.7oz (47g) of protein of which only ¼ is of animal origin. In Denmark, on a diet of meat, dairy produce, cereal products, vegetables, and fruits, the average intake is perhaps 3,300 Calories including 3.3oz (95g) of protein (2.2oz-62g-of animal origin).

Diets also vary greatly in their variety, their range of geographical source, and their handling and processing before consumption. Perhaps 75% of the world lives on a basic diet of one food, usually a cereal (typically rice), usually grown by themselves, and usually eaten in a simple boiled form.

Average individual grain intake on such a diet in a poor country totals perhaps 400lb (180kg) a year. In contrast, about 1,700lb (770kg) of grain enters the food chain of a North American each year — but only 30% is ever eaten as cereal products. The rest goes to feed livestock for meat and dairy produce. People in industrial societies buy widely from restaurants and vending machines, as well as from an average supermarket stock of 7,000 different food items that have been stored, transported (perhaps imported), usually processed and preserved, and wrapped for sale.

Opposite we show comparative Calorie consumption by food source for an average person in the USA (left) and in India (right). Calorie consumption in the USA is both far higher and far more varied in source.

What We Eat

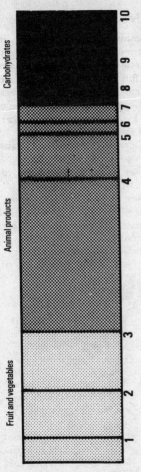

Carbohydrates

Animal products

Fruit and vegetables

USA
1 Green leafy vegetables
2 Citrus fruits and vegetables
3 Other fruits and vegetables
4 Milk and milk products
5 Meat
6 Eggs
7 Oil and fat
8 Sweetened products
9 Potatoes
10 Cereals

10 9 8 7 6 5 4 3 2 1

Average food consumption

India
1 Citrus fruits
2 Vegetables
3 Legumes (peas, beans, etc)
4 Other fruits, sugar, meat, fish, eggs, milk, oil, and fat
5 Rice

5 4 3 2 1

Average food consumption

H16

H16 The Haves and Have-Nots

The maps on the opposite page show average daily protein and Calorie intake in different countries. The patterns are very similar: most countries with high total Calorie consumption are also high in protein consumption. But a few national diets have adequate protein, though total Calories are low, while rather more have ample Calories but deficient protein. On this page we summarize the situation, but by inhabited regions rather than countries. Taking continental areas, on average:

(a) Europe, North America, and Oceania (Australia, etc) have a sizable excess Calorie intake and some excess protein intake;

(b) in South America the situation varies from country to country;

(c) the Middle East has slight Calorie and protein deficiencies; and

(d) Asia, Central America, and parts of Africa have sizable Calorie deficiencies and large protein deficiencies.

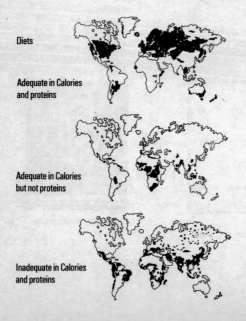

Diets

Adequate in Calories
and proteins

Adequate in Calories
but not proteins

Inadequate in Calories
and proteins

What We Eat

Calories

Over 2700

2200-2700

Below 2200

Protein

Over 1oz
(30g)

½-1oz
(15-30g)

Below ½oz
(15g)

H17-19

H17 Calorie Needs

A person's need for energy from food is measured in Calories (H06). Needs vary from person to person, depending on a variety of different factors. Age, sex, size, physical activity, and climate all affect the number of Calories that are needed.

Calories are used to maintain body functions and to provide energy for exercise (H20). An increase in weight results if a person takes in as food more Calories than are needed (H38). If Calorie intake is below requirements, fat stored in the body is converted to energy and weight is lost.

Estimates of daily Calorie needs vary — our diagram is based on statistics for 1974 from the US Food and Nutrition Board. It refers to "typical" persons living in a temperate climate, and provides a useful starting point for assessing individual needs.

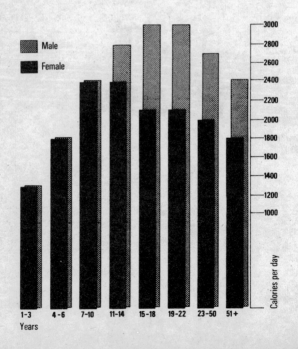

Use of Calories

H18 Calories in Childbearing

Women have higher daily Calorie requirements during pregnancy and when breastfeeding. Estimates of these increased requirements vary, but the increases suggested below should be sufficient to meet the needs of most women today.

PREGNANCY

During the second half of pregnancy, an increase to 2,250 Calories per day is suggested. This estimate assumes some reduction in the level of exercise toward the end of pregnancy.

BREASTFEEDING

A woman who is breastfeeding her child should allow 500 Calories per day above her usual requirements.

H19 Use of Calories

Calories are needed to supply energy for every activity. Approximately 1,400 Calories a day — about $\frac{2}{3}$ of her total daily requirement — are needed by a typical woman in order to maintain basic life processes such as heartbeat, breathing, and digestion. A further 600 to 800 Calories a day should probably be plenty to provide the energy needed for all her other activities at work and during recreation.

To maintain basic life processes: 1400 Calories per day

H20

H20 Calories and Exercise

People use up Calories every minute of the day. This is true even when they are asleep or lying doing "nothing." When a person is resting, most of this Calorie expenditure is used to maintain body functions. A typical woman uses about 55 Calories an hour when she is asleep. Estimating the rate of

Sleeping: 55 Calories per hour

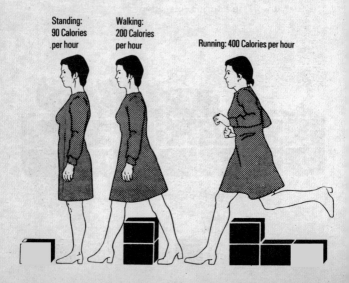

Standing: 90 Calories per hour

Walking: 200 Calories per hour

Running: 400 Calories per hour

Use of Calories

Calorie expenditure during different activities is more difficult — some people are naturally more energetic than others, even when each is doing the same thing. For example, a person walking at 4mph obviously uses more Calories than another walking at 2mph. The figures on this page are, however, of interest in that they provide an indication of likely rates of Calorie expenditure during a variety of different activities.

Walking upstairs: 800 Calories per hour

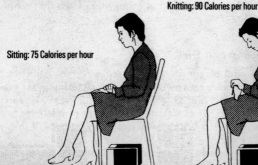

Knitting: 90 Calories per hour

Sitting: 75 Calories per hour

H21-25

H21 Nature and Nutrition

Carbohydrates, proteins, fats, minerals, vitamins, and water are all ingredients of a healthy diet. Some aspects of diet planning require special attention, but generally speaking nature is an excellent nutritionist — letting us know what our bodies require. Moreover, in developed countries, where different nutrients are readily available, most people eat more than enough different types of food to prevent any serious nutritional deficiencies.

H22 Fats and Diet

Fats form an important part of a balanced diet. But medical research into heart disease suggests that many people should take greater care over what type of fats they eat.

There are two basic types of fats — saturated and polyunsaturated. Saturated fats harden at room temperature. They occur in meat and dairy products; many solid shortening products; and also coconut oil, cocoa butter, and palm oil, which are used in many bought cookies and pastries. Medical research has shown a relationship between consumption of saturated fats and high levels of cholesterol (itself a special kind of fat) in the blood. High blood cholesterol levels are in turn associated with certain types of heart disease.

Polyunsaturated fats are most commonly consumed in the form of liquid vegetable oils (such as corn and soybean oils). Fats of this type apparently do not result in raised blood cholesterol levels. In fact, some authorities think that eating polyunsaturated fats can counteract the effect of eating other foods that are high in cholesterol.

H23 Protein and Diet

Protein is vital to growth and cell repair — yet estimates of protein needs vary enormously. An average estimate for good nutrition is about $2\frac{1}{2}$oz (70g) a day in adulthood (with protein supplying about 7% of Calorie intake). But people have been found to adapt in a healthy way to intakes under half to over twice this amount.

All this is dependent, of course, on all essential amino acids being eaten, and in the right proportions. Lack of protein can

Nutrition

be a problem in old people with little money, and in those following unusual diets.

H24 Carbohydrate and Diet

Too much carbohydrate in the diet shows itself in unhealthy weight gain. It is not, however, only the quantity of carbohydrate intake that is important. The type of carbohydrate eaten is also significant.

Traditional cereal products, such as bread and potatoes, contain other nutrients as well as carbohydrates and so can make an important contribution to total diet planning.

The current widespread replacement of traditional carbohydrate foods by highly refined and sweetened carbohydrate products has serious implications. Pastries, cakes, chocolate, ice cream, and alcohol all have high carbohydrate counts but contain little of nutritional value apart from their energy content. They provide little or no roughage.

Most important, however, are the harmful effects of too much sugar in the diet. Some scientists believe:

a) that the rush of sugar into the bloodstream causes the body to overreact — withdrawing too much sugar from the blood and so leaving us feeling tired and irritable;

b) that eventually excessive sugar intake can cause diabetes in people who would not otherwise suffer from it; and

c) that sugar has a role in producing heart disease.

Certainly sugar promotes tooth decay and destroys the appetite for more nutritious foods.

Such criticisms apply not only to white sugar, but also to brown sugar, raw sugar, honey, and molasses. But white sugar is the main culprit, simply because the amounts of sugar added in the cooking or processing of foods usually dwarf the amounts of sweetening added at mealtime.

H25 Water Requirement

The normal requirement is the equivalent of about 6 or 7 glasses of fluid a day. Thirst usually provides a very accurate indication of need, but in very hot conditions may not keep up with the intake needed to replace perspiration loss.

H26-29

H26 Minerals and Diet

Most of the body's mineral requirements are met without special diet planning. Some care, however, is needed in the following cases.

a) Sodium intake is usually far higher than necessary, but may be insufficient for very heavy work in hot conditions.

b) Calcium intake depends on ordinary consumption of milk and cheese.

c) Iron is needed for the hemoglobin in red blood cells. It is found in meat and eggs, brewer's yeast, and wheat germ. But it is only absorbed in tiny quantities, and hardly at all if vitamin C in the body is low. Women, with their regular menstrual blood loss, often develop an iron shortage (anemia), with resulting fatigue and breathlessness.

d) Iodine shortage occurs if the diet contains no seafood and only vegetables grown in iodine-free soil. A lack of iodine causes thyroid deficiencies and thyroid gland enlargement. This is less common with modern food transport and availability of iodized salt.

H27 Vitamins and Diet

Vitamins B_1 and C can by lost by bad cooking, but both have plenty of uncooked sources.

Vitamin A may be deficient if dairy produce, margarine, or green or yellow vegetables are not eaten.

Vitamin D is only much needed in the diets of children and nursing mothers. Butter, margarine, and liver are sources. Vitamin D deficiency has been found in children in poor urban areas — especially those with pigmented skin, which impedes the vitamin's formation in the body from sunlight. It can also occur in the aged and housebound poor.

H28 Excess and Deficiency

In diet planning, it is important to look at the diet as a whole. An excess of one nutrient will not compensate for a deficiency of another.

ENOUGH IS ENOUGH

Enough is enough; more is not better. You probably know that too many Calories are not good for you. But other excesses are harmful, or just useless, too.

Nutrition

It is no use eating protein above your needs: it cannot be stored. Too much of certain minerals or vitamins can cause deficiencies in others, by upsetting their absorption or storage. For example, too much B_1 can cause deficiencies in other B vitamins. And some nutrients taken in excess are positively harmful. People have killed themselves, for example, trying to get enough vitamin A and D and taking far too much. Both these vitamins are insoluble in water, and so the excess cannot just be excreted as can an excess of vitamin C. (In fact, vitamin C is the only nutrient that some scientists think may be useful to us in enormous doses — and there is far from agreement on this point.)

INTERACTION OF NUTRIENTS

Nutrients do not act totally independently of one another. The body is too complex for that. A deficiency of one nutrient can lead to a deficiency of another by affecting the body's ability to make use of the second nutrient, even if it is present in the diet.

For example, vitamin A deficiency can lead to vitamin C deficiency; vitamin C deficiency to iron deficiency.

Interactions occur not only among vitamins, and between vitamins and minerals, but also between vitamins and proteins, vitamins and carbohydrates, vitamins and fats; and there are many multiple relationships as well.

H29 Food not Nutrients

Some people set out to eat quantities of "nutrients" and build up the "perfect diet." But you cannot buy every dietary ingredient in an individual package. You have to buy food; and food is a jumble of hard-to-measure ingredients. Even drinking a glass of milk becomes a nightmare of protein, calcium, fat, carbohydrate, vitamin A, vitamin D, riboflavin, and phosphorus — together with a few other things. And if that seems too simple — what was the fat content of that hot dog? or the protein content of that lobster thermidor? Start eating for nutrients, and you will probably eat twice as much as you need to. Start buying for nutrients, and you will be trying to get, for example, your daily vitamin C out of a handful of rosehips, rather than from a morning glass of orange juice, some lunchtime potatoes, and a helping of cabbage in the evening. The search for nutrients is an excellent way of wasting time and money.

H30-32

H30 A Healthy Diet

There is no one ideal diet. First, needs differ (and so does the impact of availability, cost, taste, habit, and cooking facilities and skills).

But, more important, there are a million different ways of satisfying those needs, in healthy eating. It is possible to live healthily on a diet of milk, whole-wheat bread, and green vegetables. It would not be very interesting, though. Variety is the spice of food.

H31 Processing and Cooking

It is hard to generalize, but the more processed a food is, the less desirable it is likely to be as a regular part of a healthy diet. Canned and precooked foods, mass-produced breakfast cereals, cookies, pastries, and ready-made meals, all tend to be open to criticism. Defects include:

a) lower nutritional value;
b) added sugar and saturated fats;
c) added preservative chemicals and, often, untested colorings and flavorings; and sometimes
d) unhygienic production.

In general, the "whole food" movement is a sensible one (though, incidentally, there is no agreed evidence that "organic" vegetables have higher food value than chemically fertilized ones — even though they may taste better and contain fewer pollutants). However, nutrients can be lost in home cooking as well as in processing, and undesirable ones added. "Boiling" of vegetables should always be done by steaming in a very shallow amount of water, if vitamin C is to be preserved. (Salt should only be added at the last moment.) "Frying" should be in a tiny amount of unsaturated oil, not hard fat. (Broiling is better, where applicable.)

H32 Daily Food Guide

Included here is a daily food guide devised by a dietitian to provide a balanced diet. (Those suffering from certain illnesses, such as diabetes, may need a more carefully planned diet, about which a physician should be consulted.)

The guide divides foods into four groups, and recommended daily servings per person are given for each group.

Nutrition

NOTES
1) Group A uses 1 cup whole or skimmed milk as the basic measure. Alternatives are: 1 cup buttermilk; ½ cup evaporated milk; ¼ cup nonfat milk powder; 1oz cheddar cheese; 1½ cups cottage cheese.
2) If amounts in group A are doubled in the course of the day, not more than one serving of group C is needed.
3) Whole milk (not skimmed) and butter or margarine should be used during childhood, pregnancy, and lactation.

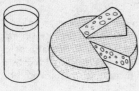

A: MILK AND CHEESE
Age 0-9 years: 2-3 cups
9-12 years: 3 or more cups
13-19 years: 4 or more cups
Adult: 2 or more cups
Pregnancy: 3 or more cups
Lactation: 4 or more cups

B: FRUIT AND VEGETABLES
Four or more servings.
Serving size examples:
a ½ cup dark green or deep yellow vegetable (served at least every other day);
b ½ cup or 1 medium-sized raw fruit or vegetable rich in vitamin C;
c 1 medium potato.

C: MEAT AND PULSES
Two or more servings.
Serving size examples:
a 2-3oz cooked meat, poultry, or fish (excluding bone and fat);
b 2 eggs;
c 1 cup beans, peas, or lentils;
d 4 tablespoons of peanut butter.

D: BREAD AND CEREALS
Four or more servings.
Serving size examples:
a 1 slice bread;
b 1 cup ready-to-eat cereal;
c ½ to ¾ cup cooked ceeal, macaroni, spaghetti, hominy grits, rice, noodles, or bulgur.

H33-36

H33 Vegetarianism

A vegetarian is a person who does not eat the meat of any mammal, bird, or fish. There are two main types of vegetarian:
a) vegans, who eat nothing at all of animal origins, and
b) lacto-ovo-vegetarians, who do allow themselves animal products such as milk, cheese, eggs, and honey.
There are also people who call themselves vegetarians but do eat fish.

H34 Reasons for Vegetarianism

Reasons for vegetarianism vary from society to society and individual to individual. It has been advocated for religious, philosophical, moral, economic, and health reasons. It has also been adopted as a necessity. Many primitive peoples have lived on a diet of fruit, nuts, and berries, with meat only when it could be obtained.

Perhaps the most powerful arguments for vegetarianism in modern society are:
a) the inefficiency of the animal food production chain (H02) in a largely underfed world;
b) the relative cheapness of the ingredients of vegetarian diet; and
c) the possible unhealthiness of eating meat that contains crop pesticides and antibiotics and hormones given to the animals, and that has been processed in many ways that are not necessarily hygienic or beneficial.

Also, many people feel that the slaughter of animals is cruel and debasing, and that vegetarianism is part of a more peaceful and harmonious way of life.

H35 Vegetarian Diet

Despite the claims of vegetarians, there is no established evidence that eating meat is unhealthy in itself. But it is certainly as possible for a vegetarian to be healthy, strong, and long-lived as it is for a meat-eater.

A person who chooses to give up meat must be careful that his diet still provides enough of the right nutrients.

There are no problems with:
a) healthy carbohydrates (grains, cereal products, potatoes, fruits);

Nutrition

b)fats (vegetable oils, dairy products, nuts, margarine); and
c) minerals and most vitamins (vegetables and fruits).
Obtaining an adequate supply of protein and certain vitamins
can, however, be more problematic for vegetarians than for
meat-eaters (see "Diet planning," H36).

H36 Diet Planning

Vegetarians must take particular care that their diet provides
them with adequate supplies of the following nutrients.
PROTEIN is readily available from eggs and dairy produce,
nuts, soybeans, raisins, grains and pulses. But a vegetarian
should be sure to get a good selection of essential amino acids at
each meal.
This is not difficult where eggs or dairy produce are eaten:
cereal and milk, bread and milk, and bread and eggs are all
good amino acid combinations. But vegans must depend on
soybeans, or on carefully planned vegetable combinations.
These include: lentil soup and hard whole-wheat bread; and
beans and rice.
VITAMINS requiring particular attention in a vegetarian diet
are:
1) cobalamin (vitamin B_{12}) — available from dairy produce and
yeast and, particularly useful for vegans, in synthetic form;
2) vitamin D — also needed in synthetic form by vegans where
sunlight is insufficient.
IRON AND CALCIUM are also worth mentioning, as they are
sometimes lacking even in the diets of meat-eaters. In fact, there
are many excellent vegetarian sources.
Iron is found in raisins, lentils, wheat germ, prunes, spinach
and other leafy vegetables, and in bread, eggs, and yeast.
Calcium occurs in dairy produce, dried fruit, soybeans, sesame
seeds, and in leafy vegetables.

$1\frac{1}{2}$ cups beans + 4 cups rice = protein equivalent of 12oz
(340g) steak

H37-38

H37 Are You Overweight?

It is not always easy to say whether a person is overweight. But there is no doubt that weight problems are on the increase in modern industrial society.

One way of learning whether you are among the overweight is to check your weight against a desirable weight table — such as the one given in H39. (Note that "desirable" weight tables give lower figures than "average" weight tables — in a society where

H38 Why People Put on Weight

Overweight is always caused by taking in more food energy than the body uses up. The bulk of food energy is taken in in the form of carbohydrates and fats. Both these supply Calories (the measure of energy); and both are converted to fat deposits if the Calories they supply are more than the body uses. The diagram shows what happens to the food energy input.

a Most of it is used to supply body energy needs — to maintain basic life processes and for all physical activity (H19-H20).

b It is still the subject of scientific controversy, but it does seem

Energy taken in as food

Excess Weight

more people are overweight than underweight, the average will be higher than is healthy.)

Even without weighing yourself, it is possible to do a quick check for overweight. Start by asking yourself the following questions. Do you have any telltale bulges? Do you look much fatter than you used to? Have your measurements increased appreciably? If you pinch your upper arm, thigh, or midriff, is there more than 1 in (2.5cm) of flesh between your thumb and forefinger?

that some people get rid of surplus input because their bodies automatically speed up their metabolism and burn up the surplus rather than store it. This burning up process is called "thermogenesis." Also, there is a rise in the body's metabolism after every meal. So two people may eat exactly the same, but one will burn up more than the other if the food is taken in several small meals rather than two or three large ones.

c Food energy that is neither needed nor burned up is stored by the body in the form of fat. In overweight people the store far exceeds any normal future demand.

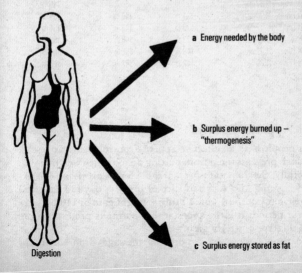

a Energy needed by the body

b Surplus energy burned up – "thermogenesis"

c Surplus energy stored as fat

Digestion

H39-41

H39 Desirable Weights

Desirable weight tables are based on statistics, usually collected by insurance companies, showing the correlation between different weights and health standards. The table included here shows desirable weights, according to height and body size, for women aged 25. Older women can expect to exceed these weights, but at age 45, for example, probably should not be much more than 12 to 18lb (5.4-8.16kg) over the weights given for age 25.

Height		Small frame	Medium frame	Large frame
4ft 9in	(1.45m)	98 lb	104 lb	114 lb
4ft 10in	(1.47m)	100 lb	107 lb	117 lb
4ft 11in	(1.49m)	103 lb	110 lb	120 lb
5ft 0in	(1.52m)	106 lb	113 lb	123 lb
5ft 1in	(1.54m)	109 lb	116 lb	126 lb
5ft 2in	(1.57m)	112 lb	120 lb	130 lb
5ft 3in	(1.60m)	115 lb	124 lb	134 lb
5ft 4in	(1.62m)	119 lb	128 lb	138 lb
5ft 5in	(1.65m)	123 lb	132 lb	142 lb
5ft 6in	(1.67m)	127 lb	136 lb	146 lb
5ft 7in	(1.70m)	131 lb	140 lb	150 lb
5ft 8in	(1.72m)	135 lb	144 lb	154 lb
5ft 9in	(1.75m)	139 lb	148 lb	159 lb
5ft 10in	(1.77m)	143 lb	152 lb	164 lb
5ft 11in	(1.80m)	147 lb	157 lb	169 lb

H40 Appetite Control

Most people have an effective appetite control — or "appestat" — which prevents them from putting on too much weight.

Generally, the appestat is remarkable for its precision. For example, eating an extra half slice of bread a day (30 Calories) above energy output, would bring a weight gain of 110lb over a 40-year period. It is the appestat that normally protects people from this type of weight gain.

Some people, however, ignore the messages from their appestats.

Excess Weight

Typical reasons are:

a) social habit or custom;

b) excessive love of food in general or of certain foods in particular;

c) habits of overeating acquired during childhood;

d) lack of exercise (see H41); and

e) eating for psychological support, whether as a general addiction or as response to shock or stress (for psychological aspects, see K20).

H41 Appetite and Exercise

Some people put on weight because their appestat (see H40) is put out of action by an excessively sedentary existence.

When physical activity falls below moderate levels, research has shown that appetite may actually increase — even though the body has no need for the extra food. Increasing the amount of exercise in such cases not only increases Calorie output, but also appears to put the appestat back into good working order.

Of course, exercise above moderate levels will increase the appetite.

H42-44

H42 When People Put On Weight

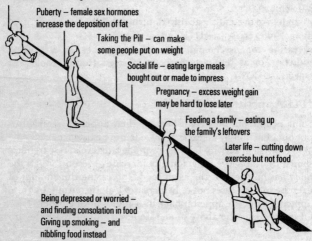

Childhood – overweight children
often become overweight adults

Puberty – female sex hormones
increase the deposition of fat

Taking the Pill – can make
some people put on weight

Social life – eating large meals
bought out or made to impress

Pregnancy – excess weight gain
may be hard to lose later

Feeding a family – eating up
the family's leftovers

Later life – cutting down
exercise but not food

Being depressed or worried –
and finding consolation in food
Giving up smoking – and
nibbling food instead

Excess Weight

H43 Excuses for Overweight

Many overweight people like to blame something outside their control — their heavy bones, heavy family, hormones, even their body water level. But:

a) variations in bone density cannot account for more than about 7lb weight difference;

b) though overweight does "run in families," it may be due more to acquired eating habits than genetic factors;

c) hormonal malfunctions can cause obesity, in very rare cases, but these show themselves clearly in other bodily symptoms; and

d) the body water level is very well regulated except in very hot weather and in some illnesses.

H44 Effects of Overweight

Overweight people are not just more tired, short of breath, and physically and mentally lethargic, with aching joints and poor digestion. They are also more likely to suffer from high blood pressure, heart disease, diabetes, kidney disorders, cirrhosis of the liver, pneumonia, inflammation of the gall bladder, arthritis, hernias, and varicose veins. They have more accidents, are more likely to die during operations, and have higher rates of mortality in general (including 3 times the mortality from heart and circulatory disease).

Some of these effects arise from mechanical causes: the burden of extra weight and its particular location as fat deposits. Others arise chemically, from the need to supply more body tissue than normal. For example, the spread of hormones over increased body tissue is sometimes a cause of infertility. It can also cause serious problems in pregnancy (eg toxemia, see D22). In many cases, reduction to desirable weight removes all the symptoms of disorder and results in increased life expectancy.

H45-47

H45 Losing Weight

Losing weight is not easy. It demands controlled eating habits, discipline, patience, and a change of attitudes. Before you start:
a) do not be tempted by any promise of easy weight loss — there are no miracles;
b) adopt a definite diet plan and stick to it;
c) if you need advice, get it from your doctor.
It is best to aim to lose weight steadily over a long period. Constant yo-yo weight changes are as bad for you as being overweight. Once weight is lost, keep a constant check, and deal with small gains as they occur.

H46 Choosing a Diet Plan

All genuine diets restrict Calorie intake. If a person's intake of food does not contain sufficient Calories to meet energy requirements, the body makes up the deficiency by burning up its stores of fat.
Three basic types of diet plan are popular at the present time. Each of them can work if you are sufficiently determined.
a) Low-Calorie plans set a numerical limit to daily Calorie intake (usually 1,000 to 1,500 Calories). Constant reference must be made to Calorie tables.
b) Low-carbohydrate plans also cut down Calorie intake, but only by reducing consumption of carbohydrates. Tables are simpler than for low-Calorie plans. Fat is unrestricted, making the diet more palatable and socially acceptable. Weight maintenance through excessive consumption of fats does not appear to occur in practice.
(A good example of a low-carbohydrate plan is described in H48.)
c) No-count plans, simplified versions of the low-carbohydrate system, divide food into three categories: high-carbohydrate food that must be avoided; high-Calorie, noncarbohydrate food that can be eaten in moderation; and unrestricted food.

Losing Weight

H47 Slimming Aids

A considerable variety of slimming aids is widely available —
but not all of them are effective or recommended.

a) Substitute meals (wafers, chocolate bars, packaged foods,
etc) have a stated Calorie content and sometimes contain
cellulose to give a fuller feeling in the stomach. Some
slimmers find them useful, but they do nothing to encourage
the eating habits needed to stay slim.

b) Low-Calorie substitute foods and drinks (eg skim milk,
slimmers' bread, crispbread) can help slimmers reduce
total Calorie intake.

c) Prescribed drugs (Apisate, Tennate) can reduce appetite.
These new drugs do not seem to be addictive, but do nothing
to encourage good eating habits.

d) Proprietary slimming pills usually contain cellulose and are
meant to suppress appetite. Amounts are so small that their
effectiveness is probably more psychological than real.

e) Saunas, Turkish baths, and reducing garments cause loss of
body water through sweating. This can reduce measurements and weight, but the effect is rapidly cancelled out
by the drinking needed to replace the fluid loss.

f) Vibrator belts and other massagers are meant to break down
fat deposits. There appears to be little evidence to support
claims made for them.

g) Machines using electric impulses to relax and contract
muscles are recommended by some slimmers.

h) Exercise will not on its own make much difference to your
weight. It would, for example, take 12 hours of tennis to lose
1lb of fat. Exercise does, however, increase the sense of well-
being that dieting brings (also see H41).

i) Attending a slimming clinic can be an effective — though
expensive — way of getting slim.

j) Many slimmers find that joining a slimming club gives a
valuable psychological boost.

H48

H48 Carbohydrate Unit Diet

The Carbohydrate Unit diet was devised by Professor John Yudkin, MD, and is described in detail in his book *Lose weight, feel great!* (published by Larchmont Press, NY, 1974). The following tables form the basis of the diet. Meat, poultry, fish, eggs, cheese, tea, coffee, butter, margarine, and fat are all zero units: eat as much as you like. Try a limit of 15 CUs a day. Lower to 10 if necessary, or raise to 20 or even 30 if weight loss is too rapid. Each day get two helpings from each of these groups:

DAIRY		CUs
Rice pudding	4oz	5
Fruit yogurt	6oz	2
Milk	½pt	3
Custard	4oz	2
Plain yogurt	5oz	2
Cottage cheese	2oz	½
Cream	1oz	0

CEREALS		CUs
Macaroni	6oz	10
Spaghetti	6oz	10
Noodles	6oz	9
Vermicelli	6oz	9
Roll	2oz	6
Breakfast cereals	¾oz	4
Buckwheat	3oz	4
Wheat flour	1oz	4
Rice	4oz	4
Semolina	1oz	4
Bread, 1 slice	1oz	3
Wheatgerm	½oz	1½
Roll, starch-reduced	1oz	½

VEGETABLES		CUs
Lentils	4oz	6
Sweet potato	3oz	5
Butter beans	4oz	4
Corn, 1 cob	4oz	4
Yam	4oz	4
Potatoes	3oz	3
Fried potatoes	1oz	3
Parsnip	4oz	2
Peas	4oz	2
Artichoke	5oz	1
Asparagus	4oz	1
Green beans	4oz	1
Beet	2oz	1
Carrot	3oz	1
Kohlrabi	4oz	1
Leeks	4oz	1
Swede	4oz	1
Turnip	3oz	1
Cauliflower	4oz	½
Cabbage, celery, chicory, cucumber, squash, mushrooms, onion		0

Losing Weight

a) milk and cheese;
b) meat, fish, eggs;
c) fruit and vegetables;
d) butter, margarine.
Drink at least ½pt of milk a day.
Note that sorbitol is not allowed.
The plan forms a very sensible basis for future healthy eating.
Typical portions are indicated for each item.

FRUITS		CUs	SWEETS, SAUCES, SOUPS		CUs	DRINKS		CUs
Banana, 1	4oz	5	Cake, fruit, iced	2oz	8	Cider	½pt	7
Dates	1oz	4	Apple pie	4oz	7	Beer, heavy	½pt	7
Raisins	1oz	4	Cake	2oz	7	Chocolate	8oz	6
White raisins	1oz	4	Doughnut	2oz	6	Beer, light	½pt	5
Cherries	4oz	3	Glucose	2oz	6	Lemonade	8oz	5
Figs, dried	1oz	3	Chocolate	2oz	5	Liqueurs	1oz	5
Grapes	4oz	3	Honey	1oz	5	Vermouth, sweet	2oz	5
Orange, 1	6oz	3	Mince pie	2oz	5	Port	2oz	4½
Pear, 1	5oz	2½	Fruit in syrup	4oz	5	Apple juice	8oz	4
Apple, 1	4oz	2	Molasses	1oz	4	Bitter lemon	6oz	4
Apricots, dried	1oz	2	Pancakes	2oz	4	Brandy	1oz	4
Melon	6oz	2	Candies	1oz	4	Gin	1oz	4
Peach, 1	4oz	2	Cookies	2 small	3	Lager	½pt	4
Pineapple, raw	4oz	2	Ice cream	1oz	3	Sherry	2oz	4
Plums	4oz	2	Sugar, white, brown	½oz	3	Wine, sweet	3oz	4
Raspberries	4oz	2	Cranberry sauce	1oz	2½	Whiskey	1oz	4
Strawberries	4oz	1½	Syrup	½oz	2½	Coca Cola	6oz	3
Apricot, 1	2oz	1	Jam	½oz	2	Fruit juices, sugared	5oz	3
Avocado, ½	3oz	1	Soups, various	8oz	0-2	Vermouth, dry	2oz	3
Grapefruit, ½	4oz	1	Peanut butter	1oz	1	Wine, dry	3oz	3
Prunes	1oz	1	Cocoa	1 tsp	1	Tomato juice	5oz	1
Tomato	1oz	1	Mayonnaise	½oz	0	Coffee, black	1 cup	0
Rhubarb	4oz	0	Salad dressing	½oz	0	Tea, clear	1 cup	0

Jo1

J01 Self-Help

The self-help movement is a recent development in the history of health care. For years women have remained ignorant of their bodies and bodily functions, and unfortunately the medical profession has done little to discourage this. Women have relied heavily on doctors for both diagnosis and treatment, but many now want to take responsibility for their bodies and to play an increasingly active part in keeping themselves healthy. As a result of this, women in many areas are now forming self-help groups where they can meet to discuss health care, sexuality, and other matters.

Many women are anxious about overdependence on drug-based treatments which deal with the symptoms but do not always tackle the cause. Resulting from this is a growing interest in branches of alternative medicine such as acupuncture (see J07).

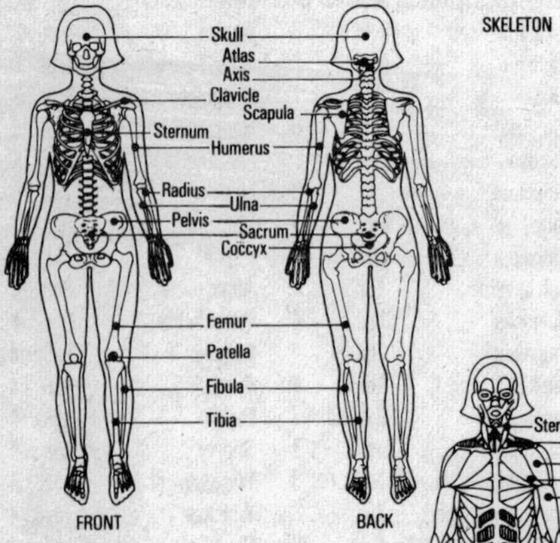

SKELETON

Skull
Atlas
Axis
Clavicle
Scapula
Sternum
Humerus
Radius
Ulna
Pelvis
Sacrum
Coccyx

Femur
Patella
Fibula
Tibia

FRONT   BACK

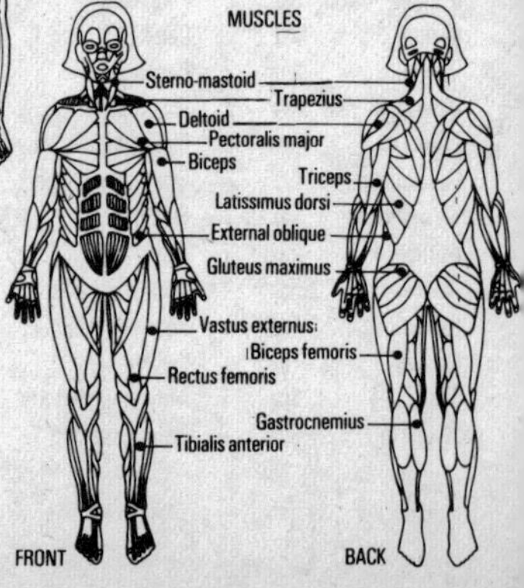

MUSCLES

Sterno-mastoid
Trapezius
Deltoid
Pectoralis major
Biceps
Triceps
Latissimus dorsi
External oblique
Gluteus maximus

Vastus externus
Biceps femoris
Rectus femoris
Gastrocnemius
Tibialis anterior

FRONT   BACK

Know Your Body

Health care and self-examination (see J02) are not just for eccentrics; if a woman really gets to know her body, she can spot any changes as they arise and get the help she needs to check up on them. She is not rejecting medical care: she is simply playing a greater part in the care of her own body. There are many measures a woman can take to establish a personal health care program.

She can ensure that she gets sufficient rest and exercise (see J08 for details of suitable exercises) and that her diet is healthy.

Above all, a woman can start to familiarize herself with her body and how it works. The simple anatomical diagrams on this page will help, and the techniques of self-examination, described in J02, will do much to increase a woman's confidence in her ability to take care of herself.

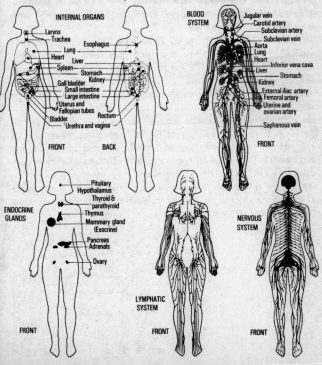

INTERNAL ORGANS

Larynx
Trachea
Esophagus
Lung
Heart
Liver
Spleen
Stomach
Gall bladder
Kidney
Small intestine
Large intestine
Uterus and
Fallopian tubes
Rectum
Bladder
Urethra and vagina

FRONT   BACK

BLOOD SYSTEM

Jugular vein
Carotid artery
Subclavian artery
Subclavian vein
Aorta
Lung
Heart
Inferior vena cava
Liver
Stomach
Kidney
External iliac artery
Femoral artery
Uterine and ovarian artery
Saphenous vein

FRONT

ENDOCRINE GLANDS

Pituitary
Hypothalamus
Thyroid & parathyroid
Thymus
Mammary gland (Exocrine)
Pancreas
Adrenals
Ovary

FRONT

LYMPHATIC SYSTEM

FRONT

NERVOUS SYSTEM

FRONT

J02

J02 Using a Speculum

A SPECULUM, the instrument used to examine the female internal reproductive organs, consists of two rounded metal or Lucite "blades" which can be separated once inserted into the vagina to give a clear view of the cervix and vaginal walls.

INSERTING THE SPECULUM is painless if the woman is relaxed. Before attempting insertion, she should familiarize herself with how it works. Next, she should arrange a mirror beneath the vulva and direct a light against it so that the internal organs will be clearly visible to the woman herself. The woman should then gently insert the speculum, blades closed, like a tampon. Lubricating cream facilitates insertion. When the speculum is fully inserted, with the handle pointing up, the blades are opened and locked in position. When the examination is over, the speculum is removed with the blades in the closed position.

WHEN THE SPECULUM IS INSERTED the cervix is clearly visible as a smooth, pink, domelike protrusion at the upper end of the vagina. In the center is the os, the opening to the uterus. The size and color of the cervix are affected by the woman's age, the stage in her menstrual cycle, and whether she has had children.

At each examination, the woman should note details of the cervix, os, vaginal walls, and vaginal secretions (and also of the vulva). In this way she will establish what is normal for her, and will be able to recognize any changes as they occur, and seek medical advice if necessary.

This does not mean that a woman should not go for regular checks by a doctor or clinic; trained examinations and tests (eg "Pap" smears) are also essential.

Self-examination

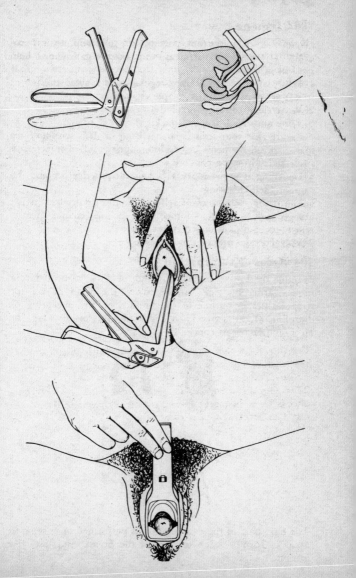

J03-04

J03 Hygiene

Hygiene is an important part of any self-help health program. There are several measures a woman can take to help prevent infection.

1 Wash vulva and anal area regularly, and avoid the use of irritating soaps and other people's towels.

2 Wear clean cotton pants daily.

3 Wipe anus from front to back.

4 Ensure that your sexual partner is clean. It is sensible for a man to wash his penis before intercourse, and, if infection is suspected, to wear a condom.

5 Douching is unnecessary as a general practice because the vagina is self-cleansing.

6 Learn the techniques of self-examination described in J02 and consult a doctor immediately if any change in the reproductive organs or secretions is noted.

7 Vulval deodorants are unnecessary.

J04 Breast Examination

Examine the breasts regularly for lumps. First, stand before a mirror arms by side, undressed to the waist. Look for irregularities in outline of the breasts, or any puckering or dimpling of the skin. Then check nipples for discharge or bleeding (see breast cancer L44).

The next part of the examination is performed on 5 separate areas in turn — each quarter of the breast, and lastly the armpit.

Self-examination

1 Lie on bed, folded towel under
right shoulder, right arm behind
head. With flat of fingers, feel
upper, outer quarter of right breast.
2 Repeat on lower, inner quarter.
3 Bring right arm to side, and
examine lower, outer quarter.
4 Repeat on upper, outer quarter
and area between breasts and armpit.
5 Examine armpit.
6 Move towel under left shoulder,
and repeat the examination on the
left breast.

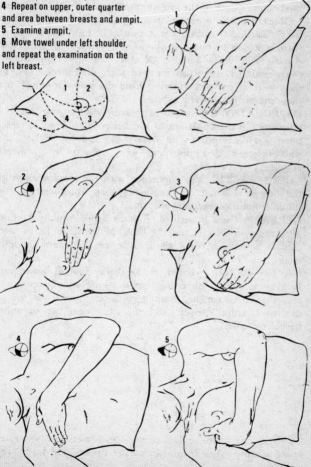

J05-06

J05 Alternative Treatments

An increasing interest in preventive medicine and self-help, combined with a growing reluctance to rely on the predominantly drug-based treatments of orthodox medicine, has led many women to explore the possibilities of "alternative medicines." Some of the most important are described below.

HOMEOPATHY operates on the principle that "like cures like." Particular substances produce certain symptoms — such as a rash or raised temperature — in a healthy person. Almost 200 years ago, a German, Samuel Hahnemann, discovered that small amounts of such substances could be used to treat patients suffering from the very symptoms that these substances would produce.

OSTEOPATHY is a system of treating disease based on the massage and manipulation of the bones. This form of treatment was developed by an American, Andrew Taylor Still, who believed that disorders were caused by incorrect alignment of the bones.

CHIROPRACTIC, also concerned with the manipulation of the bones, is based on the theory that adjustment of the spinal column cures many ailments.

HERBALISM is a branch of "folk medicine" rapidly gaining acceptance in Europe and the USA. Many of the herbs used contain substances, eg digitalis, now used in many modern drugs.

NATUROPATHY is based on the theory that ill health can be avoided by hygienic living, and is a program of prevention rather than treatment. Among its recommendations are a diet of "natural" foods, and the occasional use of some herbal remedies.

Alternative Treatments

J06 Massage

Massage — the manipulation of muscles or other parts of the body — has long been used in the treatment of various joint injuries. But apart from its purely medical aspect, massage is also used, with great effect, as a means of relieving body tension and aiding relaxation.

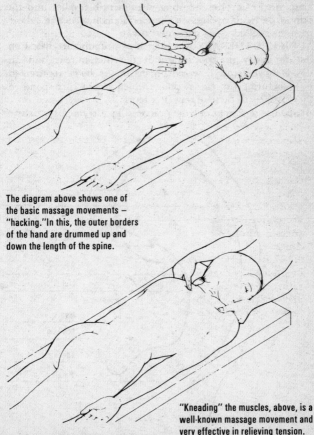

The diagram above shows one of the basic massage movements — "hacking." In this, the outer borders of the hand are drummed up and down the length of the spine.

"Kneading" the muscles, above, is a well-known massage movement and very effective in relieving tension.

J07

J07 Acupuncture

Acupuncture is an ancient Chinese system of healing. It is based on the theory that good health depends on the correct balance between the two energy forces within the body — Yin and Yang. These energies are thought to flow through the body along "meridians" (see right). The practice of acupuncture involves inserting acupuncture needles into the skin at particular points on the meridians in order to relieve pain, or swelling, in a particular organ.

AURICULOTHERAPY is a branch of acupuncture based on the similarity in appearance of the human ear and an upside-down fetus. Diseased organs in the body are treated by puncturing the ear at points which would correspond to the positions of these organs in a fetus.

Acupuncture should only be practiced by a trained specialist.

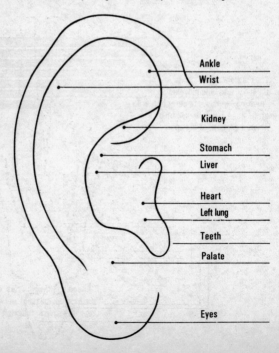

Ankle
Wrist

Kidney

Stomach
Liver

Heart
Left lung

Teeth
Palate

Eyes

Alternative Treatments

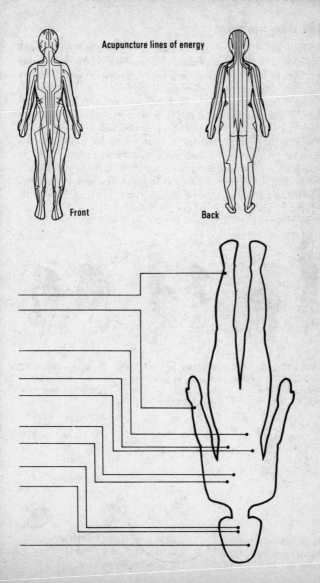

Acupuncture lines of energy

Front

Back

J08

J08 Keeping Fit

A daily exercise program — even a gentle one — can work wonders for almost everyone. Automobiles and labor-saving equipment have made our lives easier in many respects, but by reducing general levels of physical exercise, they have helped produce a population that is chronically unfit. A body that is short of exercise is stale, sluggish, and generally inefficient. But the situation can be remedied — easily, and even enjoyably. There is no need to embark at once on an intensely vigorous exercise program — indeed, such a course of action would be positively unwise for most people today. Exercising regularly is the real key to improving fitness levels. A few simple exercises — such as those described here — can prove dramatically effective if they are carried out every day.

Stand feet apart — raise arms above head — bend and touch ground between feet.

Stand feet together — grasp raised leg by knee and shin — stand — repeat with other leg.

Stand feet apart, hands to sides — side bend to left — repeat with bend to right.

Large circles with left arm, forward then back — repeat using right arm.

Sit on floor grasping knees — bring knees toward chin and rock back — hold for 5 seconds.

Keeping Fit

Lie face down, arms by sides, legs together — raise upper body and legs into position shown.

Lie on back, knees bent, feet on floor, arms back — swing arms forward to sit and touch toes.

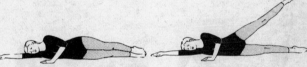

Lie on side in position shown — raise one leg — legs together — roll onto other side and repeat.

Lie face down with hands under shoulders — push body off floor, keeping knees on the floor.

Lie on back, legs together, arms by sides, palms down — raise leg — lower leg — repeat with other leg.

J09

J09 Yoga

Many thousands of women are now discovering the physical and mental benefits to be gained from the pursuit of yoga. This ancient discipline, developed in the East over thousands of years, has in recent decades won many enthusiastic followers in North American and European countries. Illustrated on these two pages are representative examples of popular yoga postures. Combined with breathing control, the attainment of such postures acts to produce deep levels of relaxation in both body and mind. Because of the precise nature of yoga postures, potential students are strongly recommended to attend classes to ensure that all postures are correctly learned. Hard work and dedication are essential for the serious yoga student, but the results will prove well worth the effort.

Examples of standing yoga postures

1 Stand erect, feet together, with weight on both feet **2** Feet apart, legs straight, arms stretched, side bent to clasp ankle **3** Similar to 2 but with one arm above head and one knee bent **4** Feet apart, legs straight, hands behind back, head touching leg

5 Arms above head, one leg bent forward, other leg stretched behind **6** Similar to 5 but with body turned to side and arms outstretched **7** Feet together, legs straight, body bent, head touching legs, hands on floor behind feet **8** Stand on one leg, other leg bent to side, hands together

Yoga

Examples of sitting and resting yoga postures

1 Basic sitting posture **2** Sitting posture, legs raised straight and together, hands at back of head **3** Sitting, legs to side, back twisted, one hand behind back **4** Shoulder stand, back straight

5 Lying posture, arms straight by sides, hands palms down, feet touching floor beyond head. **6** Lying posture, arms straight behind head, hands palms up, feet touching floor beyond head **7** Resting posture, whole body relaxed – used with breathing exercises to end each session

A combination of yoga postures forming a short sequence

1 Stand, hands and feet together **2** Inhale, adopt posture shown **3** Exhale, adopt posture shown **4** Inhale, adopt posture shown **5** Exhale, adopt posture shown **6** Inhale, adopt posture shown **7** Exhale, return to first posture

Jıo

J10 The Facts of Rape

Rape is a violent, aggressive, and hostile crime, usually committed by men against women, but also against children and
sometimes against men. For many people, "rape" is "rape" only
if it is committed in a dark alley by a complete stranger; but as
these diagrams show, quite the reverse is true. (Figures are
taken from one of the few serious studies of rape in the USA,
Patterns of Forcible Rape by M. Amir — a useful book if read
carefully.)

Forcible rape against women is increasing — from 37,900
reported in the USA in 1970 to 55,200 reported in 1974. But
these figures probably account for only 10-20% of rapes which
actually occur.

PREVAILING ATTITUDES

The causes of rape and its treatment reflect society's attitudes
both to sex and women. In general society still regards women as
passive sex objects who, if they do not "belong" to a specific
man, secretly desire or invite rape, and either get what they
want or deserve what they get.

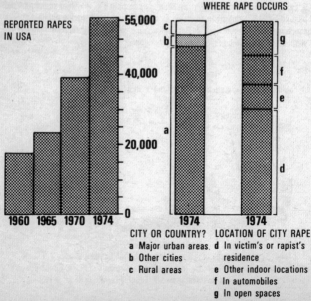

WHERE RAPE OCCURS

REPORTED RAPES
IN USA

55,000

40,000

20,000

0

1960 1965 1970 1974

1974

1974

CITY OR COUNTRY?
a Major urban areas
b Other cities
c Rural areas

LOCATION OF CITY RAPE
d In victim's or rapist's
  residence
e Other indoor locations
f In automobiles
g In open spaces

Rape: Facts and Myths

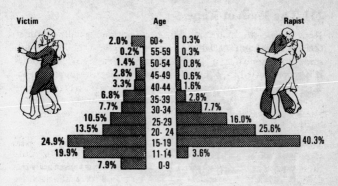

Victim	Age	Rapist
2.0%	60+	0.3%
0.2%	55-59	0.3%
1.4%	50-54	0.8%
2.8%	45-49	0.6%
3.3%	40-44	1.6%
6.8%	35-39	2.8%
7.7%	30-34	7.7%
10.5%	25-29	16.0%
13.5%	20- 24	25.6%
24.9%	15-19	40.3%
19.9%	11-14	3.6%
7.9%	0-9	

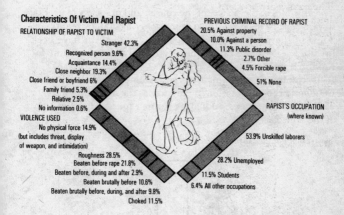

Characteristics Of Victim And Rapist

RELATIONSHIP OF RAPIST TO VICTIM
Stranger 42.3%
Recognized person 9.6%
Acquaintance 14.4%
Close neighbor 19.3%
Close friend or boyfriend 6%
Family friend 5.3%
Relative 2.5%
No information 0.6%

VIOLENCE USED
No physical force 14.9%
(but includes threat, display
of weapon, and intimidation)
Roughness 28.5%
Beaten before rape 21.8%
Beaten before, during and after 2.9%
Beaten brutally before 10.6%
Beaten brutally before, during, and after 9.8%
Choked 11.5%

PREVIOUS CRIMINAL RECORD OF RAPIST
20.5% Against property
10.0% Against a person
11.3% Public disorder
2.7% Other
4.5% Forcible rape

51% None

RAPIST'S OCCUPATION
(where known)

53.9% Unskilled laborers

28.2% Unemployed

11.5% Students
6.4% All other occupations

MARITAL STATUS OF VICTIM (rapes per 100,000 of the population in that category)

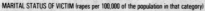
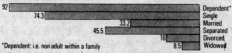

92	Dependent*
74.3	Single
33.2	Married
45.5	Separated
16	Divorced
8.5	Widowed

*Dependent: i.e. non adult within a family

J11

J11 The Myth of Rape

"RAPE IS MAINLY INTERRACIAL"

a **93%** Rapist/victim same race

b **4%** White rapist/black victim
c **3%** Black rapist/white victim

The attitudes of the police, of the courts, and of society in general toward rape have been formed more by myths than by reality.

Some of the myths are shown here. Many of them have been used to try to excuse rapists' behavior, and to lay the blame for rape on women.

It is commonly, but incorrectly, assumed that black men frequently rape white women. In fact, as the diagram shows, in 93% of the rape cases studied by Amir, rapist and victim were of the same race.

"WOMEN PROVOKE RAPE"

a **95.6%** Rape unprovoked

b **4.4%** Partly set off by
victim's behavior

Time and time again women are blamed for provoking rape, for leading men on, either by their appearance or their behavior. Again, studies show this to be incorrect. Only 4.4% of rapes are even partly sparked off by the victim's behavior — a lower rate than for homicide or even robbery.

Rape: Facts and Myths

"WOMEN CREATE DANGEROUS SITUATIONS"

a 47.8% Rape by
    "trustable" people

b 15.7% Rape by strangers
    encountered at home

c 36.5% All other rapes

It is often said that women invite rape by putting themselves into dangerous situations — by walking home alone, by hitch-hiking, by going alone to a bar. In fact, ⅔ of rapes could happen to a woman who never left home unless accompanied by someone she knew.

"RAPE IS SPONTANEOUS"

ALL RAPES
a 33% Planned single rapes

b 13% Planned pair rapes

c 24% Planned group rapes

d 30% Spontaneous rapes

Sexual aggressiveness in men is often excused by the myth of a spontaneous "uncontrollable" sex drive. In fact, most rapes are premeditated, whether they involve one attacker (**a**), two (**b**), or several (**c**). Altogether, 70% of rapes are premeditated.

UNFOUNDED ALLEGATIONS

It is often argued that many women use the accusation of rape simply for revenge purposes. But in the USA only 15% of rape charges are dismissed by police as "unfounded" — a technical term, often just meaning unsuitable for prosecution.

J12-14

J12 Legal Definition

Rape is typically defined as intercourse occurring forcibly and against the victim's will. (Statutory rape applies to those crimes of intercourse where the victim is judged incapable of consenting — eg being under age or mentally subnormal.) "Force" includes duress or intimidation, not necessarily physical violence. But the courts may require actual resistance by the victim to be proved — not just a refusal to consent.

RESISTANCE

The map below shows the degrees of resistance expected by the courts in the different US states for rape to be established.

RESISTANCE REQUIRED BY COURT TO ESTABLISH RAPE

☐ Slight or none or enough to demonstrate unwillingness
▥ Victim must have resisted unless resistance futile or victim terrified
▩ Victim must have resisted until overcome or for as long as possible

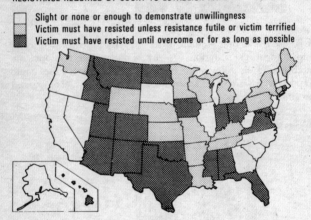

J13 Evidence Required

In a rape case the judge will instruct the jury to weigh the victim's testimony very carefully on the grounds that sexual charges are "easy to make but difficult to prove." (In the USA this guidance applies to all sex cases.) As the map opposite shows, the evidence required to prove rape varies. In some states the victim's testimony only is sufficient; in others corroboration is needed either as a matter of course or whenever the victim's testimony is not considered credible. Corroboration is generally medical — signs of intercourse, physical injury, etc.

Rape and the Courts

EVIDENCE OF RAPE

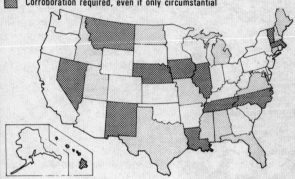

☐ Testimony of victim is sufficient
▦ Testimony of victim if credible; otherwise corroboration needed
▨ Corroboration required, even if only circumstantial

J14 Chances of Conviction

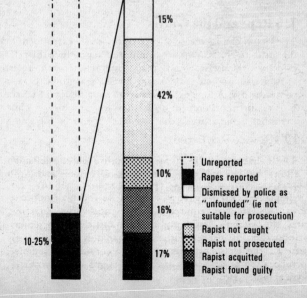

15%

42%

10%

16%

10-25%

17%

▢ Unreported
■ Rapes reported
☐ Dismissed by police as "unfounded" (ie not suitable for prosecution)
▨ Rapist not caught
▨ Rapist not prosecuted
▨ Rapist acquitted
■ Rapist found guilty

J15 Penalties for Rape

MINIMUM PENALTIES

In some states the minimum prescribed penalty is death.

☐ At discretion
☐ 1-5 years
▦ 7-20 years
■ "Life" or death

MAXIMUM PENALTIES

☐ At discretion
▦ 10-30 years
▨ "Life"
■ Death

J16 Rape and the Courts

The victim in a rape case often receives harsher treatment than the suspect. The reasons are complex. They include the rules of evidence themselves and their interaction with society's attitudes to women and to sex. Society's attitude to rape is contradictory. At one extreme are the penalties — 14 US states provide life imprisonment or death as top penalties — while at the other is the attitude that assumes rape to be the woman's fault.

ISSUES

The main issues in a rape case are to prove that the defendant is the rapist, to prove the victim's lack of consent, and to prove resistance by the victim (see J12).

RULES OF PROCEDURE

In a rape case, as in all criminal cases, "the defendant is innocent until proven guilty." Burden of proof falls on the prosecution for whom the rape victim is the complaining witness. Because of its nature, there are rarely any witnesses to rape and the outcome may well depend on who is the more credible — rapist or victim.

Rape and the Courts

DEFENSE TACTICS

Nothing can be said in court about any prior arrest of the defendant for similar offenses or about his sex life. The victim, however, can have her credibility attacked in any way. Defense tactics rely largely on the idea that rape is a woman's fault and reflect the types of social mythology mentioned in J11 or the sexual double standard applied to rape. That is, an unaccompanied woman, an unmarried woman, or one with some sexual experience (eg on the Pill) is either asking for rape or has not been raped at all.

In effect, a woman has her character and personal life put on trial to such an extent that she may well begin to doubt or blame herself.

GOING TO COURT

To cope with these attacks, a woman who brings charges should:

a) get advice and support from a women's group and rape center;

b) memorize details of the rape;

c) stress the force or duress used; and

d) stress lack of consent.

J17 Medical Examination

A woman who has been raped should see a doctor immediately afterward, however distressing it might be. This is both for her own protection (internal injuries, venereal disease, etc) and to provide medical evidence, should it be needed.

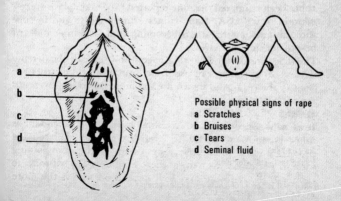

Possible physical signs of rape
a Scratches
b Bruises
c Tears
d Seminal fluid

J18-19

J18 Prevention

AT HOME windows should be kept locked and hallways and entrances kept well lit. Outside doors should be fitted with bolt locks and chains. A woman living on her own should use initials rather than full name in the telephone directory and on the mailbox. Half of all rapes happen in the home.

WHILE OUT a woman should keep to well-lit and peopled areas. Nonrestrictive clothing should be worn for ease of movement in case of pursuit. As she approaches her home, a woman should have her door key ready to avoid delay in entering.

WHEN HITCHHIKING a woman should know the license number of the car, check for inside door handles, and know how to get out quickly. Lifts with more than one man in a car should be refused, and a woman should avoid getting into the back of a 2-door car.

IF TROUBLE THREATENS panic must be avoided. No woman should fight if she can escape — but if she cannot, she should not be afraid to cause hurt. Loud yells — "fire" not "help" — may bring people. If overcome, talking, though unlikely to stop rape, may prevent extra violence.

J19 Self-Defense

It has been estimated that one reported rape takes place every 7 minutes in the USA. Rape is increasing rapidly, and to cope with this growing threat it is becoming vital for women to learn how to defend themselves.

The diagrams on the following pages show some of the defense tactics that a woman can use if she is attacked from either the front or the rear. Also shown are the most vulnerable points to aim for if attacked.

WEAPONS
No woman should carry weapons that can be used against her. But she can carry some articles which, if used fast, are effective:
a Pepper shaker
b Artificial lemon juice container full of vinegar
c Hairspray

Preventing Rape

POINTS TO AIM FOR

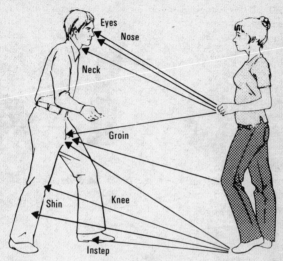

Eyes
Nose
Neck
Groin
Shin
Knee
Instep

DEFENSE TACTICS IF APPROACHED FROM THE REAR

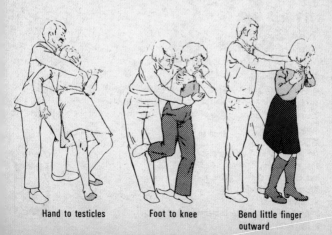

Hand to testicles   Foot to knee   Bend little finger outward

DEFENSE TACTICS IF APPROACHED FROM THE FRONT

Double fist to
bridge of nose

Thumbs into eyes

Fist to side of neck

Knee to groin

Hand to testicles

Foot to groin

Preventing Rape

J20 Effects of Rape

Rape is traumatic and can be both physically and emotionally damaging. Possible reactions include fear of, or hostility to, men; depression; loss of self-respect; and suicidal tendencies. It has been noticed, however, that women who talk out the experience with others do recover more quickly.

IF RAPE OCCURS

A woman who has been raped and who wants to bring charges must:

a) stay in the same clothes and not wash away evidence of rape;

b) call the police as soon as possible;

c) go directly to a hospital or doctor, whether prosecuting or not;

d) get support from a friend, rape center, or women's group;

e) prepare herself for possible skepticism and humiliation, both from the police and, later, the courts.

IMPROVEMENTS

Although true improvements are not possible without a change in social attitudes, some changes are beginning to occur:

a) Rape centers and units are being set up by women in various countries to provide advice, support, and emergency facilities. Likewise, some police departments are beginning to set up specially staffed 24-hour rape units.

b) Legal changes are slow — eg the law still does not recognize that a woman can be raped by her husband. Changes that have been suggested are that the need for medical evidence be removed and that questions about a victim's sexual life be prohibited. This has already happened in Iowa and California, and in Florida such questions are screened by the judge. In some states, the penalties for rape also need changing: "life" or "death" minimum penalties just make conviction harder to obtain.

K01

K01 Stress Situations

Stress is nervous tension. It may be concious or unconscious — that is, the person may or may not be aware of feeling tense. It may be environmental or psychological: the person may be reacting to a physical threat or a mental threat. And it may be acute or chronic (the threat may be a single event or a continuing situation). But whatever the cause, stress depends on the person's reaction, not on the outside event.

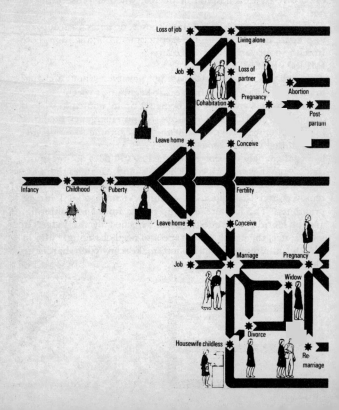

Stress Situations

The life pattern of most women is dotted with potential stress points. Some of these, such as puberty, motherhood, and menopause, are associated directly with the biological aspects of woman as a childbearer. And many women who follow the traditional roles of wife and mother may find that it creates additional stress within the context of marriage and the family. Today, indeed, an increasing number of women are choosing not to follow these patterns. But this decision can itself cause considerable stress, given the prevailing attitudes and structures of society.

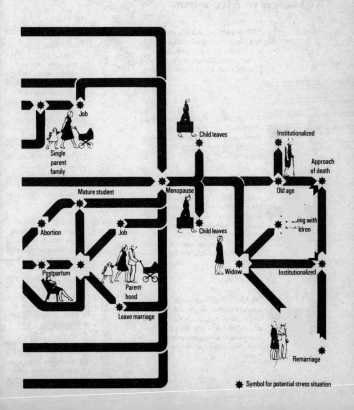

Job

Single parent family

Mature student

Abortion

Postpartum

Job

Parent-hood

Leave marriage

Child leaves

Menopause

Child leaves

Widow

Institutionalized

Old age

Approach of death

Living with children

Institutionalized

Remarriage

✱ Symbol for potential stress situation

K02-05

K02 Dependencies

Stress threatens everyone to some extent; the conditions of our society make it hard to escape. Despite this, many maintain an independent and intelligent approach to life — stress need not be something that defeats us. But others seek refuge in some form of dependence, a false center around which their lives can revolve. Some of these patterns of dependence are encouraged by our society. Others are frowned upon, and yet others dismissed as superficial rather than treated as symptoms of an underlying escapism.

K03 Stages in Alcoholism

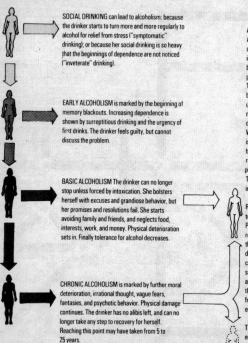

SOCIAL DRINKING can lead to alcoholism: because the drinker starts to turn more and more regularly to alcohol for relief from stress ("symptomatic" drinking); or because her social drinking is so heavy that the beginnings of dependence are not noticed ("inveterate" drinking).

EARLY ALCOHOLISM is marked by the beginning of memory blackouts. Increasing dependence is shown by surreptitious drinking and the urgency of first drinks. The drinker feels guilty, but cannot discuss the problem.

BASIC ALCOHOLISM The drinker can no longer stop unless forced by intoxication. She bolsters herself with excuses and grandiose behavior, but her promises and resolutions fail. She starts avoiding family and friends, and neglects food, interests, work, and money. Physical deterioration sets in. Finally tolerance for alcohol decreases.

CHRONIC ALCOHOLISM is marked by further moral deterioration, irrational thought, vague fears, fantasies, and psychotic behavior. Physical damage continues. The drinker has no alibis left, and can no longer take any step to recovery for herself. Reaching this point may have taken from 5 to 25 years.

ALCOHOLISM
Alcoholism is the most serious drug problem in modern industrial society — involving between 1% and 5% of the population of most countries. The point at which drinking becomes alcoholism is not decided by the quantity drunk, nor even by how far drinking dominates a person's social life. What distinguishes the alcoholic is the fact that the drinking has become compulsive — in response to a psychological or physical dependence on alcohol. This chart shows typical stages in alcoholism.

RECOVERY Procedures of treatment are detailed in K06. Psychologically, the patient regains the desire to be helped, thinks more rationally, and develops hope, moral commitment, outside interests, self-respect, and contentment in abstinence. Finally she recovers the respect of family and friends, and the confidence of employers.

TERMINAL ALCOHOLISM is the end result if drinking continues. Irreversible mental and physical deterioration usually ends in death.

Dependencies

The socially acceptable female roles traditionally encourage dependency in women, a situation which has caused conflict both in themselves and in their relationships with their partners and their children. Today some women are redefining these roles in terms of their own fulfillment. They have recognized that not only is suppression dangerous for themselves, but that it can lead to too great a burden of dependence and resentment on their lovers, husbands, and children. Without a sense of self, many women are also forced into the routine of using their sexuality for identity or as a weapon.

K04 Women and Alcoholism

Alcoholism was long thought of as primarily a male problem. But in recent years there has been a dramatic increase in the number of women alcoholics. It is estimated that between one-sixth and one-third of all alcoholics are women. Inveterate drinking accounts for some of these women alcoholics — young girls keeping boyfriends company or older women moving in the business world.

However, most women who become alcoholics begin by symptomatic drinking — turning to alcohol in response to stress. Thus, among the reasons for drinking often given by women alcoholics are physical troubles such as premenstrual tension, miscarriage and infertility, and emotional troubles associated with sexual roles and needs, such as boredom, frigidity, divorce, etc. But case studies show that their alcoholism is often part of a general picture of depressive illness. In fact, many have emotional problems dating back to disturbed childhoods — often typified by the loss, absence, or inadequacy of one or both parents.

K05 Physiological Effects

The effects of alcoholism on the body include:

a) constant inflammation of the stomach and later the intestines, with severe risk of ulceration;
b) malnutrition and vitamin deficiency diseases — such as pellagra and beriberi — caused by neglecting diet for drink;
c) cirrhosis of the liver — in which the organ shrivels, its cells are largely replaced by fibrous tissues, and functions deteriorate;

K05-07

d) degeneration of muscles — including those of the heart;

e) destruction of brain cells and degeneration throughout the nervous system — sometimes resulting in pneumonia, heart or kidney failure, or organic psychosis;

f) delirium tremens — a condition involving extreme excitement, mental confusion, anxiety, fever, trembling, rapid and irregular pulse, and hallucinations, which characteristically occurs when a bout of heavy drinking is followed by a few days' abstention.

K06 Treatment

Treatments for alcoholism are similar to those used for other types of drug addiction.

DETOXIFICATION

Treatment begins with a period of detoxification in a clinic or hospital. The patient is deprived of alcohol (or the other drug to which she is addicted). This produces severe withdrawal symptoms: sweating, vomiting, body aches, running nose and eyes, convulsions, fits, and hallucinations. Sedatives are used to bring relief during this period — but must be withdrawn before new addictions are formed. Any physical problems are treated, and the patient's health restored by good diet.

THERAPEUTIC TREATMENTS

After detoxification, attempts are made to identify and treat the underlying psychological reasons for addiction. The patient's motivation, self-confidence, and trust must be constantly supported. Treatments vary greatly, but the following are widely accepted:

a) Aversion therapy tries to create conditioned reflexes of sickness and aversion to the addictive substance. Techniques include electric shock therapy, and sensitizing drugs that produce unpleasant symptoms when taken together with alcohol.

b) Individual psychological therapy aims at removing the underlying psychological reasons for addiction by bringing them to light and getting the patient to accept and face up to them.

c) Group therapy aims at giving the patient objective outside views of herself, with which she must come to terms; and at the

Depressants

same time helps her to overcome her isolation, by giving her personal relationships and contact with fellow sufferers.

ALCOHOLICS ANONYMOUS
This organization provides group therapy and guidance by former alcoholics. Meetings provide important support in rehabilitation and continued abstention.
Treatment is long term, and success depends above all on the patient's desire to be cured.

K07 Barbiturates

Barbiturates (nicknamed "barbs," "candy," or "goof balls") are made from barbituric acid. Like all depressants, they reduce the impulses reaching the brain. Because of this, they have been medically prescribed for many years to relieve anxiety and tension and induce sleep; some have also been used as anesthetics. But with greater realization of their dangers, prescription is becoming less common.
TYPES
Barbiturates vary in their immediacy and duration of effect, depending on the rate at which they are metabolized and eliminated; eg Seconal is a short-acting drug, Phenobarbital a long-lasting one.
SYMPTOMS
Someone who has taken some barbiturates may well show signs of drowsiness, restlessness, irritability and belligerence, irrationality, mental confusion, and impairment of coordination and reflexes, with staggering and slurring of speech. The pupils are constricted and sweating increases. The person experiences initial euphoria, followed by depression.
When an excessive amount is taken (an "overdose"), the depressive effect upon the nervous system is such that unconsciousness occurs, followed in extreme cases by death from respiratory failure.
WITHDRAWAL SYMPTOMS
The barbiturates create tolerance and physical dependence. The effects of withdrawal in a chronic user can be worse than those of alcohol or heroin. They include irritability and restlessness, anxiety, insomnia, abdominal cramp, nausea and vomiting, tremors, hallucinations, severe convulsions, and sometimes death.

Ko7-09

TYPES OF ABUSE

Addicts are attracted by:

a) the possibility of escaping from emotional stress, through sedation;

b) the feelings of euphoria on initial ingestion, when large amounts of the drug are tolerated;

c) the ability of barbiturates to counteract the effects of stimulants. This cyclical use of "uppers" and "downers" can lead to dependence on both.

The common prescription of barbiturates to induce relaxation and sleep has resulted in the largest group of dependent people being the middle aged, especially housewives. The same ready availability also makes the drug a common suicide weapon, while the combination of barbiturates' depressive effects with those of alcohol has brought many accidental deaths through taking barbiturates after heavy drinking.

OTHER TRANQUILIZERS

Drugs such as Valium and Librium are increasingly prescribed in place of barbiturates to relieve anxiety and tension. They differ in derivation and mode of action, and an overdose is rarely fatal. But they do sometimes give rise to tolerance and physical dependence, and are subject to the same forms of abuse.

K08 Barbiturates

Drug	Description (but this can vary with dose and source)		Nickname
Amobarbital		Green blue	Blues, blue devils
Pentobarbital		Yellow	Yellows, nembies
Secobarbital		Red	Reds, red devils, red bird
Tuinal		Red blue	Rainbows, tooeys
Thorazine		Orange	
Miltown		White	
Librium		Green white	
Valium		Various	Goofers

Depressants

K09 Opiates

The opiates are known in drug-taking circles as "the hard stuff." Opium itself and its derivative heroin are, in fact, the archetypal drugs of addiction. However, codeine and morphine, which are also derived from opium, are better known for their medical uses.

GENERAL ACTION

All depressants inhibit the activity of the central nervous system, impairing coordination and reflexes, etc, but opiates especially affect the sensory centers, reducing pain and promoting sleep. As with alcohol, this nervous action may cause initial excitement, as inhibitions are removed.

In larger doses, the opiates act on the pleasure centers of the hypothalamus, producing feelings of peace, contentment, safety, and euphoria.

General symptoms of opiate use include loss of appetite, constipation, and constriction of the pupils. An overdose of an opiate is likely to cause convulsions, unconsciousness, and death. All opiates create tolerance and physical dependence. The symptoms of withdrawal from abusive use begin with stomach cramps, followed by diarrhea, nausea and vomiting, running eyes and nose, sweating, and trembling. These are accompanied by irritability and restlessness, insomnia, anxiety and panic, depression, confusion, and an all-consuming desire for the drug.

OPIUM

Opium is the dried juice of the unripe seed capsules of the Indian poppy. The plant is cultivated in India, Persia, China, and Turkey, and opium is then prepared in either powder or liquid form. The poppy possesses its psychoactive powers only when grown in favorable conditions of climate and soil. Poppies produced in temperate climates have only a negligible effect.

Opium is traditionally smoked, using pipes, but it can also be injected or taken orally.

CODEINE

Codeine (methyl morphine) is the least effective of the opiates. It is white and crystalline in form, and is often used with aspirin for treating headaches. Because of the inhibiting

K09-10

effect on nervous reflexes it shares with all opiates, it is used in many cough medicines, and sometimes in the treatment of diarrhea, since it reduces peristalsis (the automatic rhythmic contractions of the intestine). The risk of tolerance and abusive use are very small because of the large amounts necessary to produce pleasant effects.

MORPHINE

Morphine is the basis of all opiate action — it is opium's main active constituent. It was isolated from opium in 1805, and since then has been medically important as a painkiller. It is 10 times as strong as opium, and must be administered with great care to avoid tolerance and physical dependence. However, instances of abuse are not too common, as drug users prefer heroin.

HEROIN

Heroin (diamorphine) was first isolated in 1898. It is 3 times as strong as morphine, and has a quicker and more intense effect, though a shorter duration. Among drug takers it is often known as "H," "horse," or "smack." In the USA it is not used medically. Its production, possession, and use are all connected with drug abuse. A grayish-brown powder in its pure form, for retail purposes it is mixed with milk or baking powder to add bulk. This results in a white coloring. The high cost of the drug, and its necessity to those who have become dependent on it, account for the high crime rate associated with its users.

The powder may be sniffed but is usually injected — normally into a muscle when use begins, but then into a major vein ("mainlining") as tolerance develops. Mainlining gives more immediate and powerful effects. Constant injection into the same vein causes hardening and scarring of the flesh tissue and eventual collapse of the vein. Unhygienic conditions and use of unsterilized needles can also cause infection, often resulting in sores, abscesses, hepatitis, jaundice, and thrombosis. Almost immediately upon injection, intense feelings of euphoria and contentment envelop the user. The strength of these depends on the purity and strength of the heroin, and the psychological state of the user — the higher the previous tension and anxiety, the more powerful the subsequent feelings of pleasure and peace. It is the force of the initial pleasure that makes heroin more popular than morphine. In a chronic user, the ritual of

Stimulants

injection is also important in the creation of pleasure.

Physical dependence on heroin is reached if one grain (60mg) of heroin is used in a period of up to two weeks. Withdrawal effects will then begin four to six hours after the effect of the last shot has worn off.

K10 Amphetamines

The amphetamines ("pep pills" or "uppers") generally stimulate the sympathetic nervous system, which mobilizes the body for action with the "fight or flight" syndrome, including increase in epinephrine production, heart rate, blood sugar, and muscle tension.

EFFECTS The user experiences a sense of well-being and, with strong doses, euphoria. Alertness, wakefulness, and confidence are accompanied by feelings of mental and physical power. The user becomes talkative, excited, and hyperactive. Accompanying physical symptoms include sweating, trembling, dizziness, insomnia, and reduced appetite. Mood effects are probably due to stimulation of the hypothalamus, and sudden shifts to anxiety and panic can occur.

DEPENDENCE Amphetamines create tolerance, but are not considered physically addictive. However, psychic dependence is easily produced. The extra energy is "borrowed" from the body's reserves: when the drug's action has worn off, the body has to pay for it in fatigue and depression. This creates the desire for more of the drug to counteract these effects.

MEDICAL USAGE has become rarer since realization of the dangers. But amphetamines are still used for some purposes, eg to prevent sleep in people who have to be alert for long periods; to treat minor depression; to counteract depressants; and to suppress the appetite in a few cases of obesity.

ABUSE of amphetamines is common because of the feelings of euphoria and alertness they give. The dangers include not only psychic dependence, but also: physical deterioration due to hyperactivity and lack of appetite; induced psychotic conditions of paranoia and schizophrenia, resulting from prolonged overdose; suicide due to mental depression following large doses; and death from overdose.

Kɪɪ-13

K11 Amphetamines

Drug	Description (but this can vary with dose and source)		Nickname
Benzedrine		Red pink	Bennies
		Pink	Bennies
Dexadrine		Orange	Dexies
		Orange	Dexies
Methadrine		White	Speed, meth, crystal
Biphetamine		White	Whites
Edrial		White	
Dexamyl		Green	Christmas tree

K12 Nicotine and Caffeine

NICOTINE is a stimulant of the sympathetic nervous system. It is found in tobacco.

CAFFEINE is a stimulant of the central nervous system, found in coffee, tea, cocoa, and cola drinks. Its action combats fatigue, but it is a comparatively mild drug. It is also a "diuretic," ie it increases the urine output of the kidneys. Medically, caffeine is often included in headache pills, to counteract the dulling effect of the painkilling ingredient. Abuse is unlikely because of the large quantities necessary, but those who drink considerable amounts of coffee probably have a mild psychic dependence, because of the feelings of tiredness experienced when the stimulation wears off.

K13 Cocaine

COCAINE (often nicknamed "coke" or "snow") is a white powder obtained from the coca plant found in South America. Synthetic derivatives are also available.

Stimulants

EFFECTS Cocaine stimulates the central nervous system, dispelling fatigue, increasing alertness, mental activity and reflex speed, and inducing euphoria. After an initial "rush," the effects become more steady. Accompanying physical symptoms include dilation of pupils, tremors, loss of appetite, and insomnia.

MEDICAL USE Although it is a stimulant, local application of cocaine has anesthetic effects.

It is used for minor operations on the eye, ear, nose and throat, and can also be used to anesthetize the lower limbs by injection into the spinal fluid.

DEPENDENCE Cocaine does not create physical dependence, but psychic dependence easily develops for the same reasons as with amphetamines.

ABUSE is the main use found for cocaine. As a powder, it is inhaled, which eventually results in deterioration of the nasal linings and finally of the nasal septum separating the nostrils. Injection of a liquid form is an alternative, but using cocaine alone is unpopular, because of the violence of the sudden effects. So heroin and cocaine are often injected together. Cocaine is a short-acting drug and must be taken repeatedly to maintain the effects.

Dangers of prolonged use include insomnia, paranoia, hallucinations in the sense of touch known as "the cocaine bugs," and loss of weight and malnutrition through lack of interest in food. An overdose causes convulsions, and a dose of 12g or more at one time causes death by respiratory failure.

K14-16

K14 Summary of Drug Effects

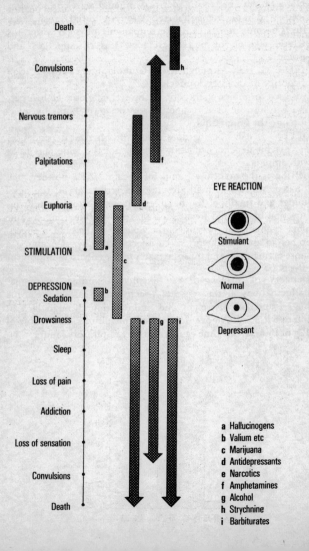

EYE REACTION

Stimulant

Normal

Depressant

a Hallucinogens
b Valium etc
c Marijuana
d Antidepressants
e Narcotics
f Amphetamines
g Alcohol
h Strychnine
i Barbiturates

Anorexia Nervosa

K15 Anorexia Nervosa

True anorexia nervosa has been described as the "willful pursuit of thinness through self-starvation." It is a serious disorder mainly affecting adolescent women.

SYMPTOMS AND BEHAVIOR

Dieting begins because the anorectic either is or believes herself to be overweight. It develops into a morbid fear of fatness and continues to the point of extreme emaciation (rarely recognized by the anorectic). Loss of weight is accompanied by loss of menstruation, constipation, discoloration of skin, and the growth of a fine body hair. Despite the extreme loss of weight, most anorectics are hyperactive. True loss of appetite is rare and starvation is interspersed with secret eating binges followed by self-induced purging.

BACKGROUND AND CAUSES

Anorexia nervosa and the reasons behind it are highly complex. It has been noticed that many anorectics suffer from an overwhelming sense of ineffectiveness. Continuous starvation and refusal of food represents a gesture of independence, possibly from an overdominant mother, while thinness is seen as a desirable achievement in itself.

K16 Age of Onset

The onset of anorexia nervosa typically occurs during adolescence. The diagram below shows the percentages of a sample group of anorectics who became ill at different ages.

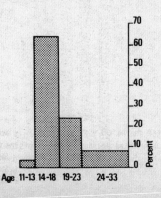

K17-19

K17 Pattern of Development

The development of a typical case of adolescent anorexia nervosa is described in the diagram below — from initial carbohydrate starvation until medical diagnosis.

Response to treatment varies considerably. At the two extremes are obesity and starvation. More typically a patient responds to treatment and attains normal weight.

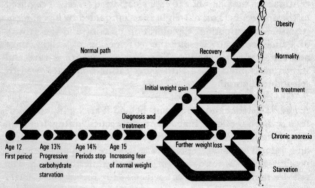

Normal path · Recovery · Initial weight gain · Diagnosis and treatment · Further weight loss

Obesity · Normality · In treatment · Chronic anorexia · Starvation

Age 12 First period · Age 13½ Progressive carbohydrate starvation · Age 14½ Periods stop · Age 15 Increasing fear of normal weight

K18 Self-Image

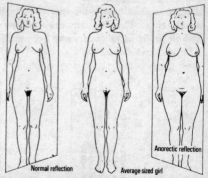

Degree of distortion in the perception of body size:

Normal reflection · Average-sized girl · Anorectic reflection

All people have a distorted view of their own body proportions, but whereas the normal person underestimates face, chest, and hip size, while slightly overestimating waist size, the anorectic grossly overestimates each of these sizes even when severely emaciated.

Anorexia Nervosa

Degree of distortion in the perception of body size:

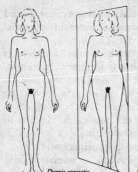

	Normal %	Anorectic %
Face	94.7	157.6
Chest	95	134.2
Waist	100.2	146.6
Hips	96.6	128.8

(100% equals actual size)

Chronic anorectic   Anorectic reflection

K19 Treatment

Treatments for anorexia nervosa include the following:

DRUG THERAPY AND BED REST

The patient is hospitalized and kept in bed. Drug therapy is combined with encouragement to eat a high-Calorie diet. The patient is allowed up only after reaching a near normal weight (usually in 1 to 3 months).

BEHAVIOR MODIFICATION REGIMES

Similar to the treatment already described, but with a system of rewards for meeting daily and weekly weight-gain targets.

PSYCHOTHERAPY

The patient and her family receive psychotherapy before and after the patient's release from hospital.

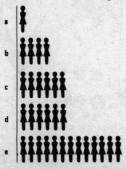

The diagram summarizes follow-up information on a group of anorectics. Follow-up material was available on 30 of the original sample of 45 patients.

a Obese (1)
b Dead (4)
c Anorectic (6)
d In treatment (6)
e Recovery (13)

K20-22

K20 Who Becomes a Compulsive Eater?

Compulsive eating is a common problem among women — and with the resulting obesity can cause considerable distress. Many women indulge in occasional bouts of "stuffing," but these are rarely significant. The compulsive eater, however, is addicted to food. She may use it to relieve feelings of loneliness, isolation, frustration, dissatisfaction, or boredom. She may use it to comfort herself if she feels guilty, depressed, or unattractive. During adolescence she may overeat to stifle her emerging sexuality, and later in life she may use her obesity to avoid contact with the opposite sex. Overeating — a secret and solitary activity — needs handling with sensitivity and understanding. To help overcome the problem, a woman should avoid being alone for longer than necessary, ensure that only low-Calorie snacks are kept in the house, and divert herself with physical activity when the craving for food starts. Severe cases often need clinical help.

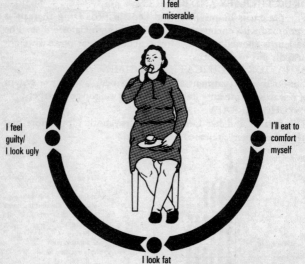

I feel
miserable

I feel
guilty/
I look ugly

I'll eat to
comfort
myself

I look fat

Reasons for compulsive eating vary,
but the vicious circle illustrated
above is common to many women.

Compulsive Eating

K21 Typical Pattern of Weight Gain

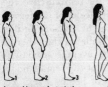

A case history of a typical compulsive eater is described here.
1 Age 12: 135 lb (61kg)
2 Age 13: 165 lb (75kg) after distress caused by deaths in the family
3 Age 14: 145 lb (66kg) following treatment at a reducing salon
4 Age 15: 110 lb (50kg) after a strict diet

5 Age 16½: 200 lb (91kg). Tired of dieting and of "watchful" parents the girl stopped paying attention to what she ate
6 Age 17: 220 lb (100kg) — highest weight despite psychiatric treatment
7 Age 18: 180 lb (82kg) after another reducing treatment and diet

8 Age 19: 130 lb (59kg) after treatment involving amphetamines to which the girl became addicted. The addiction was cured and the girl's weight increased slightly over the next 20 years
9 Age 40: 140 lb (64kg)

K22 Effects

Obesity — the well-known consequence of compulsive eating — results in some external bodily changes and the increased risk of certain diseases.

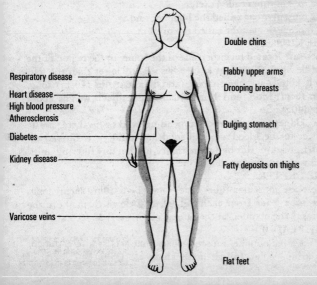

Double chins

Flabby upper arms

Drooping breasts

Respiratory disease

Heart disease

High blood pressure

Atherosclerosis

Bulging stomach

Diabetes

Kidney disease

Fatty deposits on thighs

Varicose veins

Flat feet

Lo1-02

L01 Illness

This chapter concentrates on disorders of the reproductive and urinary systems. On the one hand, the complexity of the female reproductive tract, and its proximity to the urinary outlet, make this an especially vulnerable area; while on the other, it has been difficult, until recently, for the average woman to educate herself about the special problems of the female body, or to get qualified attention from others of her own sex. Yet the causes of disorder in this area only illustrate those at work in the body in general: infection, inborn defects, metabolic disorders, developmental changes, degenerative processes, nervous conditions, and external irritations (whether mechanical, thermal, chemical, or from radiation).

L02 Urinary System

The female reproductive system is considered in B02. The urinary system consists of those organs that produce and excrete urine:

a) a pair of kidneys;
b) a pair of tubes called ureters;
c) a muscular bag called the bladder; and
d) another single tube called the urethra.

THE KIDNEYS

These are located on either side of the spine, in the region of the middle back. The right kidney lies slightly lower than the left. Each kidney is bean-shaped, and is about 4in (10cm) long, $2\frac{1}{2}$in (6cm) wide, and $1\frac{1}{2}$in (3.8cm) thick. Each weighs about 5oz (140g).

The kidneys are chemical processing works. In them, waste matter in the blood — both solid and fluid — is filtered off under pressure, through more than 2 million tiny filtering units. This waste matter is called urine.

THE URETERS

These are muscular tubes, each one about 10in (25cm) long. One tube leads from each kidney, and down them the urine passes to the bladder, at the rate of a drop every 30 seconds.

THE BLADDER

This is a balloonlike, muscular bag that acts as a reservoir for the urine. When full, it holds about 1.2(US)pt (.57 liters) of

Urogenital System

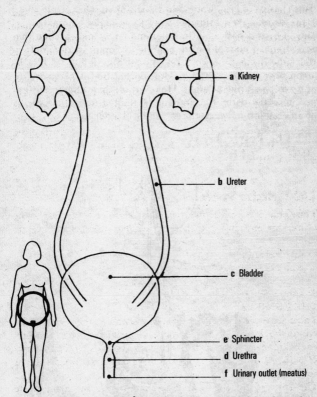

a Kidney

b Ureter

c Bladder

e Sphincter
d Urethra
f Urinary outlet (meatus)

urine — though the desire to urinate is usually felt when about half that amount is present.

A muscular ring (sphincter) surrounds the exit from the bladder into the urethra. When this is contracted, it prevents leakage of urine out of the bladder. Upon urination the sphincter is relaxed, and the urine passes into the urethra.

THE URETHRA

This is a muscular tube, about 1½in (3.8cm) long in a woman (compared with 8in—20cm—in a man). It leads from the bladder to the exterior, and it is along this tube that urine leaves the body ("urination," also called "micturition").

L02-05

URINE

Urine consists of 96% water and 4% dissolved solids. Only 60% of the water taken into the body is normally eliminated as urine. The rest passes out in sweat and feces, and through the lungs. Urine is normally straw or amber colored. In 24 hours an adult usually passes between 1¾ and 3(US)pt (0.8 to 1.4 liters), spread over 4 to 6 occasions. Most do not find it necessary to get up to pass urine at night. However, all these characteristics vary normally with: the amount of fluid drunk, and when; the amount lost in sweat; the size of the bladder, etc.

L03 The Pelvic Area

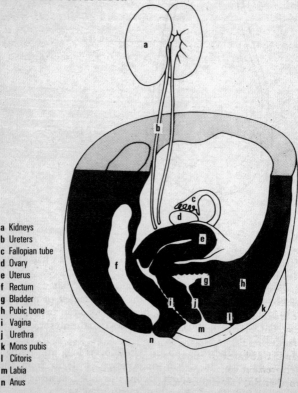

a Kidneys
b Ureters
c Fallopian tube
d Ovary
e Uterus
f Rectum
g Bladder
h Pubic bone
i Vagina
j Urethra
k Mons pubis
l Clitoris
m Labia
n Anus

Disorders of the Uterus

L04 Prolapse

Prolapse of the womb is not an uncommon condition — the uterus sags down into the vagina, and may even protrude out between the legs. The symptoms include frequent and difficult urination; incontinence; vaginal discharge; low backache; a feeling that something is coming out of the vagina; and, especially, that all the above symptoms immediately disappear on lying down.

The condition is produced by weakening of muscles that support the uterus. The cause is usually damage done in childbirth; 99% of women with prolapsed wombs have given birth. But aging and heavy physical activity also contribute, and the symptoms often appear only after the menopause, when the affected muscles may lose tone and ligaments atrophy. Mild cases require no treatment, but more serious or troublesome ones need a pessary inserted by a doctor, or sometimes surgery.

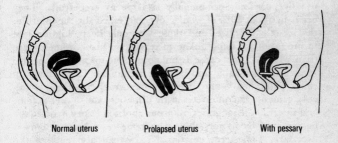

Normal uterus   Prolapsed uterus   With pessary

L05 Retroversion

In most women, from puberty on, the upper end of the uterus is tilted forward in the body, and moves backward only as the bladder fills or when the woman lies on her back. But in about 10% of women the uterus is always retroverted (tilted backward). Once blamed for many ailments, in fact this may be troublesome only in pregnancy, when the enlarging uterus may fail to rise into the abdomen. Urine retention in the bladder results. A doctor can usually correct the situation by hand. Untreated, it could cause cystitis, and even miscarriage. Retroversion can also start after childbirth. Doctors disagree whether this can cause backache, etc. If it seems very trouble-

L05-08

some, surgery is needed. Other causes of displacement can include: pelvic tumors (such as ovarian cysts); and connective tissue joining to other structures. Surgery can deal with these if necessary.

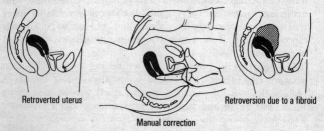

Retroverted uterus

Manual correction

Retroversion due to a fibroid

L06 Fibroids

These are lumps of fibrous tissue, growing in the muscle wall of the uterus, sometimes singly, sometimes in large groups, usually pea-sized, occasionally as large as grapefruits. They occur in about 20% of women over 30, especially the infertile, the sexually inactive, and those who only bear children late in life (also, for some unknown reason, in black women more than white). Their cause is unknown, but may be hormonal. Most give no trouble and need no treatment. Large ones can cause pain, heavy and irregular menstrual bleeding, womb enlargement that interferes with urination and bowel action, and infertility through spontaneous abortion. They can usually be removed by surgery, but in extreme cases hysterectomy is necessary. Long-term emotional stress can also enlarge the uterus and give heavy periods. This has occasionally resulted in unnecessary surgery.

Polyps are another type of lump found, also usually harmless, but developing from mucus tissue and forming dangling shapes.

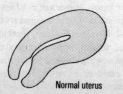

Normal uterus

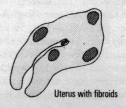

Uterus with fibroids

Disorders of the Uterus

L07 "Cervical Erosion"

The cells lining the cervical canal sometimes extend down till they show as a reddened area at the head of the vagina. This happens naturally in puberty and first pregnancy, and needs no treatment unless it persists over 6 months after childbirth and causes much vaginal discharge. It then needs electric cauterization, which produces a heavy, discolored vaginal discharge for 4 to 6 weeks till healing is complete. It may also occur in women on the Pill or using IUDs. Again, it usually disappears without symptoms or treatment, but needs regular "Pap tests" (see L43) against cancer.

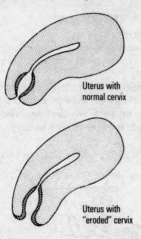

Uterus with normal cervix

Uterus with "eroded" cervix

L08 Endometriosis

Endometrial cells (see B02) can grow in the wrong place, forming cysts in the uterus muscle, the ovaries, or other parts of the pelvis. This is commonest in unmarried or infertile women in their thirties. On menstruation these cells bleed a little, so the cyst swells, causing pain in the lower abdomen, especially before or at the end of menstruation, and sometimes pain on intercourse. Where ovaries or Fallopian tubes are blocked, infertility results. Treatment involves hormones or surgery (eg removal of the cyst, or part of an organ, or in severe cases hysterectomy).

Lo8-11

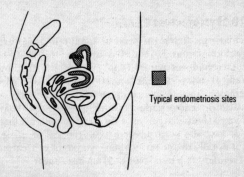

■ Typical endometriosis sites

L09 Dilation and Curettage

Also called "D&C," this involves:
a enlargement of the cervical opening, using dilators; and
b gentle scraping of the uterine wall with a metal curette.
It is used:
to diagnose cancer, pregnancy outside the uterus, or causes of abnormal bleeding or discharge; to clear waste from incomplete delivery or abortion; to help fertility (see D68); to cause abortion (see E03); and, sometimes, as routine preparation for gynecological surgery.
Anesthetic is needed. Recovery takes 6 hours to 2 days.

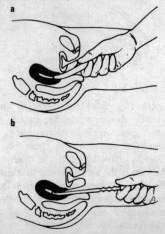

Hysterectomy

L10 Hysterectomy

This is surgical removal of the uterus (womb). It can be:
a subtotal (removal of the uterus except for the cervix);
b total (removal of uterus and cervix); or
c radical (removal of uterus, surrounding tissue, and part of the vagina).
With any of these, ovaries and Fallopian tubes may also be removed (see L14).
If the uterus is not enlarged by disease, removal can be via the vagina. Otherwise, an incision is necessary: a vertical one below the navel or a horizontal one just above the pubic region. (The scar left is almost invisible.) The operation takes less than an hour.

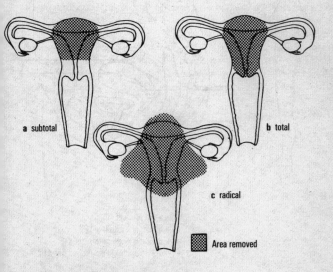

a subtotal

b total

c radical

Area removed

L11 Reasons for Hysterectomy

In the USA, 25% of all women aged 50 and over have had hysterectomies. The diagram overleaf shows some valid reasons for the operation; but very often it occurs for no good reason (eg for removal of small fibroids). Some US doctors even favor routine

Lɪɪ-ɪ3

hysterectomy once childbearing is over, to forestall any risk of cancer; but many others view this as a surgical racket. Some American doctors have also urged hysterectomy as combined abortion and sterilization, for poor women with large families. But again, most doctors are against this, because:

a) hysterectomy within 13 weeks of conception can endanger the mother's life; and

b) the patient cannot afford the hormone therapy necessary to combat the resulting severe menopausal depression if the ovaries also are removed.

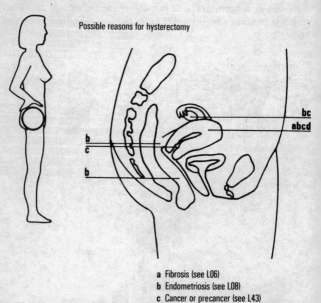

Possible reasons for hysterectomy

a Fibrosis (see L06)
b Endometriosis (see L08)
c Cancer or precancer (see L43)
d Metropathia hemorrhagica (see A18)

L12 Physical Aftereffects

The diagram opposite shows how the immediate effects of the operation wear off. Other considerations are long term:

a) Menstruation ends immediately, and with it fertility and the need for contraception.

Hysterectomy

b) Subtotal hysterectomy usually has no sexual effect. With other forms, some women claim loss of sexual pleasure after cervix removal. Some also complain of shortened vaginas.

c) If the ovaries remain, female hormone production continues. If they have been removed, severe menopausal symptoms result. Hormone therapy may be given to combat these (see F13).

d) Obesity does not follow hysterectomy unless the patient eats too much and exercises too little (but psychological factors may encourage this).

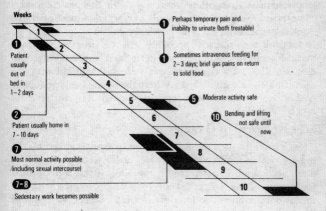

Weeks

- **1** Patient usually out of bed in 1–2 days
- **2** Patient usually home in 7–10 days
- **7** Most normal activity possible (including sexual intercourse)
- **7–8** Sedentary work becomes possible
- **1** Perhaps temporary pain and inability to urinate (both treatable)
- **1** Sometimes intravenous feeding for 2–3 days; brief gas pains on return to solid food
- **5** Moderate activity safe
- **10** Bending and lifting not safe until now

L13 Psychological Aftereffects

Hysterectomy affects different women differently. Some enjoy the relief given from heavy bleeding or threat of disease, feel more active and healthy, and are happy that they can no longer conceive accidentally. But younger women often resent the loss of fertility, and many become depressed. Research shows that hysterectomy patients in the USA:

a) grow more dissatisfied with the operation as time passes;

b) are more likely to be dissatisfied if the ovaries are also

L13-15

removed (blaming the operation for hot flashes, lethargy, and obesity);

c) are 4 times likelier to become depressed in the 3 years after the operation than other women;

d) are likely to remain depressed for twice as long (2 years on average);

e) are especially liable to depression if under 40 when operated on; and

f) are 5 times more likely to make a subsequent first visit to a psychiatrist than other women — with the peak period 2 years after surgery, and the bulk of cases from those operated on for other than a serious physical condition.

In fact, all such statistics probably reflect a situation in which many hysterectomies have been performed unnecessarily; and even so, 41% of a typical sample were still satisfied with the operation 4 years afterward . Where the operation is genuinely necessary, serious or long-term psychological disturbance is much less likely.

L14 Removal of Ovaries

This is usually used to deal with or prevent cancer of the ovaries, which eventually affects 1% of US women over 40. It often accompanies hysterectomy, especially if this is performed for cancer of the uterus (about 10% of US women with the uterus only removed do later get ovarian cancer). Removal of large cysts can be another reason for the operation.

Where one ovary needs removal, the other may also be taken out to prevent it being a future site of disease (eg in cancer cases or postmenopausal patients). Postmenopausal women who lose both ovaries experience no special effects. Younger women have a menopause, often with severe symptoms, but this is treatable by hormone therapy.

L15 Vaginal Discharge

Apart from the contribution of the uterus at menstruation (see A13), normal vaginal discharge consists of:

a) clear watery mucus from the cervix (especially midway between periods);

b) clear fluid that has "sweated" through the walls of the vagina (usually only a small amount, but more in pregnancy or emotional upset, and a great deal during sexual excitement);

Vaginal Disorders

c) dead cells from the vaginal wall; and

d) a small contribution from the Bartholin glands at the vaginal entrance during sexual excitement. The resulting discharge is transparent or slightly milky, with little or no odor, slippery in feel, and perhaps yellowish when dry. It keeps the vagina moist and clean, and may be more noticeable at certain points in the menstrual cycle than at others.

SIGNS OF DISORDER

What is significant is not increased amount, but irritation, unpleasant odor, or unusual color. Irritation includes itching, chafing, soreness, or burning of vagina, vulva, or thighs.

CAUSES

For abnormal menstrual discharge, see A18. There are several possible causes of other abnormal discharge:

a) Forgotten foreign bodies, eg tampons or contraceptive caps. These can cause a very thick, odorous discharge, which clears up when the cause is removed and the vagina washed out.

b) Chemical irritation. Disinfectants in bathing water can cause soreness; vaginal deodorants, contraceptive foams, and even some soaps can cause soreness and discharge. Symptoms may take time to clear after the cause is eliminated.

c) Postmenopausal atrophy (see F11).

d) "Cervical erosion" (see L07).

e) Infection, including candidiasis (see L17), trichomoniasis (L16), gonorrhea (L30), and NSU (L32).

INFECTION

Many bacteria live harmlessly in a normal healthy vagina. Some help keep its surface a little acidic, and this restricts the development of other, harmful organisms. Factors favoring infection include:

a) generally lowered resistance (due to lack of sleep, bad diet, other illness, etc);

b) cuts, abrasions, etc (eg from childbirth or intercourse without sufficient lubrication); and

c) potentially, all factors which affect the quantity and acidity of the vaginal mucus, including: menstruation and pregnancy; taking birth control pills, other hormones, or antibiotics; excessive douching; diabetes or prediabetes; and the menopause. (For ways of preventing vaginal infections, see J03.)

L16-18

L16 Trichomoniasis ("Trich")

Trichomoniasis vaginalis is a one-celled animal parasite and the most common infectious cause of vaginal discharge. Perhaps 50% of women carry it at some time; about 15% develop symptoms at least once. The discharge is often greenish-yellow or grayish, thin and foamy, but may be thicker and whiter if other infection is also present. Other symptoms are: itching and soreness of vagina and vulva; clusters of raised red spots on cervix and vaginal walls; and an unpleasant odor. If it spreads to the urinary tract, it can cause cystitis; if to the Fallopian tubes, infertility. Transmission can occur sexually (men carrying it generally have no symptoms), and also very occasionally via moist objects such as towels, washcloths, and toilet seats (the parasite can live briefly outside the body). It cannot be passed on to a baby in childbirth. Qualified medical treatment is vital, especially as it often occurs in conjunction with gonorrhea (this should be checked for once the symptoms of trichomoniasis clear up). Both partners should be treated. But the usual treatment is with oral metronidazole (Flagyl) or tinidazole, both thought suspect drugs by some. (Prescribed vaginal suppositories or gels may be adequate alternatives, though infection may recur.) Especially avoid oral metronidazole if you are pregnant, have peptic ulcers or another infection, or have a history of blood or central nervous system disease. Also do not take alcohol with it. Avoid intercourse until tests show clear. (For measures to help prevent recurrence, see J03.)

L17 Candidiasis ("Thrush")

This is caused by a yeast organism (a type of fungus). It can be passed on sexually, men usually having no symptoms. But it often occurs in the vagina anyway, kept at bay by the acidic conditions, and only thriving if these get milder. Itching and soreness of vagina and vulva then result, especially when the body is warm (eg in bed at night). There may also be a thick creamy discharge that smells of yeast and looks like cottage cheese.

Self-treatment may help (eg one or two yogurt treatments; or vinegar douches twice a day for 3 days), but will not usually clear up an established infection. Normal treatment is with nystatin suppositories, inserted to the top of the vagina — one a

Vaginal Disorders

night for one or two weeks. (These have fewer side effects than oral doses, and can be used during pregnancy.) Tampons cannot be worn, as they will soak up the medication; but a pad and old underpants are needed, as nystatin gives a yellow stain.

Other suppositories have also begun to be used recently. Also, creams are still sometimes prescribed for direct application to the vagina, cervix, and vulva; but these destroy all vaginal bacteria, so when treatment ends it is important to re-create acidic conditions in the vagina, to encourage normal bacterial growth.

Very recurrent infection suggests: lack of hygiene by the partner (eg thrush can live under the male foreskin); or developing sugar diabetes; or the effects on the vaginal mucus of taking oral contraceptives and/or antibiotics. If a woman with thrush gives birth, the baby may have the infection in its digestive tract, and should be treated with nystatin drops.

L18 Other Infections

NONSPECIFIC VAGINITIS This is the name for any unidentified vaginal infection. Cystitislike symptoms may be the first sign of disorder, followed by a discharge that is often white or yellow and may be streaked with blood. The vaginal walls may be puffy and coated with pus, and there may also be lower back pains, cramps, and swollen glands in abdomen and thighs. The usual treatment is with sulfa creams or suppositories (eg Vagitrol, Sultrin, or AVC cream).

HEMOPHILIS VAGINALIS This bacterium has now been identified, and in some areas is found to be more common than trichomoniasis or candidiasis. Symptoms are similar to trichomoniasis, and it is often misdiagnosed; but the discharge is usually white or grayish, creamy in consistency, and smells especially unpleasant after intercourse. It is often transmitted sexually, and treatment of both partners is necessary: for women, with nitrofurazone (Furacin) in suppository or cream form, or with sulfa suppositories; for men, with tetracycline or ampicillin.

Lɪ9-2ɪ

L19 Vaginal Organisms

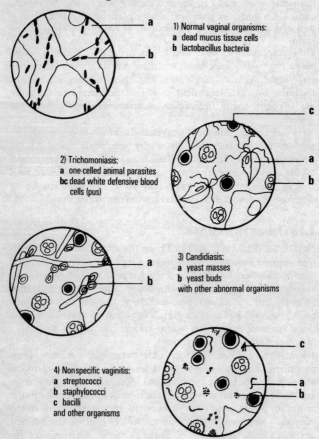

1) Normal vaginal organisms:
a dead mucus tissue cells
b lactobacillus bacteria

2) Trichomoniasis:
a one-celled animal parasites
bc dead white defensive blood
cells (pus)

3) Candidiasis:
a yeast masses
b yeast buds
with other abnormal organisms

4) Nonspecific vaginitis:
a streptococci
b staphylococci
c bacilli
and other organisms

L20 Symptoms of Disorder

For a doctor, the urine and urination are among the most useful signs of disorder — relating sometimes not just to the urinary system, but to the general health of the body.

Urinary Disorders

Characteristics of urination that may interest a doctor include: changes in quantity and frequency (including rising at night); slow and weak, or unusually forceful flow; stopping and starting, and dribbling; difficulty in beginning or continuing; inability to restrain (incontinence); sudden stopping; and, of course, pain or other unusual sensation on urinating, or inability to urinate at all.

Characteristics of the urine that may be of interest include unusual color, odor, cloudiness, frothiness, and content. Abnormal chemical content can include albumen (which may indicate kidney disorder) or sugar (diabetes). Chemical testing can be carried out very easily, using a treated paper that changes color when moistened with urine. Other abnormal contents can include bacteria, parasites, kidney tube casts, bile pigment, and especially blood or pus.

However, many unusual characteristics of the urine or urination will more usually be due to insignificant causes than to disorder. For example, having to get up from bed to urinate is often due to drinking tea or coffee last thing at night. Strikingly unusual colors can be produced just by certain medicines and foods.

OTHER SYMPTOMS

Other symptoms of disorder include: itching, redness, or stickiness at the urethral opening; any discharge of fluid from the urethra; pain or swelling in the area of the kidneys, and shivering, temperature, or fever.

L21 Types of Disorder

INFECTION

This can reach the urinary system in two ways: "downward," via the bloodstream and then the kidneys; or "upward," via the urethral opening in the genitals. An example of the first can be tuberculosis. But the second is much more common in women:

a) because in women the closeness of anus and genitals helps bacteria pass between them; and

b) because the shortness of the female urethra allows bacteria to reach the higher parts of the tract more easily.

Most bacteria entering the tract from outside are killed by the urine; but 5% of women (both adults and children) do have active bacteria in the bladder. Often there are no symptoms.

L21

If there are, frequency of urination and pain on urinating are typical. Diagnosis is by bacteriological examination of a urine sample. Treatment is with an antibiotic.

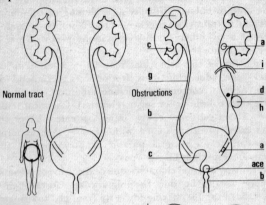

Normal tract

Obstructions

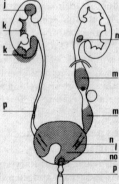

OBSTRUCTIONS include:
a stones,
b strictures,
c tumors,
d blood clots,
e foreign bodies, and
f TB fibrosis.
Also external pressure from:
g pregnancy,
h tumors, and
i congenitally displaced arteries.
INFECTIONS include:
j TB, and
k kidney infections.
Also especially, bacteria:
l in the bladder,
m in stagnant or obstructed urine,
n in stones,
o in foreign bodies, and
p in structural inflammations.

Sites of infection

Urinary Disorders

INFLAMMATION

Inflammation of the tract is mostly caused by infection, but also by: dietary irritation (eg alcohol, and perhaps food allergy); use of chemicals (vaginal deodorants, contraceptive foams, etc); and tissue damage during sexual activity, childbirth, or surgery. Even when not caused by infection, it can offer a favorable site for infection. Inflammation of the urethra is called "urethritis," that of the bladder "cystitis" (see L23). Symptoms again include pain on urinating. Treatment depends on the cause, but drinking large quantities of fluid usually helps.

FLOW ABNORMALITY

This includes obstruction of flow, complete or incomplete; also apparently normal flow that nevertheless leaves stagnant pools of urine in the tract. Causes include:

a) blockage by extraneous objects (eg stones, blood clots, etc);
b) malfunction of the tract itself (eg through congenital controlling malformation, tumors and other growths or tissue changes, and temporary spasm); and
c) outside pressure on the tract (eg from fibroids, displaced uterus, or pregnancy).

Stagnant urine is always a likely site for infection. When there is flow blockage as well, pressure builds up behind the obstruction, and that section of the tract may be stretched and dilated. Eventually the pressure and dilation may reach back up the ureters toward the kidneys. Kidney infection may result, and rapid surgical treatment is needed before the kidneys suffer permanent damage.

INCONTINENCE

This is inability to control urination. For incontinence in the old, see M16; but it also occurs in younger women. Causes include: psychological stress (eg severe fright); disorders of the bladder; congenital defects; tissue damage occurring in childbirth or surgery; and impairment of the nerves due to injury or disease. Two types are fairly common:

a) urgency incontinence, where there is a shortened time gap between the desire to urinate and uncontrollable urination — it occurs quite often in women over 40; and
b) stress incontinence, typified by small amounts of urine escaping when the person strains, coughs, or laughs — whether the bladder is full or virtually empty. This is usually

only seen in postmenopausal women; special exercises, or sometimes surgery, are needed.

L22 Kidney Disorders

These include: congenital defects; tumors; stones; damage through injury; inflammation without infection; and infection.
INFECTION is especially common in women. It can arrive via the bloodstream or the urinary system. In acute attacks, bacterial infection via the urinary tract is typical. Symptoms are shivering and fever, acute pain in loin or under ribs at back, and frequent urination.
Qualified medical attention is vital: prescribed antibiotics, bed rest, and plenty of fluids. Long-term infection may follow acute infection, or arise from urinary obstruction or blood-borne infection. (Stones are frequent sites.) Symptoms include dull back pain, painful and frequent urination, tiredness, headache, nausea, loss of appetite, and fever. Treatment depends on causes. In neglected cases, kidney damage may result, with possible high blood pressure and blood poisoning.

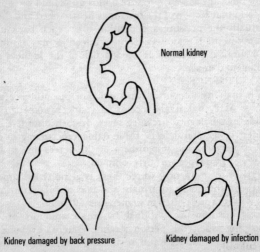

Normal kidney

Kidney damaged by back pressure

Kidney damaged by infection

Cystitis

L23 Cystitis

Strictly, this means inflammation of the bladder. However, it is now generally used for a certain collection of symptoms, usually in women, which can arise in a variety of ways. The main symptoms of an attack (acute cystitis) are:

a) great frequency of urination (perhaps every few minutes);

b) pain on urination — often extreme; and yet

c) a recurrent or even continuous desire to urinate even when there is no urine to pass.

As the attack continues, there may also be increasing incontinence, and often blood in the urine. Other associated symptoms can include: pain just above the pubic bone or in the loin; and a foul smell from, and perhaps debris in, the urine. Also, extreme pain may be felt if sexual intercourse is attempted.

This syndrome is very common: perhaps 80% of women suffer from it at some time in their lives, and it is often recurrent (chronic cystitis) and hard to eradicate. In its extreme forms it can bring depression, disrupted career and home life, and even (since it can both derive from sexual intercourse and interfere with it) broken emotional and marital relationships.

L24 Causes of Cystitis

There are two main alternative causes:

a) infection;

b) inflammation without infection (though infection may also set in later).

INFECTION

This is usually by Escherichia coli (E.coli) bacteria from the rectum finding their way into the urethral opening. E. coli are often found on the perineum (the skin between anus and genitals). Their progress toward the vulva is often helped mechanically by careless use of toilet paper or by sexual activity (petting, or just the movement of the penis).

Other sources of infection are:

a) similar cross-infection from the vagina (eg candidiasis, trichomoniasis, or gonorrhea);

b) lack of male hygiene (eg when uncircumcised — see N07); and

c) infections from the kidneys that pass downward (eg tuberculosis).

L24-25

Infection may be aided by: stones; stagnant pools of urine due to retention (see L21); lowered resistance, as in anemia; and (for bacteria preferring nonacidic urine) diabetes.

INFLAMMATION

For general causes of this, see L21.

In cystitis, the normal cause (apart from infection) is bruising or skin cracking through sexual activity. Relevant here are: frequency of intercourse (hence "honeymoon cystitis"); insufficient lubrication; use of certain positions (depending on the individuals); and overforceful petting. Other relevant causes are:

a) tissue irritation through use of vaginal deodorants, foam contraceptives, unsuitable lubricants, etc;

b) strain on the bladder due to prolapse of the uterus;

c) damage through childbirth or surgery; and possibly

d) allergic reaction of the urinary tract to certain foods.

Inflammation can, in turn, provide a breeding ground for infection (and an entry for infection into the bloodstream).

CHRONIC CYSTITIS

This is usually a case of repeated attacks of acute cystitis, but there may be long-term tissue changes also involved, including changes in the urethra due to the menopause, and changes in the bladder lining from bacterial or other infection. Occasionally there may be psychological factors.

L25 Investigation

The sufferer should always see a doctor — and always try to get proper tests made to pinpoint the cause. First step should be laboratory testing of a urine sample for infection and (if present) responsiveness to drugs. The patient should drink before going to the doctor, so as to be ready to pass urine for this. A clean sample is important: the vulva should be swabbed, and only a small midstream sample (ie from halfway through urination) taken. During menstruation, a tube (catheter) inserted into the urethra should be used. The patient may also be able to give useful information, eg the amount of time between the attack and the last previous intercourse. (Cystitis due to inflammation alone will follow intercourse sooner than that due to infection, since bacteria need time to multiply. Unfortunately, estimates vary — from "very soon after" for

Cystitis

inflammation and 12-24 hours after for infection, to 24 hours after for inflammation and 36 for infection.)

If no infection is found, or if it fails to clear after a course of drugs, hospital investigations may be needed, such as:

a) physical examination by a specialist;

b) taking of bacteria samples from vagina and perineum;

c) early morning urine samples;

d) blood samples;

e) X rays of the urinary tract, often using injections of dye into the bloodstream to show up obstructions, or introducing dye into the bladder to show its action; and

f) cystoscopy, which is the surgical inspection of the inside of the urethra and bladder, using a "periscope tube" inserted into the urethra under general anesthetic.

The diagrams show "intravenous pyelograms" (IVPs): X rays of the urinary tract taken after iodine dye has been injected into the bloodstream. The iodine passes out through the urinary system.

IVP showing normal functioning of the kidneys and urinary tract

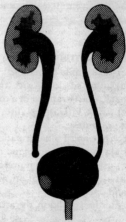

IVP showing blockage in one ureter, distention above the blockage, and a growth in the bladder

L26-29

L26 Treatment

Depending on the cause of trouble, treatment may include:
a) antibiotics and similar drugs, to combat urinary and/or kidney infection;
b) increase of the patient's fluid intake;
c) drugs to relax the muscles of the bladder;
d) drugs to combat vaginal infection;
e) hormone therapy to restore mucus and tissue characteristics;
f) surgery for urinary blockages;
g) surgery to deal with other causes of inflammation, eg repair for a prolapsed uterus.

When on a course of drugs:
a) the symptoms may vanish soon after starting the course;
b) there may be side effects, eg nausea or depression.
But it is very important to finish the whole course.
Drinking a vitamin C source may be requested, to bring urinal acidity into a range where the drug works best.

L27 Self-Help in an Attack

Cystitis attacks still have to be dealt with, despite medical help and preventative precautions (see J03). At the first hint of trouble:
a) pass a urine specimen into a clean, closed container, for the doctor;
b) drink 1(US)pt (½ liter) of cold water;
c) take a mild painkiller;
d) lie or sit down with two hot water bottles, one against the back, one (wrapped in a towel) high between the legs;
e) drink ½(US)pt (¼ liter) of water or diluted fruit juice every 20 minutes;
f) (but not if a heart patient) take a teaspoon of bicarbonate of soda in a little water, and repeat each hour for 3 hours;
g) use diuretic pills if prescribed; and
h) after every urination, wash the skin between anus and vulva and dab it dry.
After half an hour, the attack should begin to ease.

Sexual Infections

L28 Venereal Disease

The term venereal disease (VD) is used for certain infections which are almost always passed on by sexual contact. This happens because:

a) the microorganisms that cause them usually live in the infected person's genitals — or in some other place (such as mouth or anus) where they have been put by sexual activity; and

b) to infect another person, they usually have to enter the body through an orifice (such as the genital opening, anus, or mouth), and sexual activity gives them this chance. The first symptoms of disorder appear on the part of the body that has been in contact with the infected part of the infected person.

Otherwise, these disorders have little in common. Some are caused by bacteria, some by viruses, some by other microorganisms. Some are rare in our society, others epidemic. Some may only be painful or troublesome; others, if untreated, crippling or fatal. And at the same time, there are also a number of other infections, not officially classified as VD, but typically passed on by or associated with sexual activity.

Some kinds of venereal disease have been known since medicine began. Syphilis, the most notorious, may have been brought back to Europe from America as a result of Columbus' expedition in 1492. Cases of VD increased rapidly during World War II, and in the last 20 years cases in many countries have multiplied 3 or 4 times. The frequency of gonorrhea, for example, is now second only to that of the common cold.

L29 Syphilis

Syphilis is sometimes nicknamed "the pox" or "scab." It is the most serious of sexual infections. Its prevalence varies. In the USA, it is the third most common reportable disease. In the UK, for example, it is comparatively rare. Worldwide, there are about 50 million cases.

CAUSES

Syphilis is caused by tiny bacteria shaped like corkscrews: "spirochetes." These thrive in the warm, moist linings of the genital passages, rectum, and mouth, and can live in concentrated sites (sores) on the skin surface, but die almost immediately outside the human body. So the infection always

L29

spreads by direct physical contact, and in practice almost always by sexual contact. Whether the probing organ is penis, tongue, or (occasionally) finger, and whether the receiving organ is mouth, genitals, or rectum, a syphilitic site on either one can infect the other. Very occasionally syphilis does occur from close nonsexual contact (and cases have occurred in doctors and dentists from their professional work); but it cannot be spread by physical objects such as lavatory seats, towels, or cups. It can, however, be inherited from an infected mother, resulting sometimes in stillbirth or deformity, and in other cases in hidden infection that causes trouble later.

INCUBATION

There is an "incubation period," between catching syphilis and showing the first signs — always between 9 days and 3 months, and usually 3 weeks or more. About 1,000 germs are typically picked up on infection. After 3 weeks these have multiplied to 100 to 200 million. If the disorder is untreated, they can invade the whole body, eventually causing death.

Syphilis has 4 stages. Each has typical symptoms, but these can vary or be absent.

PRIMARY STAGE

The first symptom is in the part that has been in contact with the infected person: genitals, rectum, or mouth. A spot appears and grows into a sore that oozes a colorless fluid (but no blood). The sore feels like a button: round or oval, firm, and just under $\frac{1}{2}$in (1.27cm) across. A week or so later, the glands in the groin may swell — but they do not usually become tender, so it may not be noticed. There is no feeling of illness, and the sore heals in a few weeks without treatment.

SECONDARY STAGE

This occurs when the bacteria have spread through the body. It can follow the primary stage immediately, but usually there is a gap of several weeks. The person feels generally unwell. There may be headaches, loss of appetite, general aches and pains, sickness, and perhaps fever. Also there are breaks in the skin, and sometimes a dark red rash, lasting for weeks or even months. The rash appears on the back of the legs and the front of the arms, and often too on the body, face, hands, and feet.

It may be flat or raised, does not itch, is not infectious, and looks like many other skin complaints. Other symptoms can include: hair falling out in patches; sores in the mouth, nose,

Sexual Infections

throat, or genitals, or in soft folds of skin; and swollen glands throughout the body. The sores — like the original primary-stage sore — are very infectious. All these symptoms eventually disappear without treatment, after anything from 3 weeks to 9 months.

LATENT STAGE

This may last for anything from a few months to 50 years. There are no symptoms. After about 2 years, the person ceases to be infectious (though a woman can still sometimes give the disease to a baby she bears). But presence of syphilis can still be shown by blood tests.

TERTIARY STAGE

This occurs in about $\frac{1}{3}$ of those who have not been treated earlier. The disease now shows itself in concentrated form and often causes permanent damage in one part of the body.

Common are ulcers in the skin and lesions on ligaments, joints,

Primary sore

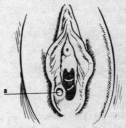

a The primary stage syphilitic sore is hard with a clearly defined edge.

or on bones. These are painful, but tertiary syphilis is more serious if it attacks heart, blood vessels, or nervous system. It can then kill, blind, paralyze, cripple, or render insane.

TESTS

Syphilis is not easy to diagnose. Its symptoms are often mild or indistinct. Testing sores for bacteria, or blood for antibodies, is necessary. Neither always works, so repeat tests are important.

TREATMENT

This involves antibiotics — usually penicillin. Given in primary or secondary stages, it completely cures most cases. Tests and examination often last more than 2 years afterward, to make sure the cure is complete.

In the latent and even tertiary stages, syphilis can still be eradicated and further damage halted; but existing tertiary-stage damage often cannot be repaired.

L29-30

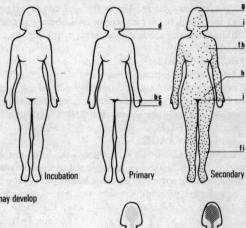

Incubation   Primary   Secondary

The primary sore may develop
in or on the:
b genitals,
c anus,
d mouth, or sometimes
e hand.
Secondary stage symptoms include:
f skin rash,
g patches of loose hair,
h swollen lymph nodes, and
i secondary sores in the mouth,
   nose, throat, genitals, or skin.
Tertiary syphilis can attack almost
any part of the body.

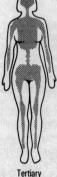

Latent   Tertiary

L30 Gonorrhea

Gonorrhea (sometimes nicknamed "the clap") has become epidemic in recent years — partly because it is so easy for a woman to have it without knowing it. There are now nearly a million reported cases in the USA every year, and the true figure is probably many times that. Several infections in a person in a single year is not too uncommon. Worldwide, there are about 150 million cases.

Sexual Infections

CAUSES

Like syphilis, gonorrhea:

a) is caused by a bacterium that thrives in the warm moist lining of urethra, vagina, rectum, or mouth;

b) is normally only passed on by sexual contact, but may be sometimes by close body contact or by inheritance from an infected mother; and

c) cannot be picked up from objects (though perhaps it can be carried by pubic lice, which can sometimes be picked up from objects such as lavatory seats).

Unlike syphilis, the form of sexual contact involved is normally only genital or anal intercourse. Oral contact does not often pass on gonorrhea; if it does, it is usually fellatio, rather than cunnilingus, that is responsible. (But some scientists even allow possibility of infection through kissing.)

SYMPTOMS IN MEN

These are considered first, as they are more noticeable. Incubation is usually under a week, but can be up to a month. It is followed by:

a) discomfort inside the penis;

b) thick discharge, usually yellow-green, from the penis tip; and

c) a burning feeling on urinating. Later there may be swollen glands, urethral abscess, and swollen infected testes (with danger of sterility).

SYMPTOMS IN WOMEN

In women, incubation is longer, and the eventual symptoms, if any, are much less severe or identifiable. There may be discomfort on urinating, more frequent urination, and vaginal discharge. The discharge is distinctively yellow, and unpleasant in smell — but this may be unnoticed due to the typically small quantities involved. Often there are no symptoms. So up to 90% of cases in women occur without the woman being aware of the disease. But she is still just as infectious — and just as much at risk. For if untreated, the infection may spread (see diagram overleaf) to:

a) glands around the vaginal entrance, making them swell, sometimes as large as a golf ball;

b) the rectum (because of the closeness of the two openings), causing inflammation and perhaps a discharge; and/or

L30-32

c) the cervix, uterus, Fallopian tubes, and pelvic interior.
Fallopian infection can result in fever, abdominal pain, backaches, sickness, painful or excessive periods, and pain during intercourse. If not treated quickly, sterility can result. It can also kill mother and fetus, by causing any pregnancy to be ectopic (see D06). Even where gonorrhea does not affect the Fallopian tubes, it can result in premature birth, umbilical cord inflammation, maternal fever, and blindness in the child. Finally, gonorrhea can spread to the bloodstream and infect bone joints, causing arthritis.

If oral contact results in infection, it is mainly as a throat disorder that is often not recognized as gonorrhea. It is also unlikely to infect others, because the lymph tissues where the bacteria can survive are deep in the tonsil area.

TEST AND TREATMENT
Gonorrhea is diagnosed by laboratory analysis of any discharge or of a smear from an affected part. Treatment is with antibiotics — usually penicillin, though many forms of gonorrhea are becoming more resistant to it. Qualified medical surveillance is vital. Alcohol can interfere with cure.

Spread of infection through the reproductive tract

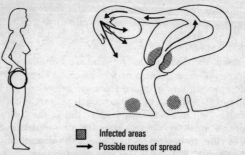

▨ Infected areas
➡ Possible routes of spread

L31 Other Venereal Diseases

The other officially designated venereal diseases are much less common in temperate climates.

SOFT CHANCRE (CHANCROID) is caused by a bacillus (a rod-shaped bacterium), and is contracted sexually (usually by intercourse). After 3 to 5 days' incubation, it generally produces an ulcer on the genitals and painful swollen glands (but

Sexual Infections

either sex can carry the infection without symptoms). Treatment is with antibiotics and other drugs.

LYMPHOGRANULOMA VENEREUM This is caused by a very small bacterium, and can be contracted from infected bedding and clothing as well as (more usually) from sexual intercourse. After 5 to 21 days' incubation, it produces a small genital blister or ulcer. Later there can be internal complications. Treatment is with antibiotics.

GRANULOMA INGUINALE This is caused by a bacillus, and is contracted sexually (usually by intercourse). After 1 to 3 weeks' incubation, it produces bright red painless genital sores. Treatment is with antibiotics.

In the USA, soft chancre cases do turn up in northern city clinics, but the others are seldom found outside the south.

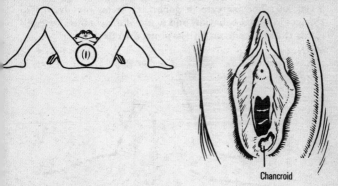

Chancroid

L32 Nonspecific Urethritis

NSU is the most common of all sexual disorders in men, but in women the symptoms are often insignificant or hard to diagnose. Also, it is not a venereal disease in the strict sense, or even necessarily an infection, since it does not always seem to require intercourse with an infected person to develop. In fact, its cause is uncertain — as its name implies. It may be due to an unidentified microorganism, or possibly just to a reaction between the penis and the chemistry of the vagina. Certainly it can develop in two people who have never had intercourse with anyone else. It often seems linked with changes in sex habits.

L32-34

Symptoms in men resemble gonorrhea: discharge and discomfort when urinating. It can be very recurrent, and untreated it can spread to other parts of the body, sometimes even causing permanent damage to joints and eyes. But such complications are very rare in women.

L33 Incidence of VD

The graphs show the changing incidence of gonorrhea and syphilis in the USA and UK, in terms of the number of people with reported infections in every 10,000 of the population. (Figures are for men and women combined.)

But the actual number of cases is always far higher than the reported number: eg, total US reported gonorrhea figures for 1974 were 874,000, but the actual number was possibly about 2,700,000. The increase in gonorrhea seems mainly due to changes in sexual behavior, and to use of the contraceptive pill rather than the condom with its protective effect.

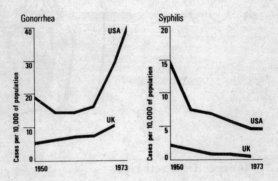

L34 Symptoms

The diagrams show possible signs of venereal disease in women. All these symptoms usually have some other cause — not venereal disease. But do not delay in getting proper medical advice. If symptoms disappear, it may just mean that the infection has progressed naturally to its next stage. You may still have a venereal disease; and you may still be able to infect others.

Sexual Infections

Possible symptoms in the genital area include:

a a sore, rash, or ulcer, on, in, or around the genitals;
b similarly, a sore, rash, or ulcer, on, in, or around the anus;
c unusual vaginal discharge;
d pain or a burning feeling on urinating;
e increased frequency of urination;
f itching or soreness of vagina or vulva; and
g swollen glands in the groin.

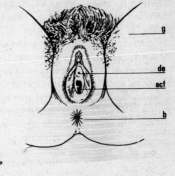

Possible symptoms on the head and body include:

h a sore, ulcer, or rash on or in the mouth (or sometimes the nose);
i an eye infection;
j loss of patches of hair;
k persistant sore throat after fellatio;
l a rash on the body;
m sores in soft folds of skin;
n swollen glands in the armpits;
o a sore, ulcer, or rash on the fingers or hand.

Possible symptoms if infection spreads up the reproductive tract include:
p nausea;
q backache;
r abdominal pain;
s pain during intercourse;
t painful or excessive periods; and fever.

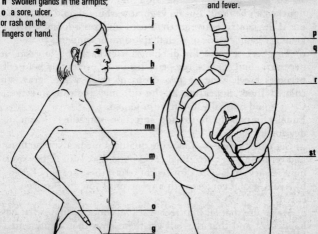

L35-36

L35 Prevention

There is no immunity to VD or vaccine against it. But various measures can help reduce the chances of infection:

a) use of some contraceptive foams (Delfen, Emko), some contraceptive creams (Cooper, Ortho), and some contraceptive jellies (Cortane, Ortho-Gynol, Milex Crescent, Koromex AII, suppositories, Progonasyl antiseptic);

b) use of some noncontraceptive vaginal products (Lorophyn suppositories, Progonaryl antiseptic);

c) use of a condom by the male partner;

d) inspection of the male penis, for an ulcer or sore, or for infectious discharge from the penis tip;

e) use of a "morning after" antibiotic dose, under prescription from a doctor or clinic (but this may be very difficult to obtain);

f) urinating immediately after intercourse; and possibly

g) washing the genitals before and after intercourse.

In practice the first two methods are probably the best.

Note that:

a) As an anti-VD measure, a condom needs to be put on before any sex play begins. It then guards fairly effectively against gonorrhea and NSU but not against syphilis.

b) To wash out the vagina after intercourse, a low-pressure douche can be used. But no vaginal washing should be carried out if the contraceptive method used involves a foam, jelly, or cream, whether alone or with diaphragm or condom.

c) To check a penis for discharge, roll back the foreskin, if necessary, and squeeze the penis firmly — preferably before it becomes erect. One or two drops of thick white, gray, or colored fluid, appearing at the tip, may indicate infection. Clear liquid is usually just urine or semen.

Equally important is to stop infection spreading if you do develop it:

a) Get cured properly, following qualified medical instructions, and returning for prescribed checks and tests even if they seem unnecessary. In fact, ask for repeat tests if these are not offered.

b) Avoid sexual contact with anyone until you are sure you are cured.

c) Make sure that all your recent sexual contacts know what has happened, and that they all get themselves thoroughly tested and, if necessary, treated.

Sexual Infections

L36 Other Sexual Infections

These include genital versions of two common skin disorders — warts and cold sores; infestation by certain minute insect parasites; and trichomoniasis and candidiasis (see L16).

GENITAL WARTS are fairly common and very contagious. They are spread by sexual contact, perhaps caused by a virus, and appear, after 1 to 6 months' incubation, on, in, or around genitals or anus. They are usually cured by repeated use of a resin application. If this fails, they may have to be burnt off with chemicals or electricity.

GENITAL HERPES, or cold sores, are not very common, though contagious. The virus responsible is thought to lie dormant in the skin for long periods. When activated, it causes a genital or anal sore that weeps colorless fluid and forms a scab. There is no sure treatment (though bathing in salt solution may help), but it usually disappears after about 10 days.

INFESTATIONS are passed on by sexual or sometimes other close body contact, and are not especially common.

a Scabies, or "the itch," is caused by a tiny mite, which mainly lives on or around the genitals. The female mite burrows beneath the skin to lay her eggs. The symptoms — itchy lumps and tracks — become noticeable after 4 to 6 weeks' incubation. They can occur between the fingers, on buttocks and wrists, and in the armpits, as well as on the genitals. The itching is worse in warm conditions (eg in bed).

b Pubic lice, or "crabs," are genital versions of lice that can also occur in other hairy parts of the body. They feed on blood, and cause itching that can be severe. Treatment of both parasites involves painting the hair-bearing parts with appropriate chemicals.

a Scabies mite, very highly magnified

b Pubic louse, highly magnified

L37-38

L37 What Is Cancer?

Cancer is one of several disorders which can result when the process of cell division in a person's body gets out of control. Such disorders produce tissue growths called "tumors." A cancer is a certain kind of tumor.

Cancer attacks one in every five people.

NORMAL CELL DIVISION

The body is constantly producing new cells for the purposes of growth and repair — about 500,000 million daily. It does this by cell division: one parent cell divides to form two new cells. When this process is going correctly, the new cells show the same characteristics as the tissue in which they originate. They are capable of carrying out the functions that the body requires that tissue to perform. They do not migrate to parts of the body where they do not belong; and if they were placed in such a part artificially they might not survive.

TUMORS

In a tumor, the process of cell division has gone wrong. Cells multiply in an uncoordinated way, independent of the normal control mechanisms. They produce a new growth in the body, that does not fulfill a useful function. This is a tumor, or "neoplasm." A tumor is often felt as a hard lump, because its cells are more closely packed than normal.

Tumors may be "benign" or "malignant." A cancer is a malignant tumor. That is, it may go on growing until it threatens the continued existence of the body.

BENIGN TUMORS

In a benign tumor:

the cells reproduce in a way that is still fairly orderly;

they are only slightly different from the cells of the surrounding tissue;

their growth is slow and may stop spontaneously;

the tumor is surrounded by a capsule of fibrous tissue, and does not invade the normal tissue;

and its cells do not spread through the body.

A wart is a benign tumor. Benign tumors are not fatal unless the space they take up exerts pressure on nearby organs which proves fatal. This usually only happens with some benign tumors in the skull.

Cancer

MALIGNANT TUMORS

In a malignant tumor, the cells reproduce in a completely disorderly fashion.

The cells differ considerably from those of the surrounding tissue (generally, they show less specialization);

the tumor's growth is rapid, compared with the surrounding tissue;

the tumor has no surrounding capsule, and can therefore invade and destroy adjacent tissue;

the original tumor is able to spread to other parts of the body by metastasis (see L39) and produce secondary growth there.

A malignant tumor is usually fatal if untreated, because of its destructive action on normal tissue.

BIOPSY

A biopsy is the most certain way of distinguishing between benign and malignant tumors. A piece of the tumor is surgically removed, and then studied under a microscope.

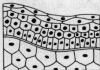
Normal body tissue

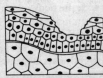
Damaged body tissue

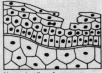
Normal cell replacement

Abnormal malignant growth

Loss of basement membrane integrity

L38 Causes of Cancer

CHROMOSOME DAMAGE

In cancerous cells, the characteristics of malignant growth are passed on from one generation to another. This means that the genetic code must have been damaged. This, in fact, is seen, if the chromosomes of cancerous cells are examined. Normal cells have 46 chromosomes arranged in 23 pairs. Almost all cancer cells are abnormal in the number and/or structure of these chromosomes.

L38-39

NORMAL DEVIANCE

Cells with genetic defects appear in the body every day; so many millions of cells are being made, that some mistakes are inevitable. But most die almost immediately, because they are too faulty to survive, or because they are recognized as abnormal and eaten by white blood corpuscles. Others are only slightly defective, and not malignant. Only very rarely do malignant cells survive and reproduce successfully.

Appearance of cancer in a person may simply be due to this unlucky chance. Alternatively, it may be that the body has "immunity" to such malignant cells, and that this sometimes breaks down. This would explain why cancer can sometimes remain "dormant" in a person for many years.

SPECIAL FACTORS

A few factors have been recognized that make genetic damage in cells more likely. But they only explain a tiny proportion of cancers.

a) Certain chemicals can cause cancer to form, if they are repeatedly in contact with the body over a period of time. Such chemicals are called carcinogens; but apart from tobacco smoke, they usually only affect workers whose job brings them into regular contact with them. (However, atmospheric pollution may also be slightly carcinogenic.)

b) Certain viruses can pass malignant tumors from one animal to another, and the same may occur in humans. But so far only one very rare form of cancer is thought to be caused this way. Apart from this, human cancer seems not to be virus induced — and therefore not infectious.

c) Ionizing radiation. Without correct protection, X rays can cause skin cancer, and radiation can cause leukemia. Also ultraviolet rays (as in sunlight) may cause skin cancer in some circumstances.

d) Continued physical irritation. There is disagreement over this, but some experts believe that continued physical disturbance of the skin or mucous membrane can cause cancer (not just accelerate it).

CORRELATIVE FACTORS

Some individuals are more likely to develop cancer than others.

a) Heredity. Actual cancerous growths are not inherited. But a predisposition for cancer can be passed on. It may be that

Cancer

some inherited characteristics make a person's cells more likely to become malignant.

b) Age. Most cancers occur in the 50 to 60 age group. However, children and adolescents are susceptible to leukemia, brain tumors, and sarcomas of the bone.

c) Sex. In almost all countries, cancer occurs more frequently in men than in women.

d) Geographical location. Eg for some unknown reason, gastric cancer is most frequent in coastal countries with cold climates.

e) Cultural habits. Eg cancer of the penis is much less common in societies where circumcision is usual.

L39 Cancer Growth

CELL DIVISION

Generally, cancerous cells cannot divide faster than normal cells. But normal cell division reaches its maximum rate only in times of injury and repair. Cancerous growths are continually producing cells at this maximum rate without check. They are less successful than normal tissue could be, because many of the faulty cancerous cells die. Nevertheless, the result is that cancerous growths grow faster than normal tissue.

METASTASIS

Metastasis is the process by which cancerous cells travel from the original (primary) cancer site to other parts of the body. It occurs when cancerous cells get caught up in the flow of blood or lymph. The cells are carried along in the vessels, until they lodge in another part of the body. If they succeed in establishing themselves there, this becomes a new (secondary) cancer site. If a secondary site gets large enough, it can also metastasize in turn.

Cancer that has metastasized along the lymph vessels normally sets up its secondary sites in the glands.

Cancer that has metastasized in the bloodstream sets up secondary sites in the bones, lungs, and liver.

Cancers in the brain do not metastasize but cancers elsewhere can metastasize to the brain. Some sites are more receptive than others. Commonest locations for secondary growths are the bones, brain, lungs, kidneys, and adrenal glands. Others are much rarer. A cancer can also spread through the body simply by the process of growth.

L40-42

L40 Sites of Cancer

Cancers can grow almost anywhere in the body, but the most common sites are shown in the diagram. Cancers are classified by the kind of tissue in which the primary growth occurred. Tumors originating in the "epithelial" cells (eg skin, mucous membrane, and glands) are called carcinomas; those in connective tissue (eg muscle and bone), sarcomas. Secondary tumors are classified by the kind of primary tumor that they came from. This is possible because metastasized growths still show some of the characteristics of the tissue from which they originally came. Cancer in general has become vastly more prevalent in the present century: in 1900 it was the seventh main cause of death in the USA, today it is the second. (Some experts believe this is simply because people are living longer — for likelihood of cancerous growths increases with age.)

Nevertheless, some types of cancer have shown a dramatic fall in recent years, eg stomach cancer. This particular example may be linked with changes in techniques of food preservation.

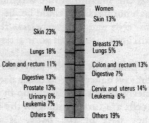

Men
Skin 23%
Lungs 18%
Colon and rectum 11%
Digestive 13%
Prostate 13%
Urinary 6%
Leukemia 7%
Others 9%

Women
Skin 13%
Breasts 23%
Lungs 5%
Colon and rectum 13%
Digestive 7%
Cervix and uterus 14%
Leukemia 6%
Others 19%

L41 Symptoms

a) Any unusual bleeding or discharge from mouth, genitals, or anus (including, in women, bleeding from the breast and menstrual bleeding between periods).

b) Any lump or thickening or swelling on the body surface, or any swelling of one limb.

c) Any increase in size or change in color or appearance in a mole or wart.

d) A sore that will not heal normally.

e) Persistent constipation, diarrhea, or indigestion that is unusual for the person.

f) Hoarseness or dry cough that lasts more than three weeks.

g) Difficulty in swallowing or urinating.

Cancer

h) Sudden unexplained loss in weight.

If you develop any of these symptoms, you should visit your doctor. Nearly always, the cause will be something else, not cancer. But do not delay. If it is cancer, quick diagnosis is essential.

L42 Treatment

Treatments for cancer have a good chance of success only if the tumor is still localized. Early diagnosis is vital. Once a tumor has metastasized, successful treatment is almost impossible.

SURGERY Surgical removal of localized malignant tumors at an early stage is the only completely successful form of treatment known at present. In later stages, surgery may be attempted in conjunction with other techniques.

RADIOTHERAPY Cancer cells are killed by radiation more easily than normal cells. Radiotherapy seeks to destroy cancerous tissue by focusing a stream of radiation on it. This can be done only if the cancer is still localized, and can be destroyed without causing radiation damage to the rest of the body.

The rays used are either X rays or those of radioactive materials such as radium or cobalt.

CHEMOTHERAPY This is treatment by the administration of chemicals. Again, the major difficulty is finding drugs that will destroy cancer cells without harming normal cells. Three main types of chemicals are used:

those that interfere with the cancer cells' reproductive processes;

those that interfere with the cells' metabolic processes;

those that increase the natural resistance of the body to the tumor cells.

These chemicals can affect the whole of the body, specific regions, or the tumors themselves, depending on how they are applied.

HORMONE THERAPY is used mainly for tumors of the endocrine glands and related organs. It is also useful in the treatment of metastases originating from these areas (eg in women, against disseminated breast cancer). Success depends on whether the cancerous cells still have the specialized relationship with the hormone that the original tissue had. In women, hormone therapy may include removal of the ovaries.

L43

L43 Cancer of the Reproductive Tract

CERVIX

Cervical cancer is on the decline. Nevertheless, about 2 women in 100 get it, and one of these dies from it. It can occur at any age, but 45-50 is most common. A possible symptom is unusual vaginal bleeding, eg between periods, after intercourse, or more than 6 months after the menopause. But analysis of the cervical tissue is the only sure evidence. The well-known "Pap" smear test involves the painless gathering of a few sample cells on the end of a wooden spatula (the physician may well do a pelvic examination to check the uterus and ovaries at the same time). The sample is sent to a specialist laboratory, fixed in alcohol, stained in solution, and examined for abnormal cells. In 1,000 smears, 20 might show some abnormality, and perhaps 3 the early signs of cancer. (The other abnormalities will include signs of vaginal infection, etc.)

A woman should have had such a test by the time she reaches 25 (or when she first becomes pregnant, if this is earlier). It should be repeated twice in the first year, and thereafter every year till she is 65. (Occasionally cancer can appear after a recent negative smear; but this is rare.)

If possible signs of cancer are found, a repeat smear may be taken, followed by a larger specimen using curettage (see L09) or a tiny punch. If cancer is confirmed, the alternatives are:

a) conization, in which cervical tissue is cut away (the cervix is stitched, and rapidly heals with little pain and usually no after-effects); or

b) hysterectomy (see L10).

Which is used depends on the state of the tumor. Hysterectomy is necessary once malignant growth has begun. It gives almost 100% success, but a few very advanced cases may need radiation therapy or further surgery.

UTERUS

Cancer here is less common; it usually only occurs in older women (typically 50-60). The diabetic and obese are susceptible, and it can run in a family. Tumor growth is slow; bleeding symptoms are significant. Diagnosis is by curettage of the uterus under anesthetic; treatment by hysterectomy and X-ray therapy. If treated early enough, 80% of patients survive more than 5 years.

Cancer

OVARIES

Ovarian cancer accounts for 5% of cancers in women. It is more frequent after 40, and especially after the menopause. Its slow growth is hard to detect. The first sign is enlargement of the ovary, showing up on pelvic examination — but only 5% of ovary enlargements are cancerous. Pelvic examinations every 5 years should catch them in time.

VULVA

Cancer of the vulva is rare, and usually only found in old women. It is typically preceded by long-standing vulval itching, and sometimes an ulcer (but in 99% of cases these symptoms do not signify cancer). Diagnosis is by examination of tissue samples taken under anesthetic.

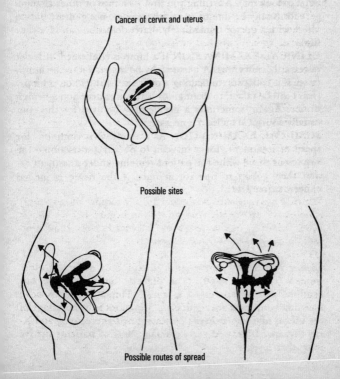

Cancer of cervix and uterus

Possible sites

Possible routes of spread

L44-45

L44 Breast Cancer

Almost a quarter of cancer in women is breast cancer, and 5% of women contract it. If it is caught before metastasis, 9 out of 10 survive. But metastasis can occur within a month of the tumor appearing. Despite medical advance, the death rate from breast cancer has been steady for over 40 years.

WHO GETS BREAST CANCER? The disease is commonest in women aged 40 to 60. Heredity, diet, and estrogen levels in the body are all under investigation as possible significant factors. Research suggests that early first childbirth, and breastfeeding, may both make breast cancer less likely in the mother.

SELF-EXAMINATION It is vital to check the breasts once every month for any changes (see J04 for the procedure and what to look for). Anything you find — lumps or other changes — will usually be due to some other cause, not cancer; but do check with a doctor immediately. Early detection can save your life.

CLINICAL EXAMINATION If a lump is confirmed, it is not necessarily cancerous. A needle may be inserted into the lump, to see if it collapses (indicating a cyst: see L45). If not, a biopsy (L37) will be taken, to distinguish between cancer and a benign tumor. Again, sometimes a needle may be used for this, but usually a surgical incision is necessary.

SURGICAL EXAMINATION As a result, it is common, for speed of treatment, for a surgeon to obtain and examine the suspicious tissue while the patient remains under anesthetic — and then go on to operate at once if the tissue is judged cancerous (see L47).

Cancer

L45 Noncancerous Disorders

Other disorders have symptoms similar to breast cancer.

FIBROADENOSIS (CHRONIC MASTITIS) features a permanent increase in the breast's glandular content, due to hormonal imbalance. The breast may feel lumpy or rubbery, all over or in patches, and there may be some pain, particularly before menstruation or after heavy lifting. Most common between the ages of 40 and 55, fibroadenosis is a normal bodily change for many women. Treatment may not be needed — but always check with a doctor.

CYSTS AND BENIGN TUMORS Perhaps 75% of breast lumps are nonmalignant. Breast cysts are small sacs in the breast tissue, filled with liquid, and usually harmless. Most common in women aged 35 to 45, they do not always need treatment. Benign tumors (see L37) may swell until pressure on nerves or neighboring tissues causes pain and requires their removal; but they cannot invade or destroy other tissue as cancer can.

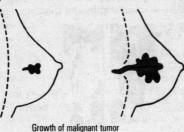

Growth of malignant tumor

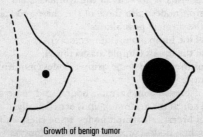

Growth of benign tumor

L46-47

L46 Screening Techniques

MAMMOGRAPHY This X-ray technique is often used as an aid in the diagnosis of breast cancer. It involves placing the breast in direct contact with the X-ray film. Usually two views of each breast are taken. Any malignancy shows up as an irregular opaque patch in the breast. One run of 2,000 mammograms detected 92% of cancers present. Mammography alone is not usually thought sufficient for certain diagnosis, but in combination with clinical examination and biopsy, around 97% of lumps examined can be correctly diagnosed.

THERMOGRAPHY This is another method helpful in the detection of breast cancer. In a normal person, 45% of the heat given off by the skin is infrared radiation.

Thermography is the technique used to record in a photograph the way in which this heat is given off. A malignant growth emits more heat than the surrounding tissue, and so shows up as a light patch on the photograph. Thermography, however, is less successful than mammography and clinical examination.

Typical thermographs

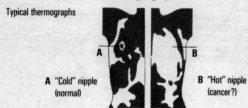

A "Cold" nipple (normal)

B "Hot" nipple (cancer?)

L47 Treatment

Breast cancer usually spreads in the lymph system, beginning with the armpit nodes (also those of the chest and spine). This determines the surgical possibilities:

a) removal of the lump alone (lumpectomy);

b) removal of the breast (simple mastectomy);

c) removal of breast and some armpit nodes (modified radical mastectomy);

d) removal of breast, some armpit nodes, and some chest wall muscles (radical mastectomy); and, occasionally

e) removal of breast, all armpit nodes, some chest wall muscles, and some chest nodes (superradical mastectomy).

Cancer

Which is chosen depends on:

a) the decision about which to minimize — deformity or the risk of recurrence;

b) surgical opinion: eg does simple mastectomy with radiotherapy give results just as good as a "radical"? — and especially

c) information about the tumor's size, type, position and spread. This last must mainly come from actual surgical observation; and as a result a patient can go under anesthetic not knowing how much of her body she will lose. Preliminary diagnostic surgery, though, may be impossible to arrange, and take up vital lifesaving time.

Surgery may, as noted, be accompanied by drugs and/or radiotherapy (see L42). But again there are difficult issues: of effectiveness versus side effects, and timing.

The more extensive operations are followed by physiotherapy, to minimize the effects of muscle loss on arm movement and breathing abilities.

Lymph nodes near the breast, and likely routes of spread in breast cancer

Simple mastectomy: area removed and stitching

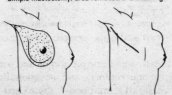

▨ Area removed

Radical mastectomy: area removed and stitching

M01-03

M01 Aging Starts Young

Everyone grows old; though some people show — and feel — their age more than others. And as the illustration shows, the process of aging begins surprisingly early. Decline in a few capabilities is already occurring in adolescence; by the middle to late 20s the main process of aging has begun. However, the most obvious symptoms of aging only become apparent late in life. It is then that profound changes in the human body go on to influence an individual's abilities, appearance, behavior, and status in society. Modern medicine can prolong the life span — but it cannot yet prolong youth. Many of the troubles of old age can be eased; but efforts to slow down the aging process itself are still simply guesswork.

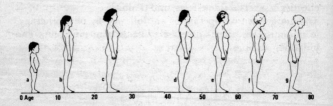

0 Age	10	20	30	40	50	60	70	80

a CHILDHOOD

b EARLY TEENS Peak of physical energy passed at 12. Eyes have begun to lose their ability to change focus.

c YOUNG ADULT Irreversible nerve cell loss starts in the brain and spinal cord. In childless women, the chances of conception begin to become less predictable.

d MIDDLE AGE Muscle strength and some mental capabilities already past their best. Female hormone production is likely to start to decline.

e AFTER THE MENOPAUSE Fertility has ceased. Body fat becomes redistributed.

f THE ONSET OF OLD AGE Weakened muscles cause the spine to droop. Hearing of high frequency sounds reduces by up to 75%. Disorders of the joints may now appear. Body weight diminishes.

g OLD AGE Decline of body's efficiency continues. Muscular strength is half that of a 20 year old. Intellectual efficiency may be reduced; character changes and organic brain disorders are possible.

The Process of Aging

M02 Why Aging Occurs

The underlying causes of aging are not yet properly understood. However, there are two tentative theories.

CELL MUTATION

This is currently thought of as the main cause of aging.

Most cells in the body reproduce to replace cells that have died. They do so by "somatic division," ie by dividing into two. In this way the exact characteristics of the original cell are preserved. However, it is possible for mutation to occur in a cell. This is any form of damage affecting the chromosomes, which are the code system built into the cell that decides how it operates.

Mutation can be caused by the gradual exposure over a lifetime to natural radiation (from the sun or from naturally occuring isotopes). Less normally, it may also be caused by disease, chemicals, or radiation from nuclear activity, exposure to X rays, etc.

When mutation occurs, a cell may become inactive, or do its job badly, or be actively dangerous (as in the case of cancer).

Moreover, because chromosomal damage is involved, the distortion is passed on whenever the original cell reproduces. Somatic division means that the number of mutated cells increases in geometric progression (1, 2, 4, 8, 16, 32, 64). In this way, areas of the body's activities become inefficient or disrupted.

NERVE CELL LOSS

From the age of about 25, there is a continuous loss of nerve cells ("neurons") from the brain and spinal cord. These cells cannot be replaced once lost; and the rate of neuron loss is accelerated in age. The consequences of this are probably a major element in the aging process.

M03 Other Factors

Some other factors have been seen to play a part in aging, but they are not "causes" in the same sense as cell mutation and nerve cell loss are thought to be.

STRESS

Psychological stress often has physical manifestations, and it has been noticed that stress of all sorts (physical danger, pain, mental strain, etc) can cause premature aging. However, the biological process whereby this happens is not known.

M03-04

METABOLISM

As people grow older, there is a drop in the basal metabolic rate: that is, the energy production of the body at its lowest waking level. For example, the body temperature of an old person is on average 2°F (1.1°C) less than that of a 25 year old. Metabolic decline is a sign of the aging process, rather than a cause, but it has a wide impact on the body's functions and abilities.

HORMONE PRODUCTION

During the menopause, the ovaries stop producing estrogen. In men, production of testosterone similarly declines after the middle years, though it never reaches zero level. It was therefore natural for gerontologists to consider using injections of the appropriate hormone to make up the body's failing supply (see F13). However, although injections of these hormones can reduce some physical signs of aging (smooth out wrinkled skin, for example), they do not seem to prevent the basic physiological process of aging going on.

In general, hormonal decline seems to be one of the ways in which aging expresses itself, but it is not a basic cause.

M04 Changes Inside the Body

As a person ages, there is a general decrease in body efficiency. However, in the absence of disease, the natural changes that bring these about only occur very gradually and do not necessarily cause discomfort.

a) From about the age of 25, there is a continuous loss of nerve cells (neurons) from the brain and spinal cord. These cannot be replaced by the body.

b) With age, the skeleton, especially in women, becomes thinner and more brittle, as calcium is lost from the bones.

c) This calcium tends to be deposited in other areas especially the walls of the arteries and the cartilage of the ribs, causing loss of elasticity. One effect can be a restriction of lung capacity.

d) Hardening and narrowing of the arteries (arteriosclerosis) is also likely. This is responsible for the rise in blood pressure (which goes up about 0.5mm Hg a year from the onset of aging). The speed of blood flow also rises — though not excessively.

The Process of Aging

e) When arteriosclerosis is combined with atheroma (fatty deposits on the arteries' inner lining), the condition is known as atherosclerosis.

f) These disorders of the vascular system speed up tissue decay, through inadequate blood and oxygen supply. This especially affects the heart and brain.

g) As aging proceeds, most internal organs — such as liver, heart, and kidneys — become reduced in size and function. This is reflected in a reduction in the basal metabolic rate (that is, the energy production of the body at its lowest waking level); eg as noted, the energy production of an elderly person is on average 2°F (1.1°C) lower than that of a 25 year old.

h) Deterioration of the vertebral disks causes a slight reduction in the length of the spine.

i) Hormonal changes during the menopause (see F04) mean that it is no longer possible for a woman to bear children, and in the subsequent years her uterus shrinks to approximately ⅓ of its former size.

j) Muscles lose much of their strength, shape, and size. Joints become worn and lose some of their ease of articulation. Combined with the degeneration of the nervous system, ease and often confidence of movement are lost.

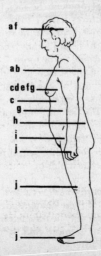

M05-06

M05 Changes in Appearance

Many of the changes that take place inside the body as it ages have an effect on the individual's appearance.

a) The main alterations are brought about by the redistribution of body fat. In later life, and especially after the menopause, fat disappears from the breasts (giving them a more sagging appearance), and from the face (deepening wrinkles). But new fat appears around the chin, waist, hips, and bottom.

b) At the same time, skin all over the body tends to become drier. It loses some of its elasticity and may chap readily in winter. It is this "drying out" process that, quite early in middle age, causes facial wrinkles to appear (see G24). Also, weakened blood capillaries beneath the skin may cause it to bruise more easily.

c) Hair is also affected by the aging process. Graying is caused by a decline in the production of natural coloring or pigment. For some, the process starts very early, while others retain their hair coloring well into old age. Balding is usually a male problem, but many women notice that their hair becomes thinner. Facial hair, though, may be more obvious.

d) The features of the face are changed not only by loss of fat, but also by atrophy of the facial bones, especially the jaw bone (making dentures harder to wear). Also, the eyes may appear dulled, because of an opaque ring outside the iris (this does not interfere with vision); and recession of the gums makes the person seem "long in the tooth."

e) Changes in the vertebrae and in muscle strength may cause the backbone to droop and the stomach to sag.

f) Some joints — especially the wrists, knees, and hips — begin to enlarge. Also, small, temporarily painful knobs may grow at the sides of the joints; but this is rare.

g) Patches of red appear on the backs of the hands and forearms, due to harmless ruptures in small blood vessels.

h) Tremor of the hands becomes common.

i) Feet frequently develop corns, calluses, bunions, and hard, thickened, ingrown or overgrown toenails.

While many of these changes are difficult, if not impossible, to reverse, several may be lessened by a sensible diet, a gentle keep-fit program, or — more controversially — hormone replacement therapy (see F13).

The Process of Aging

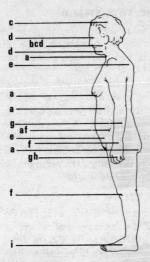

M06 Changing Abilities

It is possible to compare the physical abilities left to a person of 75 with the maximum abilities reached at her physical peak (usually sometime between the ages of 20 and 30). Factors such as work rate and hand grip show up the decline. Some of these, in an average 75 year old, are 50% less than at their peak. Underlying these changes are the declining efficiency of body processes (such as blood flow and oxygen uptake) and even declining size of body organs.

In the few examples shown, the degree of change ranges from a decline of only 10% (nerve conduction speed) to one of more than 60% (number of taste buds in the mouth).

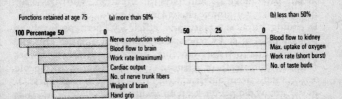

Functions retained at age 75   (a) more than 50%

100 Percentage 50   0
Nerve conduction velocity
Blood flow to brain
Work rate (maximum)
Cardiac output
No. of nerve trunk fibers
Weight of brain
Hand grip

(b) less than 50%

50   25   0
Blood flow to kidney
Max. uptake of oxygen
Work rate (short burst)
No. of taste buds

Mo7-10

M07 The Nervous System

In humans, as in all vertebrates, different levels of organization can be seen in the nervous system. The reflexes of the lowest level (the spinal cord and oldest parts of the brain) are present in the fetus.

Those of the forebrain and cerebral hemispheres develop after birth. With the onset of aging, the course of development is reversed. First, the higher levels are affected: memory, thought, and complex mental functions become slower and less reliable. Eventually the individual may pass through a "second childhood," with, finally, only basic reflexes remaining, such as eating, walking, coughing. On average, by the age of 70, the brain has lost 50% of its weight.

CHARACTER CHANGES
The frontal lobes of the brain — the first part to deteriorate — are less concerned with intelligence and intellectuality than with general personality, interest in life, deliberation, and consideration. Moreover, these higher functions often bear a repressive relationship to the lower, so that as the higher deteriorate the lower are released, in what appears an exaggerated form. Social inhibitions are removed, and the person may become increasingly selfish, inconsiderate, obstinate, and emotional.

M08 Self-image

Changes in temperament and behavior in old people may be accepted as inevitable. But how far they are really due to neurological and mental deterioration is often hard to judge. The changes may rather be a psychic reaction to the person's social, psychological, and physical situation. Old age often brings with it a dramatic change in a person's experience of life. Declining physical ability and efficiency, perhaps involving being looked after by others; the end of the working life; and isolation, due to family mobility, and disappearance of work contacts, and death of friends — all these can affect an old person's self-esteem and lead to depression and melancholia. Of course, many old people keep up a wide range of active interests — but for others it is difficult, due to lack of finance, isolation,

The Mind and Senses

physical incapacity, and lack of mental stimulation. The rate of change in modern society adds to their disorientation; and the way of life in many old people's homes does little to help. All this can result in apathy, listlessness, resentment, and mental stagnation, which others then dismiss as inevitable senility.

M09 Decline in Mental Abilities

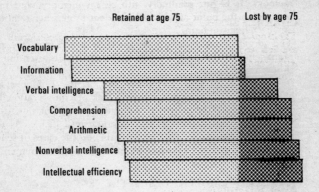

Retained at age 75   Lost by age 75

- Vocabulary
- Information
- Verbal intelligence
- Comprehension
- Arithmetic
- Nonverbal intelligence
- Intellectual efficiency

M10 Mental Illness

About 10% of people over 65 show some signs of organic brain disorder. Such mental illnesses due to old age were originally undifferentiated under the term "senility" — the loss of mental faculties with age.

However, four main conditions are now recognized.

ACUTE CONFUSION

This is one of the commonest mental disorders in old people. It is a disturbance of the brain due to physical illness elsewhere in the body, and is also known as "acute brain syndrome." Strange surroundings and other psychological factors may also play a part.

M10-12

The symptoms are confusion, delirium, and disorientation in time and place. Perception is dulled, and the sufferer is frightened, often reacting violently to situations that have been completely misinterpreted. Speech becomes incoherent and rambling. The outcome depends on the preexisting mental state and the original cause of illness, but complete recovery is rare.

SENILE DEMENTIA

This is the disorder that links most directly with the slow process of natural nerve cell loss. It usually begins to be noticeable between the ages of 70 and 80, and primarily affects the memory. It begins gradually with recent memory, and may proceed to the point at which the patient forgets her relations and even her own name.

This forgetfulness leads to incompetence in personal care and management: the person needs more and more attention as time goes on.

Disorientation in time and place also occurs. Emotions are blunted, and there is an increasing lack of consideration for others. Whether the course of the illness is rapid or slow, it is irreversible, and deterioration continues until death. As the numbers of old people rise, so inevitably do the cases of senile dementia. At present it is more common in women than men.

ARTERIOSCLEROTIC DEMENTIA

This is also due to the death of brain cells, though in this case the cells die because blockage in the arteries impairs their blood supply. The onset may be gradual, or follow suddenly upon a major stroke. In either case, the effects, in an old person, are irreversible.

Because the brain damage is restricted to the areas affected by the blockage, the basic personality may remain more intact than in senile dementia. The person usually retains more awareness and insight into her condition — though this can result in depression and fear.

DEPRESSIVE ILLNESS

This is a mental illness, but organic nervous decline plays a part

The Mind and Senses

in its appearance. It is characterized by acute feelings of sadness, inadequacy, anxiety, apathy, guilt, and fear. It may be triggered off by internal factors of mental make-up (endogenous depression), or by external events such as bereavement or knowledge of an incurable disease (reactive depression). It often results from a combination of both.

The illness manifests itself in moods ranging from apathy to despair, and in delusions, loss of appetite and weight, and a preoccupation with thoughts of suicide. It is, in fact, a major cause of suicide in the elderly. Although treatment may produce a cure, the chances of relapse are very great.

M11 The Senses in Aging

The physical atrophy that occurs with age also affects the 5 senses. As the nervous system degenerates through neuron loss, touch, taste, eyesight, hearing, and smell become less sensitive. This does not affect the body's physiological functioning, but may have dangerous consequences (eg an impaired sense of smell may mean that escaping gas is not detected). More serious sensory loss, though, comes from some illnesses brought about by, or occurring in, old age, and affecting the more complicated sense organs such as eye and ear.

M12 Hearing

PRESBYACUSIS is hearing loss due directly to age, ie to loss of efficiency in the hearing mechanisms, and to the slowing down of mental activity.

Mechanical losses especially affect the ability to detect high frequency sounds. By the age of 60 years, hearing of these has been reduced by 75%, though normal conversation and most other everyday sounds can still be distinguished with only slight distortion.

OTITIS EXTERNA (infection of the outer ear) is especially common in the aged, due partly to hearing aid earpieces that fit badly and are too infrequently cleaned.

M13-16

M13 Seeing

PRESBYOPIA is the term for the natural changes in the eye that result from old age. The most common (apart from the general loss of efficiency with age) is hardening of the lens. From the age of about 10 years onward, the lens gradually loses elasticity, and so ability to adjust focus. So, by the age of 60 years, it is often unable to focus on objects close at hand. Spectacles with convex lenses are then needed for reading, etc.

CATARACT This is caused by deficiences in the lens proteins, resulting in a special type of hardening and shrinkage at the center of the lens. The lens cracks and disintegrates, so losing transparency. Impairment of vision increases as the opaque area (the cataract) spreads outward. Cataracts occur in most people over 60 years of age, but are usually too small to affect sight significantly.

GLAUCOMA occurs mainly after the age of 50. It is caused by build-up of fluid pressure in the eye. The fluid that fills the eye (the aqueous humor) is normally being continually drained away and replaced by fresh. Drainage takes place along the canal of Schlemm, which lies at the junction of the iris and cornea. But sometimes the canal becomes blocked, through inflammation of the eye or swelling of the lens pushing the iris forward. The amount of fluid in the eye then increases as secretion of fresh fluid continues. Pressure builds up, damaging the optical disk and the visual fibers of the retina.
Loss of vision spreads gradually from the periphery to the whole visual field. Treatment is surgical.

SENILE MACULAR DYSTROPHY
The macular lutea is a small yellowish area of the retina, and the fovea lies at its center. Here visual perception is most perfect, and differentiation of minute objects takes place (for reading, etc). Senile macular dystrophy is a degeneration of this area due to impaired blood supply as a result of age. It is the most common eye disorder in the old.

Disorders of Age

M14 Disorders of Age

The atrophy of age reduces the body's efficiency, creating greater vulnerability and likelihood of malfunction. The body is still susceptible to all the usual disorders, while its maintenance, defense, and repair processes are all much weaker. Respiratory and heart disorders, for example, occur with much more frequency and intensity, skin wounds are more liable to infection, and bone fractures more difficult to heal. Cancer becomes more likely. But, in addition, the deterioration of the body and its functions produces ailments rarely found at a younger age.

M15 Nervous Disorders

The nervous system of an old person is likely to be affected by degeneration, since nerve cells cannot be replaced. Also the person is more susceptible to strokes, and liable to falls which may damage spinal cord or brain. All these may impair movement, and ability to think, see, hear, and express oneself.
PARKINSONISM occurs fairly often in old age, though less often in women than in men. It is due to degeneration of the nerve cells in one part of the brain, usually as a result of arteriosclerosis. It manifests itself in trembling and muscular rigidity, and often begins in one hand and then spreads to other parts of the body. The body's rigidity interferes with all movement, from facial expression to locomotion, and brings increasing discomfort as the disease progresses. Treatment involves drugs, exercise, physiotherapy, and possibly surgery.

M16 Incontinence

This is the inability to control the emptying of bladder and bowels. Incontinence of the bladder is usually due to infection of the urinary tract, or to damage to the controlling nerves. Atrophy of the muscles concerned also contributes. As senility and mental damage associated with old age progress, a woman may lose awareness of her bladder, so conscious control is finally lost and it empties of its own volition. Restricted mobility, emotional insecurity, and abdominal stress (caused by laughing, coughing, lifting, etc) also play their part in precipitating incontinence.

M16-19

Fecal incontinence is most often due to fecal impaction — the accumulation of a mass of feces in the rectum too bulky to be passed. This mass then acts as a ball valve, with fresh feces trickling around it and escaping in a continuous flow. In other cases it is due to the continual overflow of the original mass. It is occasionally due to diarrhea, as might occur in gastroenteritis or rectal prolapse (collapse of the wall of the rectum often due to overstraining).

M17 Spinal Disorders

SLIPPED DISK is the common name for a prolapsed intervertebral disk. The spine is built up of a column of bones (vertebrae) separated by disks of cartilage which act as shock absorbers. (The inside of the disk is made of spongy but firm elastic tissue, held in place by the strong fibrous tissue of the outer layer.) In a prolapse, one of these disks, in the lower part of the spine, slips out of position, impairing mobility and exerting painful pressure on the nerves of the spinal cord.
CERVICAL SPONDYLOSIS affects the upper part of the spinal column. Degeneration of the spine shortens the neck, forcing the vertebral artery to concertina, and so impairing the blood supply to the spinal cord and brain. Also, pressure is exerted on the nerves of the spinal cord, so their functioning, and that of all connected nerves, is affected.

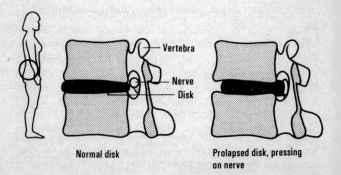

Normal disk

Prolapsed disk, pressing on nerve

Disorders of Age

M18 Hypothermia

This is when body temperature falls below 95°F (35°C). It mainly occurs in old people who cannot afford adequate heating, food, or winter living conditions. The person becomes increasingly apathetic and lethargic, and below 90°F (32°C) coma usually occurs. Direct heat must not be applied. The patient's surroundings should be warmed and a blanket wrapped around her to prevent heat loss. Because of hypothermia, deaths among old people may rise by 30 to 50% in winter, compared with summer months. The harder the winter, the worse the situation is. The trend begins even in the 50 to 54 age group, and becomes more marked over 60. Studies show that many elderly people live in temperatures that would not be allowed in factories or offices.

M19 Disorders of the Joints

Degeneration of the joints is largely due to the constant wear and tear they receive throughout life, but injuries may accentuate and accelerate any disorders.

OSTEOARTHRITIS occurs to some degree in 80 to 90% of people over the age of 60, though less in women than men. It originates from loss of elasticity in the cartilage of the joint. The cartilage breaks up with the joint's movement, and loose bits of cartilage may be deposited in the joint itself. These may grow and become calcified, increasing discomfort. The bone around the joint hardens, and cysts may develop, with spurs of bone around the joint's edges.

The knee, hip, and hand are most commonly affected. The process cannot be reversed, but can be delayed by gentle, regular exercise, to loosen the joint and strengthen the muscles.

RHEUMATOID ARTHRITIS usually begins in middle age, but its severity increases with time. It affects more women than men. The tissues of the joints thicken, so the cartilage becomes ulcerated and is eventually destroyed. There is overproduction of connective tissue, and ultimately the joint is swollen and may be fused solid.

The muscles waste with disuse. Special exercises, and rest in serious cases, are the main forms of treatment. Use of the drug cortisone is now thought to cause many problems, though it does give temporary relief.

M19-20

CONTRACTURES are deformities of the joints due to shortening (contraction) of the surrounding muscles and ligaments.
They are caused by arthritic or neurological disorders, or simply
by prolonged inactivity. If untreated they become permanent
and cause severe disability. Treatment is with muscle-relaxing
drugs and physical manipulation.

OSTEOPOROSIS is increased porousness of the bone, usually
from unknown causes, but sometimes due to severe nutritional
deficiency of calcium salts. It can also be due to hormonal
changes following the menopause (see F01). The skeleton
becomes brittle and prone to fracture. The vertebrae are most
often affected. They may collapse as they become weaker, and
as they lose weight and size the vertebral disks expand,
producing increasing curvature of the spine. The condition
may be triggered off by prolonged immobilization in bed. It is
more common in women than in men.

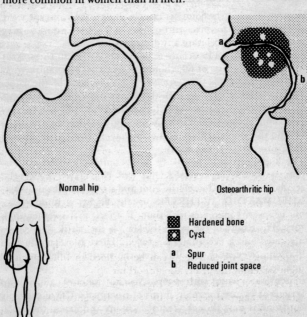

Normal hip   Osteoarthritic hip

▨ Hardened bone
▨ Cyst

a   Spur
b   Reduced joint space

The Experience of Aging

M20 Body Care

EXERCISE Lack of exercise will speed physical decline, just when maintaining the ability to get out and about is vital for self-esteem. Any exercise chosen should be started gradually, without strain, and kept up regularly. Gardening, walking, and golf are ideal. Keep-fit programs can be followed, but only after expert medical advice.

SLEEP Recent evidence suggests that sleep needs do not decline with age. Still, during old age, sleep at night is often fitful and shallow. Daytime naps, illness, anxiety, loneliness, and discomforts such as stiffness of the limbs can all contribute. An aging person may well try to accept the changed pattern of her sleep, and try to use waking hours whenever they occur. But a little exercise each day, avoidance of afternoon naps, a warm bedroom, a warm and comfortable bed, and a hot milky drink, can all help in achieving a sound night's sleep. If lack of sleep causes anxiety or depression, a doctor should be consulted.

WARMTH Adequate home heating is essential. Central heating is ideal. Open gas or electric bar heaters, or freestanding stoves, can be fire risks, while solid-fuel fires (coal, etc) can be both dangerous and difficult to maintain. Also, diminished awareness of pain may lead to self-scorching through sitting too near. With gas and oil heaters, good ventilation and regular safety checks are important. In bed, electric overblankets are safer than underblankets. Hot water bottles should always be cloth covered, never overfilled, and never used with electric blankets. Hot water bottles and blankets can also be a tremendous daytime help.

MOVING ABOUT THE HOUSE Reaction speed and balance decline with age, and bones and muscles weaken, so falls become more of a problem (see M19). Highly polished floors, loose mats, trailing appliance wires, frayed carpet or linoleum edges, and poor or uneven lighting are all dangerous. Strong banisters, and good bath and toilet hand supports, are important. Awkward steps can be outlined in white paint. A light switch by the bed is also important.

TESTS AND CHECK-UPS Eyes should be tested yearly, and glasses changed if necessary: increasing farsightedness is typical with age. A doctor should be consulted over any hearing difficulties. The ears can be checked for wax, and the help of a hearing aid should not be ruled out. Elderly people who still have their own teeth should brush them regularly and visit a dentist every 6 months. Denture wearers should have a check-up every 5 years, or if the dentures cause discomfort or difficulty in eating or speaking.

FEET Shoes should be fitted with care; low heels are safest. Stockings should not be too tight. A chiropodist will help with problems caused by corns, calluses, bunions, or toenails too thick to cut.

ILLNESS A doctor should always be told of any symptoms appearing, such as poor appetite, loss of weight, blood in urine, etc; also of any discomfort, for in an old person even a bone fracture may feel no more than troublesome. Medicines should be clearly labeled. Sleeping pills should not be kept by the bedside, in case of mistakes.

BLADDER AND BOWEL CONTROL The causes of incontinence (see M16) are often temporary, and control is regained naturally. Otherwise, medical treatment can often help. Pads, special sheets, and mattress covers can be used. If suitable help is available, it is usually best for the sufferer to remain at home.

M21 Diet

NUTRITIONAL NEEDS The main change is simply in quantity. With age, decreasing physical activity and falling metabolic rate lower food energy needs; calorific intake should be gradually reduced (see H17). Otherwise, the kind of food needed stays basically the same at any age, though in old age there is reduced need for protein, fat, thiamin, glucose, and calcium (but see Osteoporosis, M19). However, more foods may cause digestive problems, because of slower and therefore incomplete digestion and absorption.

DAILY DIET Ideally, two portions of meat, fish, cheese, or eggs should be taken each day, and some milk as well. Vegetables and fruit, wholemeal bread, and butter or margarine, are also important as sources of vitamins, minerals, and roughage. Several small meals during the day may be better than one or two large ones; breakfast should never be missed. Large meals late at night are best avoided, since they can interfere with sleep. Liquid intake should be at least 3 (US)pt

The Experience of Aging

(1.4 liters) daily. Also, when catering for an old person, variety and attractiveness of food count as much as good nutritional balance.

POOR NUTRITION Many old people eat badly. The lonely, impoverished, and neglected may do so through apathy, poverty, lack of facilities, lack of judgment, or general physical or mental disability. Others, unrestricted economically and practically, may overeat such foods as pastries and cakes, with a resulting weight gain that impairs health. Finally, unhealthy teeth and badly fitting dentures can encourage the old to choose comfortable rather than nutritious foods.

M22 Age and Society

Life expectancy has risen steadily in industrialized countries in this century. So, with declining birth rates, their populations are increasingly older ones. In the USA, over 10% of the population are 65 or over: almost 22 million people. Of these, almost 60% are women. It is important to realize the variety and naturalness of old age. For a working person, post-retirement can be up to ⅓ of the life span, and the majority of old people are not lonely, poor, incapacitated, neglected, or ignored.

Nevertheless, they can count it as individual good fortune or good planning if they are not. Our society does not have a good record for its treatment of the old. There is insufficient provision for their physical welfare; there is little or none for their self-esteem. After a lifetime of work, elderly people too often find they have no role to fulfill, and no social label but that of "old person." Physical and financial difficulties can reinforce this. Society's subtle message can often seem to be: you are no longer really useful, and though you are enjoying the deserved fruits of your labor, your difficulties and incapabilities are something of a problem for us. Because they live longer, there are more retired women than men — and more living alone. Still, elderly women often keep their self-respect better than men. A man's identity faces a severe crisis when he retires from work. For a woman, even if she has had a job, the home has usually remained an important sphere of activity. Her crisis of identity — the menopause, and the departure of her children — comes earlier, when her mental resources are stronger.

M 22

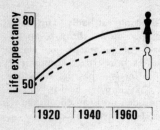

Figures for the USA show that life expectancy at birth has risen steadily in this century and that woman's advantage over man has increased.

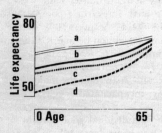

Life expectancy also increases with age, since at each age the fittest survive. Figures shown are for the USA now, for: white women (a); black women (b); white men(c); and black men (d). Expectancy for a white woman born now is 76 years; for one aged 65, over 82.

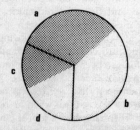

Because of female life expectancy, the retired population in a developed country consists overwhelmingly of women:
a)women living alone, 30%
b)other women, 39%;
c)men living alone, 13%;
d)other men, 18%.
(Figures for Great Britain.)

The Experience of Aging

visual defects 19%
hearing defects 21%
lack of dentures 15%
arteriosclerosis 27%
osteoarthritis 14%
genitourinary disease 14%
varicose veins 13%
feet disabilities 34%

The diagram shows the estimated extent of unrecognized medical needs in those aged 65 and over, in a typically developed country. For example 34% of the group have unattended feet disabilities.

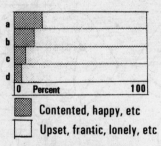

Contented, happy, etc

Upset, frantic, lonely, etc

The diagram illustrates how negative the reactions of most people are to retirement. Only 23% of people retire with any positive feelings (a); within 6 months (b) this percentage has dropped to 16% and within a year (c) to 10%. Of those who have been retired for more than 1 year (d) only 6% remain content.

N01 Male-Female Differences

In the following pages is given some basic information about the male sexual system. Apart from genital differences and the lack of breast development, other male surface differences are:

a different proportions between shoulders, chest, and hips;

b different pattern of body hair;

c greater surface prominence of the skeletal and muscular systems, due to less uniform skin fat; and

d presence of the "Adam's apple" throat bulge, from a larger larynx.

Most of these are not obvious until puberty; but the basic difference in sexual organs is established within a few weeks of conception.

Location of major
external physical
differences

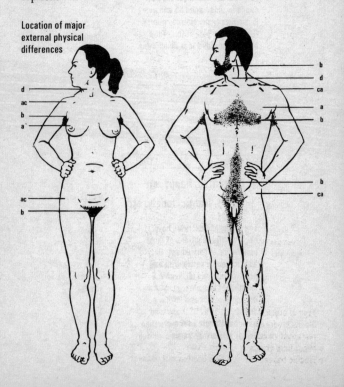

Sexual Differentiation

N02 Sexual Similarities

The male and female sexual and reproductive systems differ greatly in their structure and function. Nevertheless, they develop from the same original tissues in the embryo (see A03). So different parts of the final systems are comparable in origin and even partly in the role they play. The diagram illustrates some examples of these "corresponding organs." For example, the same embryonic tissue that goes to form the outer vaginal lips in a female child forms the scrotum in a male.

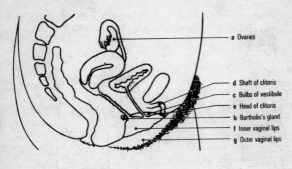

a Ovaries
d Shaft of clitoris
c Bulbs of vestibule
e Head of clitoris
b Bartholin's gland
f Inner vaginal lips
g Outer vaginal lips

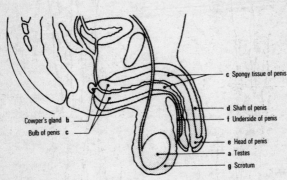

c Spongy tissue of penis
d Shaft of penis
f Underside of penis
Cowper's gland b
Bulb of penis c
e Head of penis
a Testes
g Scrotum

Type of organ
a Glands producing reproductive cells
b Minor fluid glands
c Erectile tissues
d Muscle tissue
e Sensory tissue
f Soft tissue
g Hair-bearing soft tissue

No3

N03 Puberty

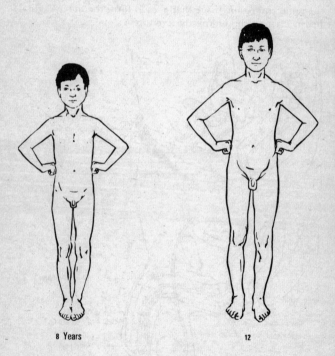

8 Years

12

TIMING

The changes of puberty usually start later in boys than in girls: the typical age is 12, rather than 11. More important, the changes happen less quickly and less simultaneously — so they are spread out over 4 years or more, rather than just $2\frac{1}{2}$ or 3. For all these reasons, boys mature later, and the changes of

Sexual Differentiation

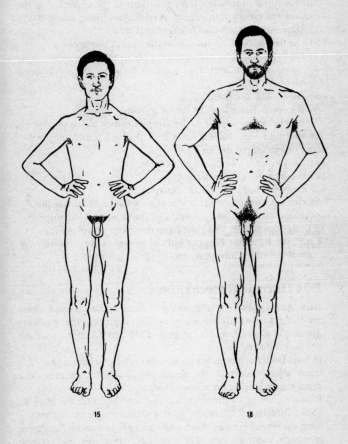

15   18

puberty in a boy, starting normally at any time from about 10 years of age to about 15, do not usually end until between 14 and 18. (For example, an average boy, 1in — 2.5cm — taller than an average girl at 9 years, is ½in — 1.2cm — shorter than her at 12, and does not catch up until he is nearly 14.)

No3-04

SEQUENCE

Although the time taken is longer, there is less variation in the sequence of events than in girls. A typical sequence would be:

1) the testes and scrotum begin to enlarge;
2) the first pubic hair appears at the base of the penis;
3) the penis begins to enlarge; and, about the same time
4) there is a sudden rapid gain in height ("the adolescent growth spurt");
5) the shoulders broaden;
6) the voice deepens as the larynx grows;
7) hair begins to appear in the armpits and on the upper lip;
8) sperm production reaches a level at which semen may quite often be ejaculated during sleep;
9) the pubic hair begins to show color;
10) the prostate gland enlarges; and
11) there is a sudden increase in strength.

As with women, other particular changes of puberty include: increased oiliness and coarseness of the skin; and development of body odor for the first time from the armpits and genitals.

Typically, by about $17\frac{3}{4}$, the bulk of growth is over. Height, for example, usually only gains another 2% after that.

N04 Hormonal Mechanisms

As in girls, puberty is triggered off in the hypothalamus where releasing factors are produced which stimulate the pituitary gland. As a result, and as in girls, FSH and LH hormones are produced (see A10).

In boys both hormones act on the testes. After about a year, LH stimulation results in the testes producing testosterone, the main masculinizing hormone of puberty.

It makes the penis grow, pubic hair develop, etc. Meanwhile, FSH stimulates the testes to start producing sperm. To keep a limit on sexual activity, both LH and FSH are under "negative feedback control" (see A10), eg LH stimulates testosterone production, which reacts back on the hypothalamus. The hypothalamus sends out a message cutting back LH production. As LH is no longer stimulating testosterone production its level falls, allowing LH to be made again. (With FSH the control mechanism is probably not the testosterone level.)

Sexual Differentiation

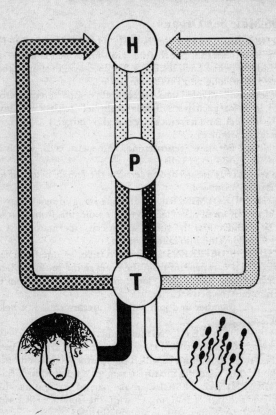

Releasing factors
Luteinizing hormone (LH)
Follicle-stimulating hormone (FSH)
Testosterone
Unknown factor
H Hypothalmus
P Pituitary gland
T Testes

N05

N05 Male Sex Organs

a THE TWO TESTES are the male reproductive glands. They hang in an external pouch (the scrotum), which is below and behind the penis. Each testis is a flattened oval in shape, about 1¾in (4.4cm) long and 1in (2.5cm) wide.

The scrotum is divided into two separate compartments (scrotal sacs), one for each testis. (Usually the left testis hangs lower than the right, and its scrotal sac is slightly larger.)

The testes produce:

a male sex hormone, testosterone; and sperm cells, which are the male reproductive cells.

The sperm cells are needed to fertilize the female ovum, if new life is to be produced.

b THE EPIDIDYMIDES are found one alongside each testis.

A number of small tubes lead to each epididymis from its testis. In the epididymides the young sperm cells (spermatocytes) are stored and develop into mature sperm.

c THE VAS DEFERENS are the two tubes — one from each testis — that carry sperm from the testes to the prostate gland. They are about 16in (40cm) long, and wind upwards from the scrotum into the pelvic cavity.

They come together and join with the urethra tube just below the bladder.

d THE PROSTATE GLAND surrounds the junction of the vas deferens and urethra tubes. Here the sperm cells are mixed with seminal fluid, the liquid in which the sperms are carried out of the body. The resulting mixture is semen, a thick whitish fluid.

e THE SEMINAL VESICLES make part of the seminal fluid that the prostate gland mixes with the sperm cells. More seminal fluid is made by the prostate gland itself.

f THE URETHRA is the tube that carries urine from the bladder to the penis. It is S-shaped and about 8in (20cm) long.

In the prostate gland it is joined by the vas deferens — so it is also the route by which the semen reaches the penis from the prostate gland.

g THE PENIS is inserted into the female vagina during copulation. Most of the penis is made up of spongy tissue, loosely covered with skin.

The urethra tube enters the penis from the body and runs inside it to the tip of the penis.

Sex organs

The external opening in the tip (the meatus) is where semen or urine leaves the body.

In its natural state, the sides of the penis near its tip are covered by a fold of skin, called the foreskin. When rolled forward, the foreskin is like a hood around the penis tip; but it can also be pushed back along the shaft. In primitive circumstances, it probably served as some protection to the penis at its most sensitive part.

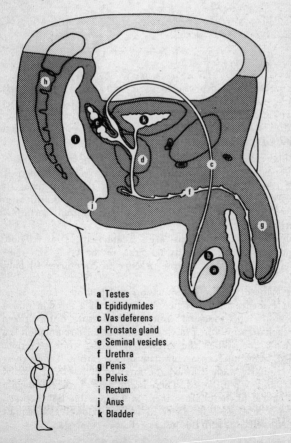

a Testes
b Epididymides
c Vas deferens
d Prostate gland
e Seminal vesicles
f Urethra
g Penis
h Pelvis
i Rectum
j Anus
k Bladder

No6-07

N06 Erection

When a man is sexually aroused, blood flows to his penis, swelling its spongy internal tissue. Instead of being "floppy" and hanging down, it becomes stiffer and longer, and juts out from the body. This is called "erection."

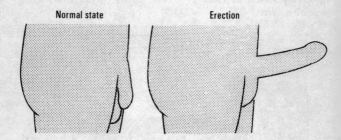

Normal state   Erection

N07 Circumcision

In many societies, the foreskin is often removed — it is cut away, in a minor surgical procedure known as circumcision. In rare cases there are medical reasons for this: sometimes the foreskin of an adult man can become very tight and difficult to move. But usually it is a religious or social custom, performed shortly after birth.

Male Jews and Moslems are circumcised as a religious requirement; and in many hospitals in the USA, and some other countries, it is routine practice to circumcise all baby boys.

The value of routine circumcision is debatable. There is no clear evidence that presence or absence of a foreskin makes much difference to sexual sensitivity, or pleasure, or time taken to reach orgasm. One practical argument for circumcision is a hygienic one. When the foreskin is intact, white secretions called "smegma" can accumulate underneath it. Unless these are regularly washed away, the foreskin can become smelly, dirty, and even inflamed. There is also a link between smegma and cancer of the penis in men; and a possible link between smegma and cervical cancer in women. However, adequate hygiene will cope with this just as well as circumcision.

Sex organs

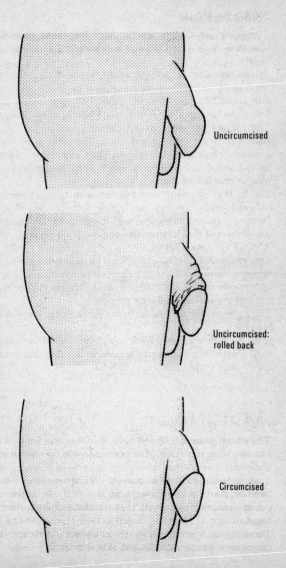

Uncircumcised

Uncircumcised:
rolled back

Circumcised

No8-10

N08 The Penis

The penis can vary in several ways, but these generally have little to do with sexual prowess or female sexual satisfaction.
SIZE
An average flaccid penis is about $3\frac{3}{4}$ in long, and most are between $3\frac{1}{4}$ and $4\frac{1}{4}$ in. An average erect penis is about $6\frac{1}{4}$ in long, and about 90% are between 5 and 7in. (In a recent survey of UK males, the smallest found was $4\frac{3}{4}$ in, and the longest 9in.) There is no clear proof that ethnic variations occur.
Body size is no guide to penis size: the erect penis has a less constant relationship to body size than any other organ. Nor is flaccid size decisive: penises which hang longer when flaccid tend to gain less on erection.
But, in any case, there is no physical relationship between penis size and sexual prowess or female satisfaction. The female vagina accommodates its size to that of the penis, and stimulation of the clitoris does not depend on penis length.
ANGLE OF ERECTION
This varies from the horizontal to the near vertical. Variations between individuals are not necessarily significant. Variations in any one person on different occasions may show different levels of immediate sexual excitement.
The angle usually declines with the decline of potency in age.
SHAPE
Some erect penises bend back in a curve toward the abdominal wall. Usually the vagina can accommodate this, but in extreme cases it may make intercourse difficult.

N09 Sexual Arousal

The sexual process takes the male sexual system from its normal inactive state to orgasm. On orgasm, semen is discharged from the penis.
The stimulus that first arouses the system can be purely psychological — the thought of sex. But the system usually needs physical pressure on the skin surface of the penis to reach orgasm.
The diagram opposite shows typical events at different stages in the process, plotted against rate of heartbeat.

Sexuality

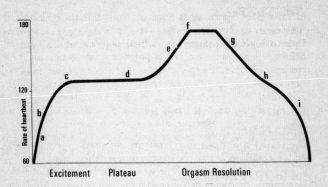

a Penis erects
b Scrotum thickens
c Testes rise
d "Sex flush" skin color may appear on chest, neck, and forehead
e Penis tip and testes swell
f Ejaculation, usually with heavy breathing and muscular spasms
g Sex flush disappears
h Loss of erection
i Penis returns to normal state

N10 Impotence

Over 90% of impotence is caused psychologically (see B31). The few physical causes of long-term impotence can be categorized into physical defects from birth, defects of development due to hormonal failure, and changes in the adult body state. The last can include:

a) some diseases of the genitals;
b) some hormonal disorders;
c) some general disorders, such as diabetes, debilitating illness, and infectious damage to the spinal cord;
d) some surgery (eg for cancer of prostate or colon);
e) continual heavy drug or alcohol use; and
f) aging.

However, none of these is certain to cause impotence.

Physical causes of short-term impotence can include almost anything that lowers the body's vitality: immediate factors like great fatigue or heavy doses of alcohol or drugs, and more mild

N10-11

ones like poor health, poor nutrition, and perhaps even lack of exercise.

There are great variations in normal potency, and almost all men experience some failure of potency at some time in their lives.

N11 Behavior of the Penis

1 EXCITEMENT
The sexual stimulus triggers off an automatic reflex, which sends blood flowing into the spongy tissue of the penis.

The spongy mass swells and presses against the sheath of skin. As a result, the penis becomes stiff and sticks out at an angle from the body, usually pointing slightly upward.

Muscular contraction pulls the testes closer in to the body. This stage can be maintained for long periods, and can be lost and regained, without orgasm, many times.

2 PLATEAU LEVEL
The testes are drawn still closer to the body. The penis increases slightly in diameter near the tip, and the opening in the tip becomes more slitlike. The tip itself may change color, to a deeper red-purple.

3 ORGASM
The muscles around the urethra give a number of rapid involuntary contractions. This forces semen out of the penis at high pressure (ejaculation).

There are usually three or four major bursts of semen, one every 0.8 seconds, followed by weaker, more irregular, muscular contractions.

4 RESOLUTION
Often there is:

first, a very rapid reduction in penis size, to about 50% larger than its normal state;

followed by a slower reduction back to normal.

But each of these stages may be prolonged, eg if the penis remains inserted in the female genitals.

Sexuality

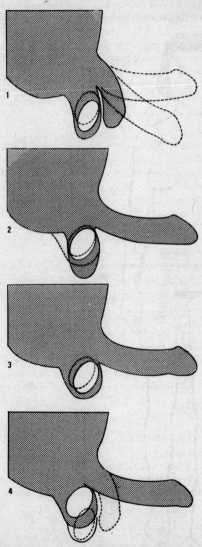

This pictorial index helps to locate descriptions of the main parts of the body; the box numbers in brackets refer to the disorders. Some organs (eg the brain, and the heart) have no central reference of their own. In these cases, references have been given for the sections in which they are mentioned under other subjects.

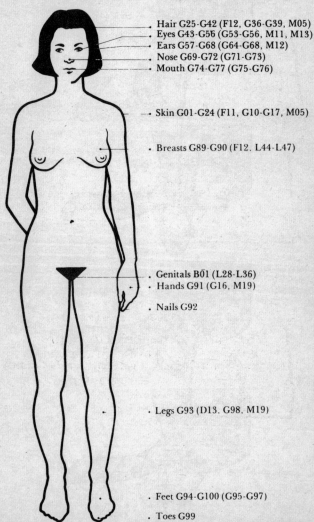

Hair G25-G42 (F12, G36-G39, M05)
Eyes G43-G56 (G53-G56, M11, M13)
Ears G57-G68 (G64-G68, M12)
Nose G69-G72 (G71-G73)
Mouth G74-G77 (G75-G76)

Skin G01-G24 (F11, G10-G17, M05)

Breasts G89-G90 (F12, L44-L47)

Genitals B01 (L28-L36)
Hands G91 (G16, M19)

Nails G92

Legs G93 (D13, G98, M19)

Feet G94-G100 (G95-G97)

Toes G99

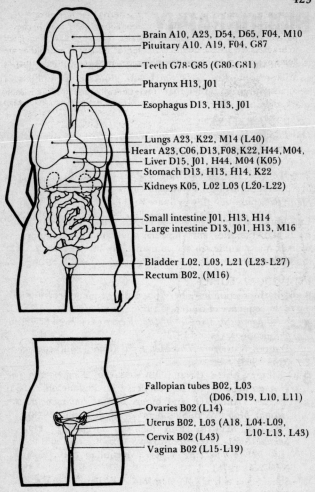

Brain A10, A23, D54, D65, F04, M10
Pituitary A10, A19, F04, G87

Teeth G78-G85 (G80-G81)

Pharynx H13, J01

Esophagus D13, H13, J01

Lungs A23, K22, M14 (L40)
Heart A23, C06, D13, F08, K22, H44, M04,
Liver D15, J01, H44, M04 (K05)
Stomach D13, H13, H14, K22
Kidneys K05, L02 L03 (L20-L22)

Small intestine J01, H13, H14
Large intestine D13, J01, H13, M16

Bladder L02, L03, L21 (L23-L27)
Rectum B02, (M16)

Fallopian tubes B02, L03
(D06, D19, L10, L11)
Ovaries B02 (L14)
Uterus B02, L03 (A18, L04-L09,
L10-L13, L43)
Cervix B02 (L43)
Vagina B02 (L15-L19)

BIBLIOGRAPHY

Some of the sources used for *Woman's Body*, and a suggested further reading list, are given below. Books or pamphlets of specialist interest, rather than for general reading, have been marked with an asterisk.

GENERAL REFERENCE

Our Bodies Ourselves (Simon & Schuster, 1976)
Life and Health (Random House/CRM, 1976)
Family Health Guide (Reader's Digest Assoc., 1972)
The Woman's Almanac (Armitage Press Inc., 1976)
Ms (pub. monthly by Ms Magazine Corp., New York)
Spare Rib (pub. monthly by Spare Ribs Ltd., London)

In addition to these general reference works, there are many medical dictionaries, encyclopedias, and home health guides, as well as many guides to the human body in the form of text designed for schools or for teaching nurses.

INDIVIDUAL TOPICS

Books in this section have been listed in a sequence corresponding to the sequence of contents in *Woman's Body*.

A   *Tanner, J. M. *Growth at Adolescence* (Blackwell Scientific Publications, Oxford 1973)

Dalton, Katherina *The Menstrual Cycle* (Pantheon, New York 1969)

B   *Kinsey, Alfred C. and others *Sexual Behavior in the Human Female* (W. B. Saunders Co., Philadelphia 1953)

*Kinsey, Alfred C. and others *Sexual Behavior in the Human Male* (W. B. Saunders Co., Philadelphia 1948)

*Masters, William H. & Johnson, Virginia E. *Human Sexual Response* (Little, Brown & Co., Boston 1966)

Hite, Shere *The Hite Report* (Macmillan Pub. Co. Inc., New York 1976)

Schaefer, Leah C. *Women and Sex* (Hutchinson & Co., London 1973)

Brecher, Edward *The Sex Researchers* (Signet Books, New York 1969)

Brecher, Ruth and Edward *An Analysis of Human Sexual Response* (Signet Books, New York 1969)

Ayers, Charlotte J. *Biology of Sex* (John Wiley & Sons, New York 1974)

Wolff, Charlotte *Love Between Women* (Duckworth & Co., 1971)

Friday, Nancy *My Secret Garden* (Pocket Books, New York 1974)

C Demarest, R. and Sciarra, J. *Conception, Birth and Contraception* (McGraw Hill, New York 1969)

D Garrey, M. M. and others *Obstetrics Illustrated* (E&S Livingstone Ltd., London 1969)

Roberts, R. and Shettles, L. *From Conception to Birth: the Drama of Life's Beginnings* (Harper & Row, New York 1971)

Kitzinger, Sheila *The Experience of Childbirth* (New York International Publication Service 1964)

Dick-Read, Grantly *Childbirth without Fear* (Harper & Row, New York 1959, 2nd ed)

Wright, Erna *The New Childbirth* (Hart Pub.,New York 1968)

F Weideger, P. *Menstruation and Menopause* (Alfred A. Knopf Inc., New York 1975)

*McKinley, S. M. & Jefferys, M. "The Menopausal Syndrome (*Brit. Journal of Preventative and Social Medicine* 28.2.1974)

Cherry, Sheldon H. *The Menopause Myth* (Ballantine Books, New York 1976)

Bart, Pauline "Depression in Middle-aged Women" (*Women in Sexist Society,* Basic Books, New York 1971)

H Krause, Marie V. & Himscher, Martha V. *Food, Nutrition and Diet Therapy* (W. B. Saunders Co., Philadelphia 1972)

Bruch, Hilde *Eating Disorders* (Routledge & Kegan Paul, London 1974)

J Rush, Anne Kent *Getting Clear: Body Work for Women* (Random House Bookworks, New York 1973)

Brownmiller, Susan *Against Our Will* (Simon & Schuster, New York 1973)

Conroy, Mary *The Rational Woman's Guide to Self-Defense* (Grosset & Dunlap, New York 1975)

K Jones, K. L., Shamberg, L. W. ,Byer, C.O. *Drugs and Alcohol* (Harper and Row, New York 1973)

Diehl, Harold S. *Tobacco and your Health* (McGraw Hill, New York 1969)

L Kilmartin, Angela *Understanding Cystitis* (Pan Books, London 1975)

M Bromley, D. B. *The Psychology of Human Aging* (Penguin Viking, New York, rev. 1974)

N Diagram Group *Man's Body* (Paddington Press, New York 1976)

INDEX

We Deliver!
And So Do These Bestsellers.

BANTAM
SHOP·AT·HOME
C·A·T·A·L·O·G

Special Offer
Buy a Bantam Book
for only 50¢.

Now you can have Bantam's catalog filled with hundreds of titles plus take advantage of our unique and exciting bonus book offer. A special offer which gives you the opportunity to purchase a Bantam book for only 50¢. Here's how!

By ordering any five books at the regular price per order, you can also choose any other single book listed (up to a $4.95 value) for just 50¢. Some restrictions do apply, but for further details why not send for Bantam's catalog of titles today!

Just send us your name and address and we will send you a catalog!